P9-CJF-714

To Susie
Happy 37th Birthday!

Love
Patti
David
Michelle

At the request of the translator
we are happy to dedicate this book
to our brothers of every color, creed and race,
in the Name of Emmanuel, God-with-us.
And with a special thought
for all the divided Christian groups
united forever in the Name of Jesus in one,
indivisible and eternal Church.
"All of you one: one body, one soul,
one prayer... Let us be one,
all of us together".

HE and I

GABRIELLE BOSSIS

H E   a n d   I

Translated and condensed by
Evelyn M. Brown

Editions Paulines

Originally published as LUI ET MOI by
Beauchesne et ses Fils, 117 rue de Rennes, Paris

Imprimatur: Msgr. Jean-Marie Fortier, Archbishop
Sherbrooke, November 14, 1969

Composition et mise en page: *Les Éditions Paulines*

ISBN 2-89039-807-2

Dépôt légal — 4e trimestre 1985
Bibliothèque nationale du Québec
Bibliothèque nationale du Canada

© Éditions Paulines
   250 Boul. St-François nord
   Sherbrooke, Qué., J1E 2B9 (Canada)

HE and I

Verified Edition
complete in one volume

Reader's Remarks

Maria Augusta, Baroness Von Trapp, Stowe, Vermont, U.S.A. "Since half a year *He and I* is my daily companion. I try to follow our Lord's will to read a passage in the morning and two in the afternoon. To me it is simply a continuation of the Gospels and I can't tell you how much I thank this book."

An Irish psychiatrist, Mary V. Hynes, M.B.D.P.M., Ballintemple, Cork, Ireland. "A woman patient let me in on the 'secret' of what had transformed her emotional life, and liberated her from a host of phobic fears, when she confided to me that *He and I* had worked where pills and psychiatry had failed. I promptly bought twelve copies of this extraordinary spiritual classic, as a mini-apostolate — keeping my original books, of course, as a great treasure!"

Dr. Conrad W. Baars, M.D., a psychiatrist of international fame. "The book *He and I* read over and over again, a few pages at a time, provides an ever-growing conviction of Christ's boundless love for each one of us individually and moves us towards a more complete confidence and surrender. Christ's compassionate words of love are a great source of both spiritual and psychological help to all troubled by fears, loneliness, depression and non-affirmation."

From an English actress, London, England. "Yes indeed, I was enchanted and bowled over by *He and I* and I think of nothing better than having the privilege of distributing the books in England. I've lent the book to several of my friends and they, too, have fallen in love with it and we find ourselves quoting bits to one another! I can say that having read the volume, I cried out, 'Lord, I suspected You were like this!' ''

The Most Rev. James J. Byrne, Archbishop of Dubuque, U.S.A. ''I have suggested *He and I* to a number of people and all of them find tremendous spiritual motivation in this book.''

From the Dean Emeritus of a university. *He and I* is a remarkable book. What struck me at once was its great practicalness. Books of devotion are so often up in the clouds but this is right down to earth.''

From a non church-goer. ''It is a fully delightful work... I read the volume this summer and found it exquisite reading. It renders Augustine's 'Love, and do what thou wilt', and 'we go toward God, not by walking, but by loving' ... It cannot be read rapidly; like Traherne's *Centuries of Meditation* one must stop after each thought and allow that thought to travel inside to redeem the necessary externality of words''.

From an Irish religious. ''How often I have stopped in reading *He and I* in the last four years and asked, Am I really reading this; is this book really in print? I would love to see it done in leatherette, gilt edges, like some of the old manuals of devotion: *The Imitation*, etc. *He and I* will be around for 100 years.''

From the leader of a world-wide Protestant Crusade. ''I cannot adequately tell you how much this book means to me... Every page is filled with inspiration and gives its own authentic message straight through from the Lord. I have been reading it with great delight and have been receptive to the wonderful inspiration which fills it.''

Note:
   As some of these remarks were taken from the translator's private correspondence, we have not revealed the name of the writer.

Preface

"A fresh restatement, that is the point,"[1] *was Father McCorry's appeal in his challenging article on the state of spiritual writing in the post-conciliar year of 1967. And taking a case in point, he went on to say, "The vital religious problem of prayer is discussed and discussed and discussed yet again; and can anyone remember when he encountered an original and truly helpful suggestion in the matter?" I can. There are several in the pages of this volume, translated from a series of books entitled* Lui et moi, *alleged to contain the words of Our Lord to a French woman called Gabrielle Bossis. Here is one of them: "Give yourself a rest from saying prayers so that you may enjoy My love."*

I meditated these books for four years, dreaming all the time of translating them before I was chosen to undertake the work. And now that it is done, I am more than ever convinced of the timeliness of this document and its significance in our religious-scientific age, when in the physical-spiritual world man is exploring the vast reaches of outer space, ever seeking to widen the bounds of light.

It is the triumph of our century that man has set foot on the moon. But the journey towards its light is only a symbol of the one he must take toward the Light of Christ within him. And only the astronauts of the spiritual world who incarnate Jesus, the Way-shower, can lead us there. They are the avantgardists who venture forth audaciously on the promises of God into another dimension and they alone can guide us to that Sea of Tranquillity before the throne of God within us: to the New Jerusalem whose replica is in the human heart.

The conquest of all sidereal space is before man, but this is only a faint and far-off image of what awaits him when, through the conquest of himself and an ever-increasing awareness of his divine

---

1. *No Laughing Matter* — *America,* February 11, 1967.

origin and destiny, he emerges "from the man-kingdom into the God-kingdom". Yet man's true evolution is not on a horizontal plane at the mercy of time, but an ascension from grace to grace into the many mansions of the Christ-consciousness; and the point of departure is humility. That is why the recorded dialogue with God of a little, somewhat sentimental French woman born in the last century is of more value to us in our creative outreach than the record of the three dauntless men who reached the moon in 1969.

Man has spent his best efforts in the release of the atom in the mineral kingdom, but this is only a puny achievement compared with the release of the atomic energy of his own soul: the God-Power as both revealed and hidden in the pages of this volume.

In this book, there are hints of knowledge that will be better understood tomorrow than today. There are moments of heart-breaking beauty for the attentive reader. But he must listen to the Voice, to the silence too; for "our estranged faces" are ever wont to "miss the many splendor'd thing." And it is not literary French that I have been translating; it is the language of the mystics in a French woman's mother tongue, so treacherously simple, of such utter limpidity, that inattentive minds may miss the unfathomable depths which put it beyond all suspicion of personal invention.

The words of Our Lord? Whatever the reader may or may not believe concerning the Voice that speaks to Gabrielle Bossis in these words too shockingly tender, too anti-traditional for some good Christians for whom orthodoxy is still strictly bound to the old order of things, no one fully aware of God as the Great Lover and who has therefore had a deep, personal experience of His action in his life will doubt the truth of what the historian Daniel Rops wrote in his preface to Lui et Moi: "...here we breathe the sweet fragrance of Christ."

The fact that this French woman heard, or thought she heard a voice, a voice that smiled, and pleaded more persuasively and poignantly than the nightingale in the woods beyond her garden, should not be a reason for us to doubt the authenticity of the experience. If we can admit that Christ does speak in the soul, can we deny the possibility of a voice or at least of the impression of a voice? Gabrielle herself had doubts. The reply to one of them reveals her own suspicions:"And if these words do come from your own human nature, didn't I create that nature?" As Daniel Rops pointed out:

8

"...truly what better answer?" Indeed, what better answer from the One who is Transcendence and Immanence?

"Sometimes you doubt that it is I speaking to you," says the Voice on another occasion, "it all seems so simple, so like yourself. But aren't we one?"... "The Spirit also adopts the language of the little ones." Surely it is a mark of the divine simplicity that the Uncreated Light should transfigure the soul as sunlight does a stained glass window — in terms of the colors presented to its rays?

"The language of the little ones." It is not everyone who can comprehend the doctrine of the elaboration of the Mystical Body of Christ. But even the smallest child of God can understand the science of love, can drink from the clear flowing fountain of the same truth in this brief dialogue:

"I was giving Him a sacrifice," wrote Gabrielle Bossis, "and I said, 'It's a flower that I'm pinning to your robe'."

The Voice: "Give Me these flowers often. (Smiling). It's as though you added to My beauty. You see, when you become more beautiful, I become more beautiful. Oh! My little child, how one we are!"

"Fall in love with Me over and over again," says the Voice. And I believe that divine Love in all its seductive beauty would be irresistible were we for one fleeting moment to get a clear picture of the infinitely tender Father-Mother God, who would ransack the whole of His beautiful universe to find us a needed joy or love; or would suffer our suffering of untold fears and pains and losses to bring us the joy imperishable; to satisfy the craving of our truer, deeper selves, using our very wounds to open out a way "whence the imprisoned splendor may escape."

It is because we lose sight of the immensely tender heart of the God-Man — this Christ who is exuberance of life, this Christ described as "the most humanly human of all men", that we complicate the spiritual life. Instead of it being, as it was for Gabrielle Bossis, a voyage of discovery of a love surpassing all human loves, to many it has become what Father McCorry described as "A grim business".

A fresh restatement, yes, that is our crying need. New terms for the Unknowable that we may know and love Him more and better, terms that will "stab the spirit broad awake". Yet it is not a case of discovering something new, but of rediscovering something old, of freeing ourselves from the shackles of an outworn religious terminology that time and travesty have rendered worse than inadequate; and from all that man has done in the name of religion to disfigure the adorable face of the Father. It is a case of rediscovering the Word made flesh in the sacrament of man himself. Above all it is a case of rediscovering the divine Tenderness.

"Come to this wellspring of My love," says the Voice, "come draw living waters of constant union and levitating joy."

Here in the pages of this book, which Daniel Rops classed among "the most authentic masterpieces of spiritual literature", is the perfect answer to our needs in this age when we are breaking through the artificial forms of theology to a deeper knowledge of the Divine Being, to a new awareness of the ever-living Person of Christ and all the vastly unexplored possibilities of our atonement with Him.

Theology is the science of religion, but it is a far cry from the knowledge we gain from such science to that of faith's knowing.

"I am God," said the Indian disciple of Ramana to Lanza del Vasto, "but I do not know it."

"Since you do not know it," replied Lanza del Vasto, "why do you say that you are God?"

"I know it by hearsay," replied the disciple, "I know it in words; I believe it, but I do not know it as he knows it."[2]

People of deep faith have always heard the music of eternity beyond the mathematics of theology, but what has only kindled fires of love in the pure in heart has often proved to be a crematorium for the spiritually dead. There is a perennial and universal truth in the statement of the Upanishads, "All philosophical doctrines, all theses and principles paralyze the mind and lead it away from the profound truth."

The profound truth... "This gospel of an unchanging world beyond our senses. We Christians have always known about it," writes Lanza del Vasto, "but it has remained among us so transcendent, so strangely contrary to all that we have learned from the world and from men, that we did not know what to make of it; we imprisoned it between church walls and in the shadowy places of the heart." How true this is; we have always kept our trea-

_____

2. *Le Pèlerinage aux Sources* — Lanza del Vasto.

sures in earthen vessels; but it is overflowing, as it has always overflowed. For Love is vehement.

"I am in everything and I am all Love," says the Voice. "Be imbued with this thought."

It has been a thrilling adventure to translate Lui et moi, to listen to the still small Voice above the rumors of our restless and rapidly changing world, above the babel of voices in a church in a state of glorious but tumultuous transition. But I needed an education for this work; there was much to learn, much to unlearn. Above all I had to learn to exchange any ludicrous sense of responsibility for what has aptly been called "response-ability". This done, every thread for the weaving came to me unsought.

One great source of insight and inspiration to me, one that prepared me for the full joy and import of parts of this dialogue was the whole beautiful science and philosophy of light, knowledge concerning the cosmic rays and particularly the seven major color rays or the rainbow. From this I saw how the Light of lights ensouling matter has given an esoteric as well as an exoteric meaning to all cosmic phenomena. For I not only came across a wealth of information of scientific interest but a beautiful illuminated version of the communion of saints and one more striking illustration of the divine unity and simplicity revealing facet after facet of the Christ-Prism of truth.

The reader will easily see these references to the rays. He may not, however, be aware of the profound metaphysical significance of this revival we see today in the higher consciousness of the human race of the rainbow bridge. Radiant symbol of the dawn of a new age of enlightenment to which man is again called to arise, it shines like the secret smile of God above the present deluge of tribulation and unfaith in which our planet is seemingly submerged. And if we delve deep into its meaning, we will discover the dove with the olive leaf — harbinger of "the new heavens and the new earth which He has promised us, and in which nothing but good shall live."[3]

"Everything in nature is only an image and a sacrament," says the Voice.

Oh, everything is a sacrament, an outward and visible sign of

3. 2 Peter 3:13.

an inward invisible grace, and the entire universe is of the same authentic weave — the resplendent aura, the colorful seamless robe of the Christ of the Cosmos. To understand this is to breathe freely in our faith. It is to awaken to the Voice when It says, "Enter more gaily into your Savior-God." It is to have that "more saved expression" that Nietzsche sought in vain among the Christians he knew.

Is it not because as Teilhard de Chardin has pointed out, we have been "incapable of grasping the All", of seeing matter in "its sacred mystery and incomparable majesty" that only too often we have unconsciously worshipped a God made in our own small and trivial image? But when we realize fully that even "heaven and the heaven of heavens cannot contain Him"[4] we shall believe more readily in His imprisonment in the tabernacles of our altars. For it is only when we recognize how great He is in the great things that we see "how immense He is in the very little ones". When we have gathered up the fragments of the broken bread of mankind's entire spiritual heritage that nothing be lost; when we find that we feed upon Christ in the vast universe, we shall feed upon Him with more fervor and joy in the Holy Eucharist. When we have learned to marvel at the seven sacraments of the rainbow and the miracle of the water turned into wine in the flowers of our fields, we shall become more naturally supernatural and accept the mysteries of our faith as simply as a child accepts love. "For what is a miracle," says the Voice, "but a token of Love's simplicity."

This is a book of a Door, of doors, of many doors. I was tempted to open them for you; I have even left the door to the rainbow ajar, but I realize that no one can open these doors for another. Noah could never have seen the rainbow if it had not already been in his mind and heart. For "in Thy light shall we see light..."[5]

"As you read these words that I have spoken to you," said the Voice, "go deeper, ever deeper into their profound meaning."

It has been my joyous duty as well as an unspeakable privilege to do this. But it is not easy to translate a document of this kind from French, a language so transparent, so full of light that it seems to have been created expressly as the language of the Spirit. It is important to me therefore to let my readers know how scrupulously

---

4. 2 Chronicles 6:18.

5. Psalms 36:9.

careful I have been in this work. All passages touching on subtle points of doctrine as well as liberties I should normally take quite happily have been submitted to one or more bilingual theologians. With their approval, here and there, when even the best possible translation failed to convey the full charm or impact of the words, I have resorted to a scriptural word or phrase. I have also submitted for their approbation all important decisions concerning the vocabulary, especially the replacing of traditional terms by others simpler, more modern and closer to their pristine meaning.

While the work of condensing was infinitely more painful than would be the condensation of a Beethoven symphony, for as the Voice says, ''Love never repeats'', all anxiety was removed from this too by the sure knowledge that a Mind was thinking me.

''Take care in setting down My words,'' says the Voice, ''so that what springs from My heart may be light and joy easy to capture...'' Having done this, I can only hope and trust that the reader may find what I have found in these pages — what the Voice describes as ''a never-ending beginning again of the joy of hearing Me''.

E.M.B.

Biographical Sketch of
GABRIELLE BOSSIS

The youngest child of a family of four children, Gabrielle Bossis was born in Nantes in 1874.

From an extremely shy, fearful and tearful little girl, more often found by herself in corners than playing with other children, she grew up into a graceful, gay, high-spirited young girl, very sociably inclined, though then, as from her childhood, possessed of a secret yearning for God and the things of the spirit which led to frequent contemplation.

As her father belonged to the wealthy middle class, there was no need for Gabrielle to earn her living. Her early years passed peacefully in her home at Nantes or at their summer residence in Fresne on the Loire River. Yet she was always very active. She obtained a degree for nursing, helped out in various parish projects, embroidered church ornaments for missions and practiced the fine arts of the day — music, painting, illuminating and sculpture, while still finding time for her favorite sports, horse riding, dancing and many social activities.

When the hidden treasure of her unusual inner life came to the notice of the Franciscan priest who was directing her, he felt convinced that she had a vocation for the convent and brought pressure to bear to induce her to become a nun. But Gabrielle resisted his suggestion with great determination, feeling led by an interior guidance more impelling than this, to remain in the world. No doubt it was this same guidance and the supreme attraction of a love surpassing all human loves that led to her refusal of the many proposals of marriage that came to her.

Quite late in life she discovered that she had another talent — that of writing the kind of entertaining and thoroughly moral comedies so much in demand by church clubs, a task "not so easy as one imagines," as Daniel Rops commented. Her first play, written for a club in Anjou, in which she acted the principal part, was such a success that before long her name became known throughout France and even in far distant countries. From this time on, right up until within two years before her death, she traveled extensively, producing her own plays and continuing to act the principal rôle. Those who remember her still remark on her extraordinary youth of mind and body, the golden hair that resisted the touch of time well on into her later years, the infectious laughter and her unfailing charm.

On very rare occasions in her early life, Gabrielle had been surprised by a mysterious voice which she felt with awe, though sometimes with anxious questionings, to be the voice of Christ. It was only at the age of 62, however, while traveling to Canada on the 'Île de France', that this touching dialogue with the inner Voice began in earnest, continuing until two weeks before her death on June 9, 1950.

The journal that she kept of her tour through Canada right to the Rocky Mountains is an extraordinary revelation of the double rôle she was called upon to play on life's stage — that of a contemplative and an exceptionally active woman exposed to all the hurly burly of life in the world. For the most part this document might be the travelogue of any gay, charming woman, much younger that she, possessed of a keen sense of humor, very much alive to every aspect of life around her and delicately sensitive to beauty. It is all the more astonishing for the reader to come across those sudden interruptions where the Voice recalls her to His everpresent Presence in words that touch the very depths and heights of mystical experience, words so simple yet so august as to recall those lines from the Song of Moses: "My doctrine shall drop as the rain, my speech shall distill as the dew, as the small rain upon the tender herb and as the showers upon the grass."

At the instigation of the Voice the travelogue ends with the Canadian tour. From there on, however, we can still trace her wandering footsteps by the colorful place names recorded with the sayings: Carthage, Tunis, Algiers,

Constantine and numerous names in France, Italy and other parts of Europe. Most of the time the only retreat she had for contemplation was the inner temple of her soul, for it was on airplanes, trains, buses, in the 'metro' during the rush hour in Paris, on the busy streets of great cities, even on the stage in the midst of a performance that the Voice spoke to her.

From the Word within her Gabrielle learned of her mission: to record and publish what she heard so that people might know that the life of intimacy with Christ was not reserved for those in cloisters but for every man, woman and child no matter what his state in life might be. As the first volume of the carefully recorded sayings of *Lui et moi* was published anonymously in 1948, she lived to see its phenomenal distribution. No one guessed at the authorship and when, subsequent to her death and at the ever-increasing demand for more of her notes, a second volume prefaced by Daniel Rops revealed her identity, so well had she hidden her secret that her friends were utterly astonished. Three more volumes followed at the request of grateful and enthusiastic readers: then a sixth volume giving her biography, and at still further request, a seventh with more of the dialogue. "This little book will go to the ends of the earth," said the Voice. And in recent years, more than ever we are seeing the fulfillment of these words as translation after translation is being published and distributed far beyond the boundaries of Europe.

Thomas à Kempis once said that those who travel a great deal rarely become holy, and Our Lord Himself, that it was easier for a camel to go through the needle's eye than for a rich man to enter into the kingdom of heaven. Yet Gabrielle traveled widely and was very wealthy. The Voice had a remedy for both situations: "Don't talk about your travels any more; they are for Me," It said. And when she thought of giving some embroidered cloths for the altar: "Don't buy them; make them with your own hands."

Until the illness that carried her off, Gabrielle's health was impeccable. Yet when death came, she welcomed it as she had welcomed life — with the same high-hearted love and joy. "My heart is getting weaker every day," she wrote on

May 9, 1950. "I have taken neither food nor liquid for three days. So I shall be leaving soon. Rejoice with me. Magnificat... and there will be no more partings."

When the moment of the "great Meeting" drew near on June 9th, at the beginning of the octave of Corpus Christi, was she able, I wonder, to remember those prophetic words spoken to her by the Voice on Corpus Christi just one year previously: "The last altar of repose, you know, is in heaven"?

As her testament she left us "the peaceable record of heaven". Heaven — from the Greek word *ouranos* or *expansion* — not for tomorrow in some far off Elysian field, but an eternal now, here as hereafter, by our at-onement with Him in the Christ-consciousness.

Gabrielle Bossis' name will never go down in history for anything she accomplished, but what was accomplished in her flows and will go on flowing to us when history has been lost in eternity. She was no one and she was everyone, for in her self-effacement and receptivity she became the little wind instrument through whom the Voice speaks to each one of the readers of HE AND I. For we feel not so much that we are reading as that we are being read, watched, followed.

Each soul is My favourite," says the Voice...
"I choose some only to reach the others."

E.M.B.

PART ONE

"Be assured by My lovingkindness
that as others are blessed by these words,
your cup of joy will overflow
in the same proportion.
Every reader too will receive
the same measure of grace.
And all will become members
of one united family:
the Family of My intimate friends".

He and I

1936

August 22 — *Aboard ship. During a concert of classical music I was offering Him garlands of sounds and all the fragrance flowing from them. Very tenderly He said to me as once before:*

"My little girl…"

August 23 — *The piano was being used as an altar, and I was thinking of the seagulls and airplanes that sometimes alighted on the great liners.*

"This time it is the Christ."

As the ship was rolling: "You know that everything is for You; so I don't say so."

"You must tell Me all the same because I love to hear it. Tell Me often. When you know that someone loves you it makes you happy when he tells you so."

September 24 — *Saint-Brieux, Canada.*

The chapel is near my room, and every time I pass by I smile at Him.

"Smile at everyone. I'll make your smile a blessing to others."

October 24 — *Montreal. (In such a gentle voice)*

"When you don't go deep into the inner stillness you deprive Me."

October 25 — *Feast of Christ the King.*

This morning at Mass, Father Boulier consecrated me to

God, placing my profession of faith in the paten under the Host.

"Take care of My Love. There isn't an orphan more forsaken than I."

November 3 — *At Mass on the liner taking me back to France.*

"Believe that in My blood there is infinite power to purify."

December — *In France, on the street.*
"I'm walking beside You."
(Gently) "But you don't talk to Me very much..."

December 14 — "Try to be My smile and My kind voice for everybody..."

December 17 — "Let us begin heaven. Moment by moment, love Me while I'm loving you."
One evening.
"Wherever you find perfect beauty and perfect charm, you find Me."

December 19 — "Sometimes you doubt that it is I speaking to you. It all seems so simple, so like yourself. But aren't we one?"

December 21 — *As I was asking Him to give me and mine all the spiritual blessings that so many people refuse, He answered:*

"My blessings are given according to measure, but I am rich enough to give you still others. Am I not the infinite One? Be simple with Me, just as you are with your own family."

December 24 — "Be hard on yourself and gentle with others."

December 25 — ''Hide in Me. Let your suffering feed the world. In this way you will be My bride.''

December 26 — ''Your imagination? It's the house dog that wanders here, there, and everywhere. Is one severe with a dog that roams about? Just act as if you had never strayed away.''

December 28 — ''When you love Me, you purify yourself. Be my grace for everyone.''

''I transform your prayers into My prayers, but if you don't pray... Can I make a plant that you haven't sown bear blossoms?''

1937

January 1 — ''Here is your keynote for the year: Purely and simply.''

January 2 — ''Offer me each little moment as it passes. This will be enough, because then your whole year will be for Me.''

January 5 — ''Express your hope in Me. Come out of yourself. Enter into Me.''

February 7 — ''Can you doubt My love?''

February 12 — ''Of course... I know all your faults and failings because you are My little girl. If you only knew how touched I am by little things...''

February 14 — *In a car.*
   ''You saw My kindness in the face of that young girl? Be like that always. If My followers were good to one another, the face of the world would be transformed.''
   ''Your longing to love — this is love...''
   ''In your soul there is a door that leads to the contemplation of God. But you must open it.''

February 17 — ''Don't fail to give Me your sufferings. They help sinners.''

February 19 — *Chateau C...*
   ''You can't come to receive Me for these three days

that you are spending so far from any church. But I'll meet you. Every morning when you awaken I'll have an appointment with you.''

The next morning I was going to forget the rendez-vous, when a little golden-crested wren perched on my window sill, and sang with such piercing insistence that I suddenly remembered.

March 1 — *In the Rhone Valley. At the station.*

''You're watching the direction in which the train will come. That's the way My eyes are fixed on you, waiting for you to come to Me.''

In the train. ''Always keep busy. You will honor Me in My constant work for your salvation.''

Watching the flooded Loire River.

''Always be serene and calm. The river reflects the sky only when it is calm.''

March 3 — *In the train.*

''My sunsets are also My love. So few of My children look at them to praise Me... and yet My love is there.''

''If you didn't have little trials, how could I give you big rewards?''

''I am the One who loves the most.''

In the evening. ''Nothing is small for Me.''

Mid-Lent — *During the procession I went into a church to console Him. To my surprise, the organ was playing in the empty naves. Some musician had evidently profited by this solitude to practice. It was like an ineffably solemn ceremony, and He said simply:*

''I was waiting for you.''

''See Me in others. This will help you to be more humble.''

March 6 — *Le Havre.*

As proof of the truth of His word in me, in the confession-al He allowed me to hear His very words from the lips of Father A... de Saint-François:

"Begin heaven. Live with Him just as you do with your family. See Christ in others."

March 9 — *I was thinking of leaving at the Elevation.*

(In a tender voice): "Don't go so quickly. I couldn't give you all My grace."

March 10 — *Crossing the Saint-Nicolas, Nantes.*

"I am no longer on earth, so take My place."

March 15 — *After the play at Brest I was thinking: 'If cir-cumstances had led me to film acting, my fame...' Immedi-ately, he interrupted me:*

"I'm keeping you for Me."

March 16 — *Notre-Dame Church.*

"Be kind. Take the first step toward your neighbour, tenderly."

"And if what you write makes only one soul stop and think!"

In the train. "Don't say 'Glory to the Father and to the Son' in such a vague way, but wish for this glory in this and that action of yours."

March 18 — *In the Puy-de-Dome, I was aching under the weight of my baggage after a night of jostling in the train, and as I climbed the steps of the 'metro' I said, "I'm carrying my cross with You, but You had someone to help You." And immediately a man walking behind me relieved me of my suit-case.*

March 20 — *At the women's detention hospital.*

"Be more kind and good than usual. The bride

resembles her bridegroom... Listen to them. It does them good to talk and to have someone listen.''

Assisi. — While someone was saying grace before our meal, I was very absent-minded.

''You think a blessing is a small thing? To Me it's very important.''

Rome. — Easter. The Minerva Church.

I was thanking Him for His suffering.

''Never will your thanks be filled with as much love and joy as I had in suffering to save you.''

Taormina, Sicily.

I was watching the women who had husbands to help them in their little difficulties as they traveled.

''But since I am with you!''

March 23 — *Genoa.*
Surrounded by people speaking in foreign languages.
''This week be one with Me in My silences.''

March 30 — *Palermo.*
''You remember when you were little, you said to Me: 'Incline my heart, O Lord, to the words of Your mouth.' ''

''Listen and I'll speak to you. Would you like to be My confidant?''

From Palermo to Monreale.

''There is more of Me in you than you.''

In the Kairouan-to-Sousse Bus.

''You remember when you were little, I said to you, 'Tell Me what you did today.' But you didn't believe that it was My voice.''

April 8 — *Sousse.*
''Return good for evil. Don't lose a single opportunity.''

April 9 — *Tunis.*

"I'll be your smile today."

"Don't get the idea that a saint is a saint at every moment. But there is always My grace."

Oran. Convent of the Trinitarian Sisters. In my cell under the stairs.

"You must aim at perfection. But the perfection of your nature. This is the way you will please Me."

And he made me understand that the work of perfection of one soul is not the same as that of another.

April 16 — *Algiers. At St. Augustine church, where I had been able to receive Communion immediately after getting off the train.*

"Shorten your thanksgiving for kindness' sake."

And as I left, I found the nuns who had missed me at the train station, hunting anxiously for me.

April 18 — *At the theater.*

"Why do you talk to Me as though I were so far away? I'm very near... in your heart."

April 20 — "Don't feel sad about a distraction even if it lasts some time. Just pick up your loving contemplation where you left off."

April 30 — *In the train, going home.*

"When something needs mending, one puts it into the hands of a craftsman. Put your soul, silent and still, beneath my loving look. I repair."

In the country. While I was planting geraniums on the terrace and twining flowers around the arches.

"Together we'll make beautiful things. I wanted to make man My collaborator, to tighten the bonds of our oneness. Love leads to union."

As I was about to leave again. "Take My gospels and

keep them always with you. You will please Me by doing this.''

May 5 — *While I was meditating on the glorified wounds of Christ in heaven.*

''Bear in mind that love and the soul's intent to love are what give actions their value.''

May 8 — *Le Fresne.*

(.....) ''Lower the lamp of love into the depths of your soul. Believe more firmly in My love.

If you must pass judgement, judge according to the good rather than the evil.

Don't go to so much trouble to make plans. I am the one who does your thinking for you.''

May 12 — *Nantes.*

I was thinking of all the Masses that had been said in my house on Avenue de Launay.

''It was quite natural and simple for Me to come there since you gave Me this house.''

And I remembered how one day I had said to Him, ''It's for both of us.''

May 14 — ''The very fabric of your being is all woven of My lovingkindness.''

May 16 — (.....) *I was thinking that I ought to offer my most insignificant moments, and He said:*

''I collect atoms — the dust of time.''

May 19 — *Paris. In the 'metro'.*

''I am the Host. You are the monstrance. The golden rays are the blessings I give through you.''

May 23 — *Gevray-Chambertin, the Gold Coast, in the midst of the vineyards.*

"Pull yourself up by the roots, and plant yourself in Me."

May 25 — *Rennes, in the train.*
"Why should you create solitude for yourself if I want you before the public? *(then tenderly)*: My beloved little child, take Me, take Me to others. Be Christlike."

May 28 — *I was thinking of Corpus Christi and He said:*
"When I have first place, the first place in every soul, then it will really be Corpus Christi."

"Don't be afraid to enjoy me. You see this little insect darting straight into the sky? You do the same. Learn to look and you will learn to see Me, your Creator."

"Do you know what goodness is? Goodness is My mother."

May 30 — *As I waited for the Nantes — Paris — Lagny train.*
"You will be My work of compassion."

May 31 — *In Seine-et-Oise.*
"When you are in church, get rid of all thoughts and cares of the day. Just put them aside as you take off a garment. And be all Mine."
In a coach, as I was tempted to be sharp with a traveler who was sharp with me. He said gently:
"The more Christian one is — that is, the more one is Mine — the kinder one is. So you be the kindest of all women."

June 4 — *Feast of the Sacred Heart. In the station.*
"Today I'll take every smile of yours for Myself."
So I decided to smile at everything and everybody.

June 8 — *In the country.*

"Don't stop at life's little details. Think only of love — the love you receive from Me and the love you give Me."

June 9 — *Le Fresne.*

"Don't pay any attention to the opinion of this one or that one. Just think of pleasing Me."

June 11 — *Le Fresne. After Communion.*
"I am the Principle and the End."
During an ordeal.
"Now it's your turn to offer."

June 12 — "Divide your day into three parts. In the morning as soon as you awaken, give yourself to the Father Creator, who offers you His Son as food. After Mass, give yourself to the Son, who is in you. And fall asleep in the Holy Spirit, who is Love."

"Music lifts man right up above this world. Then why should you be amazed that contemplating Me can be sheer ecstasy? Look at everything in the perspective of eternity."

In the street. "Take careful note of what I'm saying: It's not only by words that one can do good. A look can go straight to the soul and touch it."

"To become little, don't diminish your gifts. Just realize that everything comes from Me."

June 14 — *Nantes.* "You know sometimes I ask you to sacrifice a sacrifice."

June 15 — (.....) "Even in your thoughts you should seek Me mostly and yourself very little. Think in Me, not in you, and think just as though you were living in Me. Be like those who have their feet on earth but who talk to Me with their heads and hearts. Don't have any earthly cares. Live in Me and be concerned for My glory and whatever concerns Love. Make Me your home."

June 17 — "Everything in nature is only an image and a sacrament. Haven't you felt that the magnet is the image of My love?"

"Take the little daily trials with a smile and you will dress My wounds."

"It's because you are smaller and weaker than others that I've chosen you. Be one with Me as you suffer in your body, as though I had been mocked and scourged this morning."

June 18 — *Le Fresne. After Communion.*

"Even in a season of dryness, don't interrupt our conversations."

"You admired the carpets of all colors laid down along My route at Corpus Christi? Make more beautiful ones for Me all day long by your sacrifices and good deeds..." (.....)

June 21 — "You're amazed, aren't you, when you are told that you did good to someone in such and such a country? You see, it is not you who do this good; it is I through you. If only you knew what goes on in your soul when My blood purifies it... My grace goes farther than your soul."

June 22 — *Nantes. At the movies.*

"Wherever you are, keep Me in your love. If you could know the beauty of a soul!"

June 24 — "Be happy when you can offer a little suffering to Me, the suffering One."

June 25 — (...) "Don't see sins in what are only nature's weaknesses. What makes Me suffer is indifference."

"Take your memory in your hands and offer it to Me. Do the same with each one of your faculties. In life we always have an inner store of little worries and difficulties that can be used to make amends for our sins and the sins of others."

June 26 — "Is it because I'm God that you think I have no need of tenderness?"

"Do you think I remain silent with those who want to talk with Me? Talk with Me..."

June 27 — "I asked you to wake up in the arms of the Father because each one of your mornings is a new creation."

June 28 — "I asked you to fall asleep in the Holy Spirit because your last conscious breath should be in love."

June 30 — "Sometimes you feel Me more, sometimes less, but I never change. Don't let praying tire you. Why do you give yourself so much trouble? Let it be utterly simple and heart-warming, a family chat."

July 1 — *During Communion.*
"If you could only see My splendor at this moment!"
"Give Me your suffering. No one can give it to Me in heaven. Give it to me."

July 4 — "Now that you have given Me your suffering, ponder on Mine."

July 10 — "Don't aim at saying an exact number of wordy prayers. Just love Me simply. A look of your heart. The tender smile of a friend."

July 18 — *Le Fresne. Showing me the decorations on the altar.*

''Yes, you gave Me all that, but it would be nothing if you hadn't given Me your heart at the same time.''

July 27 — *Nantes to Le Fresne. The dear Lord said to me again, as though He wanted us to make a little more progress every day.*

''Aim beyond your usual reach to think of Me.''

July 28 — *Le Fresne. As I was hesitating to recognize His voice.*

''Don't you believe in Me? *(the Host).*

I am the defenseless God.

You see these little birds alighting on your chair, in the garden, on the table, on your hat?... Before an evil person they would fly away, I don't fly away.'' (....)

''The more you give to others, the more I'll give Myself to you.''

July 30 — *Absent-minded after Communion.*

''When a beloved person is in your living room, you don't stand at the window watching the people pass by, do you?''

August 4 — *Waiting under the trees for a bus.*

''You see how imperceptibly the year passes by, its seasons slipping away. It's like that in spiritual progress. So be patient with your slow pace.''

August 10 — *Lyon.*

''To become holy, you must first of all desire to be holy. You are born for that alone.''

August 12 — *La Louvesc, Ardèche. In the confessional Father B... said the same words He had said to me:*

"You are nothingness. Give God all the glory."

"How can You come down into this little bit of wine in the chalice?"

"With so much joy..."

August 16 — *La Salette.*

"Fathom the depths of your nothingness. Wear your qualities and your gifts like jewels given to you by your Bridegroom King."

August 21 — *The water pipe had burst.*

"Why do you think so much about these little things? Try to see them as though you were looking down from above."

August 24 — "Continue Me. Smile in your soul when you look at Me."

At table, dining in front of the garden.

"You notice how the white butterflies often fly two by two. Always be seen with Me."

August 25 — *On the terrace.*

"You doubt that it is I? Then act as though it were true."

"Keep Me company. I am your intimate One. When you read, don't be with the author of the book. Be with Me. I admit no rivals.

Set Me as a seal upon your heart.

Don't be afraid to look at My wounds; they are for you. Enter into your home...

Take from Me things old and new. Don't leave Me. Never leave Me. (....)

Enter into the realm of the mirror of peace."

August 26 — *After Communion.*

I was doubting.

"Is it because I am God that I should not have the right to speak to My children?"

August 31 — "The more light you give, the more you will keep."

September 1 — *In the garden.*
"You hear those little goldfinches chatting in undertones without ever stopping? — Bird voices. — Talk to Me like that, ceaselessly, sotto voce. — Soul voices."

September 2 — *"Lord, does Your blood wash me only at the moment when I confess my sins?"*
"Your desire to wash yourself in My heart or beneath the fountain of the cross already purifies you."

September 3 — "I'll keep you young, My bride. Shouldn't the Bridegroom and the bride be like one another?"
"Ask, ask. Often it's only after a long time of asking that you receive. Act as though your eyes were behind My eyes and you saw everything through Me."
"Lord, do you want me to spend a Holy hour with You between 4:30 and 5:30 in the morning? Is this your wish?"
"My wish is to be able to reward you later on."

September 5 — "If distractions come through no fault of yours, I give you the same grace as if you had been quite attentive."

September 8 — *Lourdes. — During the High Mass for the forty thousand pilgrims assembled before Cardinal Suhard of Reims, I was thinking of the joy of the Mother of God.*
"All women are a little of My mother."
During the procession of the Blessed Sacrament I wasn't thinking of praying in the name of His merits.

"And where do I come in?"

In the church of the Rosary.

"You will take on another face. I'll give it to you marked with humility."

At home. "Try to make everything tidy around you. This is a reflection of holiness. Strive for it."

September 12 — *In a bus I was saying "My Beloved", and He replied:*

"My beloved".

It was like a litany all along the way.

"Examine the riches of My infinity. It's like all other knowledge — you have to study it."

September 14 — *In a church.*

"Look at the stained glass windows. Some are in the shadow and have kept all their colors to themselves. Others have surrendered to the sun and are completely lost in its light."

I had come back to the old home and was enjoying the solitude near Him.

"But this is not your goal. You must keep going, keep going, just as I did in My public life. You give Me your whole self better this way."

September 15 — "Who could be happier than you, My Christians? The same Father — Mine. The same mother — Mine. And I — your Brother. Try to understand then, and be full of joy."

September 17 — *Saint-Lazare station.*

A little girl said to her father: 'Give me your hand.'

"Say that to Me often."

Seine-et-Oise. — *I said,* "I don't understand how You can love poor creatures so much."

"Can you understand the heart of God?"

In the Bretagne train. "What would you say of someone who had received jewels the mere sight of which gave joy and consolation, and then kept them secretly hidden through laziness or neglect?"

He said that because instead of talking in a friendly way, I remained silent and aloof in my compartment.

As I was dismayed at the distractions of my daily life.

"A daughter doesn't think of her love for her father every minute, but it is all alive in her heart."

October 1 — "I thought only of you when I was on earth. Think only of Me and of My glory. Give Me back your life. Never stop asking that the Spirit of holiness, the Holy Spirit, may come and take possession of you. Ask this through the one He covered with His shadow, My mother, your mother."

At Mass. "Would you have the humility to hide yourself in such a little piece of bread and in such a pittance of wine?"

"Today is Thursday. Live for the Host like another host. When your feelings are inadequate, take Mine."

"Weave the fabric of your soul, the one that will clothe it for eternity."

"It's in loving Me that one learns to love Me."

"Make Christ your whole life."

October 3 — "Your measure will be to love Me beyond measure. I'll pay you with love.

Portion off your day in order to be more sure of offering it to Me. Offer Me this visit, that letter, this piece of work. See more of Me and less of you. Rise above these little earthly cares until you think of Me alone."

October 7 — "My merits are great enough for your sinner. Ask for his conversion in the name of My merits."

As I was considering the difference between my good desi-

res and my deficiencies, He said tenderly: "My poor little girl.... Call, keep on calling the Spirit of holiness."

October 8 — *In the train, reciting the rosary.*
"Honor My mother in the Father's eternal thought because her life was the perfect unfoldment of the divine pattern for her."
"My meat was to do the will of My Father."

October 13 — *The Bordeaux station. Five o'clock in the morning.*
"Let your life be one perpetual feast... the feast of the will of God."

October 20 — *Le Fresne.*
(.....) "I want to keep you hidden beneath My arm, upon My heart."
I said, "I should like to be the wretched little donkey that carried You on its back."
"Keep in mind that it was in God's own image that you were created."
"Quicken your love of God and your neighbor. Cultivate it. Use all your wit to make it grow. This is My children's life-work.
I'm building a house in you, — a temple for My glory. Don't expect anything of yourself. Look to Me for everything."

October 25 — "Even when you are suffering intensely, there is a part of you where you can take refuge. During My passion there was nothing but torture in My whole body and soul. Pain to the quick..."
"The three equal Persons are for you, for everyone. Try to think often of their presence in you. It is Love."
(.....)

October 26 — *After Communion.*

"Why do you talk to the tabernacle on the altar when I am in your heart? You are consecrated to Me. Serve Me only."

I said, "The Lord be with you."

"Yes, I am always with you. And you? If you knew how I wait for you... how I wait for souls... Be holy in everything you do today. Call the Spirit of holiness. Ask Him to fill you with love."

November 11 — *Nice. Alone in the crowd, He said,* "Together."

"If your sight is weakening, be one with Me at the high priest's court. I could scarcely see after the blow I had from the soldier's iron glove."

"There are people that I draw into solitude even in the midst of crowds so that they may share the intimacy of My love and give Me the joy of My most faithful ones. Oh, may they not insult and pain Me by being unwilling to understand. You, child, come."

November 19 — *Vico, Corsica. The grace of hope.*

"Hope against all hope."

"Be especially tender with little children. I was once a little child."

November 24 — *Ajaccio. — The sun was setting behind the Sanguinaires Islands.*

"Are you another Jesus Christ? This is the secret of all holiness."

"And if I acted toward you as you act toward others?"

"Receive every trial as though it came from My hand. Remember how I kissed My cross."

"When you are tired, think of My fatigue."

"To be My disciple, you must not only carry your cross; you must take it."

November 28 — *As I waited with my baggage for the train in the station at Nice, I was praying that His kingdom might come.*

"Your heart is a refuge for Me. You are the only one praying in this station."

December 7 — *After Communion.*

"Repeat this often: 'Father, may Your will be done. May Your will be done. Can you imagine a world where God's will is done everywhere'?"

December 8 — *I found myself beneath His blood flowing from the cross, and He said to me:*

"Be your Christ. Be your Christ for everyone. Make Me grow in others. Make use of the gifts you have received and you will please Me.

May My kingdom come? Prepare for the coming of My kingdom by goodness and love.

The same things are not asked of every person. But I want you to follow what is written for you.

I am beauty in all its forms."

December 17 — *La Fère, Aisne.*

"Don't wait for the big events of your life to have something to offer Me. Every tiny gesture is just as great in My eyes. Offer Me everything. Pray with all your will to pray well and I'll do the rest."

When He gave me certain good ideas for theater costumes, I said to Him, "You look after these details?" And He replied:

"In my love for you nothing can be called a detail. The fallen angel didn't believe in love and he was deprived of it. Believe in My love and you will have over and above all that you ask or think."

After Communion. "Gentleness, gaiety, charm... cultivate them. I have given them to you to give to Me. Live them still more inwardly than outwardly. A child should give back everything with love to his Creator. My little instrument!''

December 22 — *Nantes.*

"Lord, I give You my day today."

"Our day... when I shall work in you more than you work."

December 24 — *Midnight Mass.*

"Enjoy it. Nothing must be lost of what I suffered for you in My passion. Bring everything into the inner stillness. Offer Me to Myself."

I was in spirit inside the wounds of His hands and as I was astonished to find myself entirely enclosed, He said to me, "My wounds can hold the entire world. Stay there *(on His heart)*, say nothing. Let us exchange our sufferings and love in secret... I live you. My child, live Me."

Christmas — "Don't you live enfolded in Love? Give Me all. Everything...

Love Me. Make amends for all the ways others are going to offend Me tonight."

December 27 — *Feast of St. John, who leaned on His heart.*

"Tell Me that with every breath of yours you breathe the love of My heart. What priceless treasure for you!"

1938

January 1 — *Keynote for the year:*

"This year you will love Me in My brothers. Do for them what you would do for Me.

If I give you favors of tenderness, it is to encourage you to stoop to make sacrifices for your brothers. Give as you have received. I want to go down to the very heart of your heart and make My home there. It will be simple and habitual."

January 2 — *While I was mending my gloves, I was wondering, "Does this count for love?" And He replied,*

"When I was planing wood, didn't this count for the salvation of the world?"

January 4 — "Consolations? Give them to others."

January 15 — *Notre-Dame. During my stations of the cross before leaving for Brest.*

"At each of the stations you will think about My love."

In the train. "Be careful. I want you to go up higher. Hide yourself in the Cleft of the Rock." *(His heart).*

January 16 — *Brest. — On the stage during Act Three of 'The Old Maid and Thirteen Youngsters', I was repeating the words, "It's not time that makes a saint; it's the will," and He said:*

"Do you have this will? Do you have it every day?"

February 4 — *I was hurt by a lack of friendliness.*

"I allowed this so that you might understand what it is for love to be rejected."

In the evening. "Confess your faults and failings of the day to Me in the secrecy of our two hearts, and I'll forgive them."

February 5 — "Go lovingly right to the end of your suffering and your sacrifice. Don't stop of your own will. Do good deeds in order to avoid laxity."

February 6 — *In the tram, I was saying my prayers mechanically as I was eyeing the pedestrians and the shops. Gently He said to me:*

"If I were just a man I should ask, 'Are you making fun of me'?"

After Communion.

"Change your nature. Be exquisitely kind. Even when your neighbor is not present, speak well of him. Keep watch on your manner, the very little touches. This is what gives charity its charm."

As I was considering the fame of certain actresses and theatrical productions, He said:

"Let Me look after you."

Moulins. In the train.

"Desire... Desire... To desire is to increase your capacity to receive."

February 8 — *After Communion.*

"The angels had not yet seen God when they sinned. If they had seen Him they wouldn't have been able to disobey Him. So look at God as much as you can. Gaze on Him.

Gaze and gaze on Him."

February 23 — *Nantes. In the avenue at 5:30 A.M., I said, "We're all alone, Jesus." And He said:*

"Say 'My Jesus'. Don't you prefer to be called 'My Gabrielle'?"

March 1 — *Shrove Tuesday.*

"The reflection of My soul on your soul before My Father... You've heard of the aurora borealis in Canada, the reflection of the sun on polar ice... What a spectacle!..."

March 10 — *In the country. I was staying in thought with the Holy Family, near good St. Joseph, the most holy Mother, and the only Son, when He said, ever so tenderly:*

"Be the little sister."

"Don't be impressed by your impressions. Do what you should do."

March 12 — *Montauban.*

I had a trial after the success of yesterday's performance.
"That was to purchase the good done yesterday."

April 1 — *Montmartre, Friday.*

"Be My gay little friend. Speak to Me as it were with smiles. So many people look upon Me as an executioner or an inexorable judge. My heart wants to be your gentle Friend. What would I not do for those who really want to give themselves to Me in confident and childlike surrender!"

In the 'metro'. "Talk to Me. Talk to Me."

April 4 — "Oh, how difficult it is for you to flow right out of yourselves and into Me!"

Chalon-sur-Saône. "Give importance only to what is eternal."

In the train. "You are consecrated to Me. Smile always. You remember in one of your plays you said, 'I'd like to be a smile merchant'."

Angers. "If you don't listen to Me, you won't hear Me."

"Be in Me. Don't be in yourself. I give you everything that I received from my Father. Give to others exactly what I have given you."

I asked Him to take care of a treasure I had in my baggage, and He replied:

"Perhaps if you lost it and accepted the loss for love of Me, it would be a greater treasure than the treasure you have now."

April 7 — *In the train between Paris and Grenoble. A young married couple were talking tenderly in the dining car.* "If only you talked to Me with the same joy... It would be so simple... so wonderful..."

Watching the high Alps, their peaks white with snow, their foothills flushed with the rose of peach trees, I was adoring His power and tenderness. I invited Him to come down into these wild regions, and so that the ice might not freeze His feet, I laid down a carpet of love.

"From now on spend your life delighting Me. You will feel transformed. Please Me. Live for Me. This is the true meaning of your godhood."

April 14 — *In the desert before the mirages I said to Him, "Perhaps I'll see You too in a mirage?" And He replied,* "Seek truth above everything else."

April 17 — *Visiting the White Fathers.*

"Ask Me for every grace. Don't ever think 'That's impossible. He couldn't give me that'."

April 19 — *In the desert, on the way to El-Goléa.*

"Plant seeds: Glory to the Father and to the Son and to the Holy Spirit — so that these places may be sanctified in honor of the Father... our Father."

April 23 — *In the desert. Oued Ouaouseur.*

"Ask Me to give you a love for what is eternal."

"You remember when you were little you said to Me, 'If some day there is anything good in me, please keep it from showing, and keep me from knowing anything about it'."

April 29 — *Carthage.* — *As I kept myself in spirit in His heart I wondered how I should find the time to be as near to the Blessed Virgin, and He said to me,* "Be in this heart formed in My mother's womb."

May 2 — *Tunis.*

"My mother lived for God alone. There was no selfishness in her, no egotism. Her life was a perfect response to the purpose for which the Creator had fashioned her. Imitate her."

May 9 — *From Tunis to Constantine I was looking at thousands of prairie flowers.*

"Daily multiply your 'acts of love' with the thought of giving joy to My eyes."

May 10 — *Constantine. Cathedral, after Communion.*

"My delight is to be with the children of men."

May 22 — *Algiers. Notre-Dame d'Afrique, after Communion.*

"I am the Living Heart."

At the Station where Christ is stripped of His garments. "Keep a careful watch on your words. Possess your poverty."

After a little suffering. "I must recognize Myself in you."

May 30 — "When you devoted a whole day to a dear

and intimate friend, do you remember how happy you were? Give Me your times of solitude with still greater joy." (.....)

"Live in the home of your Lord and Bridegroom (*His heart*). Do you believe in Him? ... Ask Me for love. Ask Me, I am burning with desire to give it to you."

June 8 — *As I was asking the Blessed Virgin for a conversion.* "A soul is costly. It takes time, sacrifices. Suffer for it. Unite your sufferings with Mine so that they may be more pleasing to the Father."

June 10 — *Anniversary of my First Communion, as I was looking at some magnificent roses.*

"That's for you, so that you may love Me more." *I was thinking of a variety of roses that fold their petals over their hearts when the sun sets, and He said to me after Communion:*

"Fold yourself on Me."

June 12 — *Versailles.*

"When you see something reprehensible in priests, instead of criticizing them, stop and ask yourself, 'Have I prayed for them?'."

"Get out of yourself. Surrender the helm of your life to Me. Let your soul be lost in Mine. Why do you want to do everything? Give Me your trust and then just let yourself drift along wherever I take you."

June 14 — *Le Fresne.*

"Talk to Me. For Me there is no sweeter prayer."

June 15 — *After a work of charity. "Give me Your goodness; mine stops half way."*

"Take everything. My little girl, for you alone I would have come down to earth, suffered, and died" *(in such a tender voice).*

June 17 — "Say 'good morning' to Me every time you awaken just as though you were arriving in heaven."

"You remember your first Communion? You didn't dare to move, you were so sure that I was in your body? Well, I am there."

June 21 — *After Communion.*

"Certainly I am there to receive your praises, but above all I'm with you to serve you. So take what you want. All of you, come and take."

"When you say 'Sacred Heart of Jesus, have mercy on us' with love, I grant more grace than for a long-drawn-out prayer that you repeat mechanically."

As I was thanking Him for the day's songsters, the blue sky, the Loire, and all the flowers.

"You thank Me for My sun, and you do well. But be just as grateful for the dark weather. Everything comes from My providence."

June 23 — *I was thanking Him for all the Hosts since my first communion.*

"They are yours forever. A Host received is eternally given. This is the treasure of the elect."

June 24 — *Feast of the Sacred Heart.*

"All that is Mine is yours. Tell Me that you share everything with Me. Tell Me often."

June 26 — *Nantes. Corpus Christi, at Notre-Dame. Under the canopy the Blessed Sacrament was waiting for the procession to go out. Few people in the church, the crowd in the square, choir boys in line. Seeing Him come out of His tabernacle I said, "You are happy, Lord?" He showed me the people and said,*

"There are My children."

It was said so simply, in tones of infinite tenderness, inex-

pressible kindness — sadness too for those who were not there, and touching gratitude for the faithful ones.

June 29 — *As I was considering the poverty of my feelings.*

"Give Me everything that you can. Go the whole way. Have the intention of never keeping anything for yourself. Give Me... I take even your shortcomings as well as your efforts to be good."

June 30 — *Feast of the Eucharistic Heart.*

"You remember Jos.? What a power of love hers was! And Eltt. and J.? The power of My heart surpasses theirs by all the distance between God and man. Just think of it. No human being is capable of loving as I love."

As I saw my countless shortcomings, I was thinking, "I'll never succeed in correcting myself."

"No, you will never succeed. But we two — together we'll succeed."

I said, "My Beloved, when shall we see each other? You see me, but I can't see You."

"Always act as though you saw Me."

July 2 — *After Communion.*

"Nothing for you. Everything for Me. Nothing without Me."

August 17 — *From the church of Clayette seen from the train.*

"An action without an intention would be like a body without a soul. You get the picture? A body without a soul."

September 2 — *At night.*

"As you begin to act, put yourself in My presence: 'Jesus is there.' Then at the end of your action say, 'My Jesus, I love you', and put your heart into it."

September 4 — *Le Fresne. As I was thanking Him for His marvelous sunshine.*

"If only to have the joy of your thanks, I would create weather like this."

September 8 — *After Communion, I asked Him to deliver me from my instabilities and shortcomings.*

"On earth you will always have these battles. Now is the time of the Crusading Church."

September 17 — "Sometimes I create frightening situations in order to test your confidence. Give it to Me often."

Bourges. — "If you have the intention of loving Me when you pray, I'll accept your prayer even when you are distracted."

September 24 — *Combourg.*

"Live in My presence in all simplicity, without any tension. Tell the world about My love... again and again. Offer Me your death now for the conversion of sinners. Be like Me.

Don't be afraid. It will be clear to others that it's not because you deserve it that I speak to you, but because My compassionate heart needs to do so."

October 4 — "Above all, confidence! When you have an anxiety and you can do nothing about it, just think, 'He will straighten that out for me' — and go back into the peace within Me."

October 7 — "A presence... you know what a presence is. Then live in My presence wherever you go."

October 8 — *Saint-Jean d'Angély.*

"Even in the joyful mysteries, My mother found suffering and sacrifices. Give Me My share in your joys."

October 11 — *Feast of the Motherhood of the Blessed Virgin.*

"Mother... not only Mine but yours. Throughout this whole day, call her your mother."

October 19 — *Le Fresne.*

"Don't you understand that I want to be always with you? Why do you act by yourself when you are in Me? I am your intimate One. Then find it impossible to think outside of Me."

October 20 — *On the train for Tours-St-Avertin. 'Grace of the mystery of the Crowning with Thorns, descend into our souls'... He said:*

"When you call upon the grace of each mystery of the rosary in this way, believe that it enters into you."

November 7 — *Saint-Rambert-d'Albon.*

I was praising Him for these touching landscapes, and He said to me:

"They are the outflowing of My tenderness."

November 23 — *Calvi, Corsica. — I was alone in the miserable nave of the little church of the Citadelle, near the ruined house of Christopher Columbus.*

"My little girl is there and she's keeping Me company."

Bastia, Corsica. — "Every day say to Me, 'I'll be better than yesterday.' And then look for opportunities to improve."

Tempted to give up the work and stay at home. "Did the apostles retreat to their homes so that they could give themselves up to contemplation?"

November 25 — *Bastia.*

"Be glad to be little, since that's the way I love you."

November 29 — *Corte. Chapel of Christ the King. I said, "Take care of me, Lord."*

"I've taken care of you to the point of dying for you. So you may trust Me."

December 3 — *Arrival of Msgr. Llosa at the cathedral. I was praying for him.*

"When you talk to My mother, be one with Me as I poured out My heart to her on the earth."

"Use your feet, your hands, and your breath as though they were Mine. What I want most is to be one with you."

"When you pray to the Father, pray with My lips."

"If you are humiliated, remember that your humiliations complete Mine. One does not feel sorry to be sacrificed to love."

December 5 — *Ajaccio, on the Solario Mountain. I was admiring the sight of the full moon and the setting sun transfiguring the milky waters of the bay.*

"I am the sun that transfigures souls."

And He showed me how His merits belong to us.

December 6 — *Ajaccio. After Communion.*

"Don't let any cloud come between us. If you do something wrong, make amends immediately by saying 'I love you' with all your heart.

Show more tenderness and respect toward your friends."

December 18 — "Humble yourself often as My mother did."

December 23 — *Bastia.*

"Do you remember when you were little how you wrote in an exercise book, 'Speak, Lord, for Thy servant heareth'?"

Christmas — *In France.*

"Don't be amazed that I called the shepherds first. They were the image of My beloved priests, My other selves."

December 25 — *Nantes, Midnight Mass.*

I was wondering why the child Jesus didn't show himself more as God even in the manger.

"That wasn't the moment. That is reserved for My second coming." *(End of time).*

December 27 — "I am the Son of God. Through Me, you are the daughter of God."

1939

January 1 — *I was desiring His glory.*

"Don't ask Me for it as though it were something that will never come. When you ask, believe that the answer will come. Ask for My glory and My kingdom this year. Then pay attention to the little things, little vanities, little exaggerations. These will be big victories."

January 8 — *Seine-et-Oise.*

"Don't be vain about anything. What does it matter to you what people think about you? Be satisfied with the thought that I know you."

January 20 — *After receiving a favor, I was thinking, "How good He is!"*

"You say that I am good at this moment. I am always good with an unchanging goodness. You must remember this if you want to keep your love alive."

I was thinking in my solitude, "If only He were here, near me in the train."

"You don't see Me, but I'm always with you."

January 30 — *As I reread His teachings, I was lamenting the fact that I had not been faithful to them for very long.*

"There are some things that I ask for one day only, and My compassionate heart applies it to an entire life."

February 3 — "My Father... our Father, He is more

yours than the father you had on earth. If only this could be a reality to you!''

I said to Him, ''I'm so poor that I don't even know what I need.''

''Make Me your provider. Why don't you ask? Don't you trust Me, the Almighty, your Christ who is Love? You should always be as simple as a little child, and have boundless trust.''

February 12 — *Nantes. 5:35 A.M. The Way of the Cross.*
''As you meditate on the stations of the cross, look at My eyes and see in them nothing but the utmost kindness and love in the midst of the torture.''

February 14 — *Nantes, after Communion.*
''Don't you understand that I am your life? I planned it all. I'm here. I'm there. See Me everywhere.''

And in returning to the house I heard about a terrible automobile accident I had escaped the previous evening at Saint-Nazaire.

February 25 — *After Communion.*
''Trust more and more in My compassionate heart. You would save more and more souls if you did. Believe in the communion of saints. My compassion stoops to your poverty. Then understand the true meaning of trust.''

March 7 — *Rennes to Nantes.*
''*Darling Father, when the time comes for me to die, if I'm in a coma You must wake me, I should like to die completely aware of the sacrifice.*''

''It's simpler than you think. Just abandon yourself.''

''Do everything with the same joy and love that you would have if you were in heaven. Seek nothing but My glory and everything else will be given to you as well. Live wholly in the kingdom deep within you.''

March — *In the Vosges.*

"Don't say your prayers just to get them finished, but saturate your soul with love. Otherwise it would be better to say less."

"When I give you power, if you keep it for yourself, it remains with you. If you share it with others it multiplies a hundredfold. Then have the courage to pass it on."

March 29 — *After Communion.*

"Say, 'Holy Father, I offer You Jesus living in my life and dying in my death. And I offer You the heart of Jesus in each one of my heartbeats'."

I was wondering, "Can I ever be made pure?"

"Everything can be made pure in My blood."

April 1 — *I was thinking of the ugliness of humanity.*

"I love you all the same, just as you are."

"Serve. Serve others. My mother said, 'I am the servant'."

April 16 — *Sfax. Quasimodo. Mass.*

"Don't you believe that when you pray I listen to you and that I love you? Pray believing and loving. Adore and give thanks. Humbly adore, trustfully adore, with faith in Me, the all-powerful One. Adore while you are loving Me."

April 22 — "Are you fully aware that it is your soul that really matters? Why should I who am Love itself, not have My moments of mysterious, secret love, — a love of My own choosing?"

When my feelings were hurt.

"Make use of your sensitivity. It was given to you so that you might merit by it."

April 24 — *After Communion. I was saying the Lord's Prayer.*

"What other prayer could equal the one I composed myself? (.....)

Love your prayers very much, the Our Father, the Hail Mary. You who love works of art, love your prayers. When you pray, I guide the words on your lips as one guides the steps of a little child."

April 28 — *After Communion.*
"Enjoy Me. Give yourself a rest from saying prayers so that you may enjoy My love."

May 2 — "Don't you see that I'm calling you to perfection? And don't you realize that the perfection of one person is of the highest gain to the whole human race?"

"Tell people to talk with Me."

"You see how gently the rain falls on the little new leaves of May? Then you may imagine how careful I am in approaching souls."

May 5 — *As I was looking at the dust on furniture cleaned the previous evening.*
"That gives you a true picture of the daily care you should take to purify your souls."

"Live in intimate communion with your Creator as I did when I was on earth, — your mind continually occupied with the Father."

"Yes, but You saw Him, Lord."

"Be one with Me, and satisfied with the thought that your Brother, the Christ, sees Him."

"What more should I do?"

"Nothing more. But do everything with more gentleness. Be more like Me."

May 8 — *Le Fresne.*
"You ask Me to help you to discover new ways of loving Me? Be one with me. Be one with Me. Be one with Me."

May 17 — "Offer yourself to Me just as you are. Don't wait to be pleased with yourself. Be one with Me in your greatest shortcomings. I take them and restore you if you put your trust in Me. Have confidence. Who loves you the most?"

May 22 — *Genelard.*

"You like making something pretty out of a worthless object, don't you? That's the way I work in souls — so happily!"

May 23 — *Lyon. With the Sisters of Saint Joseph de l'Apparition.*

"You worry about not thinking of me constantly. You worry about your many shortcomings and are afraid to look at Me any more. You mustn't do this. Just give yourself as you are. I know all about human nature. I came to help and restore. Transplant yourself in Me not because of your worth but because of My yearning.

Unite the weariness of your face with My face disfigured by blows, to make amends for your shortcomings and those of the world. Seize upon every opportunity to be one with Me. If you only knew what a joy this union with souls on earth is to Me, you would understand that I reward those who offer Me the frequent thoughts of their hearts."

In the tram. Bellecour.

"It's because you are so unworthy to hear Me that I speak to you. My compassionate Heart is like that."

May 25 — *Lyon. Saint Joseph.*

"You don't understand the mystery of the little seed that grows into a mighty tree and gives a thousand other seeds. Nor the mystery of electricity and wave lengths. Nor of so many forces scarcely known to you. Then don't be amazed at the mysteries of God. Be in love with mysteries. They are there to prove your childlike trust in the Father."

When I found myself uglier than usual.
"Love your appearance. I gave it to you."

May 26 — *5:30 A.M.*
"From the moment you wake up, intercede for others. Claim sinners from Me. You cannot know the joy you would give Me. I died for them. It wasn't illness that made Me die. I was struck down in the fullness of life. If you don't help Me today I won't be able to save this soul or that one, and you know I love them. Then save them as though you were saving Me."

May 30 — *Lyon.* — *"Is it love when my heart beats more quickly when I think of You?"*
"Yes, it is love. But it's also love when you make an effort to be good for My sake without the slightest pleasurable feeling.

Have I ever overburdened you with work? Or taken more than you could give? I measure everything."

June 1 — *Ain.*
"Write! I don't want people to be afraid of Me any more, but to see My heart full of love and to speak with Me as they would with a dearly beloved brother.

For some I am unknown. For others, a stranger, a severe master or an accuser. Few people come to Me as to one of a loved family. And yet My love is there, waiting for them. So tell them to come, to enter in, to give themselves up to love just as they are. Just as they are. I'll restore. I'll transform them. And they will know a joy they have never known before. I alone can give that joy. If only they would come! Tell them to come..." *(Voice full of yearning).*

June 3 — *Ain.*
"When you ask, believe that I am good enough to

answer you, otherwise you will deprive Me of giving."

"Be crucified with Me. To be crucified is to be stretched against your desires, against the love of self... in poverty, obscurity, and obedience to the Father.

Remember that the crucifixion is the prelude to the resurrection, that is, to all joys."

June 12 — "Live in Me. I am your principle, your fountain of life and joy, the dayspring of your being. And that is why when you see Me you will be able to say, 'I recognize You, You whom I had never seen'."

June 15 — "Give yourself to Me as you are. At any moment in your life. Just as you are.

Of course! in an instant I can change you. But you must believe it. You must put your trust in Me."

June 22 — *In the country.*
"Be very simple with Me. You know how people act *en famille*. They kiss each other affectionately morning and evening, and this is perfectly natural. And sometimes during the day some word or gift makes them exchange a loving look. There are outpourings of tenderness! Oh, if only I were allowed to be one of the family!..."

June 23 — *In the train, as I had an unkind thought about another passenger.*
"Don't judge too quickly. Don't judge people by appearances."

June 26 — "I want to in-dwell your very being. I'll live you. I am Life. Life itself. So don't have any other will than Mine, the will of My Father, and you will be rewarded on the final day."

June 27 — *"What should I expect from Him today?"*
"Everything that you have asked for in faith."

July 1 — "Go higher, still higher. With all your strength. And when you have reached a higher level, you will see that you have not even begun your ascension."

July 2 — *I had lost my reduced-fare pass.*
"Offer Me these little annoyances like your thorns to ease the pain of My own."
In the train.
"You see, you gave them nothing but a little smile, yet you did them good. You have understood Me. Try to always understand Me, then our oneness will be more complete."

July 4 — *Le Fresne.*
"If I didn't allow you to be tempted, where would your victory be? So instead of being unhappy, you should be glad. Say to yourself, 'Now is the moment to win through.' Remember when you were little how you loved to win?"

July 5 — "Don't underestimate the Holy Spirit. If you could but comprehend His majesty!"

July 10 — "Who is your God, you or I? Then why don't you think of Me more than of yourself?"

July 17 — "Is it so difficult to talk with Me? Everything that interests you, every little detail of your life, tell me about it. I'll listen with such attention and joy. If you only knew... Tell others to act with Me as they would with the intimate Friend who knows all the secrets of their hearts."

July 19 — *After Communion.*
"For love I gave myself into the hands of men who

did with Me as they wished. Now, I give Myself up in the Eucharist, and once again you do with Me what you wish. This is for love too. Right to the end. Right to the end of time.''

July 27 — ''Yes, you may offer Me your entire day as a gift from yourself. But when you join in a crusade of prayer you are more closely united with all those who are praying the same words.''

September 2 — *General mobilization of French troops (While I was folding my blankets.)*
  ''Offer Me your most ordinary actions, the smallest of them, like a bouquet of wild flowers. Aren't they loved, these little flowers of the fields? Make a crown of them for Me; it takes many little flowers to make a crown. Don't weary of placing them on My brow lacerated by the thorns. In this way you will win strength for the poor soldiers who are leaving today. This is the communion of saints. Its fountainhead is your Christ, the first saint.'' (.....)

September 7 — *I was humbling myself before Him for my many distractions.*
  ''Offer them to Me all the same. They're something of yourself. Give so that I may restore. Keep yourself often before Me, My very little one.''

September 15 — *As I was praying.*
  ''If you only had faith you would receive in a single request what it takes you years to obtain. So believe that I am listening to you and that I always answer — in a way that you may not recognize to be the fulfilment of your prayer.''

September 19 — ''If you suffer alone you are poor. But

if you unite your sufferings with Mine, you are rich.''
(.....)

September 29 — *Le Fresne. Mass.*
"Even if you do nothing at Mass but try to drive away distractions, you please Me all the same. I understand.''

October 10 — ''Don't drag your past along with you constantly if it burdens you and hinders you from coming close to Me. Just as you are, throw yourself into My arms for your joy. Can I give you anything else?''

October 18 — (.....) *"Lord, what does it mean this atonement with You?''*
"It is to think of Me. To talk with Me as with your best and gentlest friend. To seek My interests. To suffer for My cause. To be eager for My kingdom. To remember My sufferings. To set your love adrift in My love every moment of your life. And it is everything that unfolds from all this.
Love Me as best you are able. I complete.''

October 28 — *After Communion.*
"If at each of your thanksgivings you asked My mother to help you, it would be a great joy to Me.''

November 19 — *5:30 A.M. The Way of the Cross. I was saying, "I am crying out my love so loudly that You won't hear the blows of the hammers.''*
"Condemned to death... to this death... Do you realize what this is?''
"I should like to experience it, Lord, so that I could offer it to You.''
(.....) "When the love of the cross sinks deep into

a person, he lives in a joy that the world can never know. For the world has only pleasures, but joy belongs to Me and Mine, My friend.''

November 22 — *I was weary of meditating.*

''This is another reason for vocal prayer. One way of praying rests the other and in this way you stay close to Me. You mustn't lose your gaiety. You need it to soar upward.''

Nantes. — I had sewed vestments and received three priest-soldiers for dinner.

''Thank you for preparing those clothes for Me yesterday. Thank you for entertaining Me and giving Me happiness.''

November 28 — *Notre-Dame. After Communion.*

''Today you will pay attention to everything you say. You remember: 'He who does not sin in words is a perfect man.' Seek this perfection lovingly with the thought of pleasing Me. How happy I should be to see My little girl perfect... Around noon, see how you have got along.'' (.....)

''You remember when you were little and slept with your mother, I said to you, 'Every evening you will tell Me about your day', and you chased away the thought, believing that you were imagining it.''

''Lord, how much closer I should be to You now if I had approached You every day of my life.''

''We'll make up for lost time.''

December 4 — *After Communion.*

''Seek perfection. Aim at perfection in each one of your actions. At first it seems difficult. Then you learn to recognize the fact that all happiness is in this. The joy of having more of Me brings about all other joys.''

In a conversation, I had great difficulty in restraining an unkind word. But the Voice said:

"To give Me pleasure."

After the temptation:

"You see? You are happy now, aren't you? How could you compare the pleasure of having said this unkind word with the joy of having won the victory? These little victories have eternal rewards. Think about this."

"Don't waste your time thinking about yourself. Am I not there to watch over you? (.....)

What is left of all the earthbound thoughts you have cherished? And what would your treasure not be today if they had all been transformed into upsoarings to Me. Ponder deeply on this."

December 22 — "Pray a great deal for others. Pray for bigger things — for those who govern, for missions, for nations. Pray for My kingdom to come everywhere. As for you, I'm taking care of you."

December 24 — *Moonlight in the avenues. Joyful, because in a few hours it will be Christmas.*

"Oh, yes, be full of joy. Do you know what the world was like before I came? There was God and there were men. Now God has become a man among men — one of you. What love! What potential oneness between you and Him! Do you really feel the difference? Then thank Me with all your heart and all your mind and all your soul, and be Mine more than ever."

After Communion.

"Here is the Savior, the Messiah men called and longed for. The Savior of the world and of each one of you, — your Savior. Ask Me to save you from your daily faults, your deplorable habits, all the wretched you in you, and I'll save you from them. Look for ways of multiplying loving deeds and refraining from sins of the tongue. Say to yourself, 'He'll be happy'.''

December 25 — *Christmas at the cathedral.*

''Christians of today!... Others have passed before you. Still others will come after you, soul upon soul in the Father's sight. Christians of today!... In your short time on earth, give Me the utmost of your love for My glory. Oh, may your period in the history of the world be for My heart a golden age of abundant harvest!''

December 26 — *After a meeting with young people.*

''Take your soul in your hands and look at your day. Weigh up the love you have given Me during the hours that have gone by. And remember: you will be judged according to the measure of your love.''

After Communion.

''Try to avoid the smallest faults. This is your work, since you have been called to holiness, and holiness is the absence of any wilful faults. It's a work of love. Of love... do you understand?''

Stations of the Cross. First Station.

''You would condemn Me to a kind of death if the jumble of your earthly thoughts beclouded the thought of Me.''

1940

January 1 — *After Communion, as I was asking Him for the keynote for the year:*

"Prayer... At-onement."

January 2 — *After a very mediocre day.*

"You see that you can do nothing by yourself. Throw yourself into My arms every morning and ask Me for strength to pay attention to the little details.

Life is made up of little things, you know. Don't count on yourself any more. Count on me."

January 5 — "The days that lie ahead of you are fewer than those behind you. Then you and I should spend this last period of your life like two beings in perfect accord, heart calling to heart before they come face to face.

My little friend, aren't you loved like a very little one, the weakest of all?"

January 17 — "You don't always feel Me in the same way, but don't let the darkness hinder you from going forward. Humble yourself and go on your way faithfully. Keep going. You don't see Me or feel Me, but I'm there — Love itself, holding out My arms to you. Nothing ever makes Me lose sight of My children on earth. Their ideas and thoughts are short-lived, and so they imagine I am like them in this. But I am perfect Poise, the same yesterday, today and forever. I am the Presence, the loving Look. The entire cosmos is cradled in Me. I am this second of time and I am Eternity. I am the lavishness of Love, the One who calls so that you may come without fear and throw yourself upon My heart. I call. You, at least you, My child, be the response.''

January 26 — *In the freezing cold train. Valencia.*
''If I had another way of bringing you closer to Me than suffering, I would choose it.''

Forty Hours.
''Don't you understand that the bonds of My union with a soul must be tightened as it draws near to eternity? Try to be no longer in yourself but in Me. You were touched when you read that I was in the gospels, hidden in the sacrament of the words. But how much more am I present in the sacrament of man himself. Oh, My children who live in grace, let us never leave one another.''

In a moment of doubt.
''But you readily admit that there is a soul in your body, don't you? And yet you don't see your soul. Then why have you so much difficulty in admitting that I live in you when you are in a state of grace, even though you can't see Me? I am there. Don't leave Me alone. Talk to Me.''

February 2 — *In the morning.*
'' 'Give back your soul...' How true this expression is. I gave you your soul; I enfolded it with such love. You must give it back to Me with your utmost affection and tenderness to honor Me who first loved you.

So when I come to pluck you, beloved soul, give Me your breaking like a fragrance.''

February 18 — *At the Elevation.*

"I am the one who atones. Place all your sins, beginning with the first, on the altar, and speak to the Father tenderly of your sorrow."

"Your little share in any action is your love-will. Bring it to everything you do, and you may expect all the rest from Me."

"Every Christian in a state of grace is another Christ. They sometimes say that there are several men in one. The Christ was all men. He bore all their sins. Be one with Him when He was you, when He took on Him the burden of your shortcomings. On earth you cannot understand the compenetration of Christ in each person. He was God in man. His power of salvation was infinite, His divinity never having left His humanity. Treat Me as the most intimate One who not only excuses the sins confided to Him but who takes them upon Himself in order to obtain the Father's pardon."

February 24 — *After Communion I was asking Him to engrave faith, hope, and love upon my heart.*

"I do this when you believe that I am going to do it. But afterwards you must cultivate the seeds I have sown." (.....)

March 1 — "Hasn't it ever occurred to you that this or that grace was given to you because of some prayer said for you, or some priest's blessing, or what your parents won by their efforts, or because of My divine compassion, or the goodness of My mother? Don't ever get the idea that the cause is any goodness of your own or anything in yourself."

March 5 — *After Communion.*

"When you see that your will is suddenly going to run away with you, just put your hand in Mine and look at Me and then it will go My way for My service."

March 6 — "You know how cold and sad an empty house is, how different from one that's filled with youth and life and joy. That is the difference between a soul where I cannot live because sin has driven Me out and the soul that I in-dwell. Say to yourself often, 'He is in me', and love your Host wherever you take Him. Tell Him everything that your love inspires. Tell Him simply, very simply."

March 7 — "Perhaps I created you only to console Me and to give Me a refuge in your heart where you sing Me the hymn of love. Why shouldn't I have a home on earth? Must I still have no stone on which to rest My head? Open to Me. Fling the doors of your heart wide-open, dear little one."

March 11 — *After Communion.*

"This is the test of your faithfulness to Me: When you are working, work well; when you are occupied with your business affairs, give your whole attention to them. But during the hours of prayer and love, let nothing distract you from Me. You enter into Me; there you abide, looking after Me and My interests. Follow this from now on, my faithful child."

After an unkind word.

"My little child, be afraid of being less holy than the one you are running down."

Lord, I should like to talk with you with as much grace as the first woman when you came to visit Adam and Eve in the Garden of Eden."

"But you have much more cause for loving Me than your first parents. I was only their Creator and Benefactor, the One who gave them Light, whereas I am your Savior and Redeemer, your tender Victim, Love unveiled. I do more than visit you. I in-dwell you. You partake of Me as food. I never leave you unless you drive Me away. Then find within you heart-melting words of love.''

March 12 — ''Sometimes you say, 'If only one could have several lives!'

Instead of that, every morning awaken to the thought that a new life is given to you, and make better use of it than yesterday. You see how rapid your progress in perfection would be? No, perhaps you wouldn't see it. But I know everything.''

Palm Sunday — *Nantes cathedral.*

''Is it a reality to you that I have bought you? purchased you with pain?... Then you are Mine much more than you can ever believe.''

March 25 — *Aboard the Nantes-Fresne train.*

''And now that you are coming to the end of your life, sing your hymn of thanks to Me every day. Because I gave you this life. It was a free gift, you understand? And yet I foresaw all your ingratitude. I gave it to you with the thought of all the happiness that I am preparing for you. Oh, My children, you are My extravagance of love.''

March 29 — *In the country. In the great hall: ''Perhaps I talk to You too familiarly?''*

''But since we are on family terms nothing could give Me greater pleasure. One who understands My desire opens his heart at all times. I have so much love for a soul that its faintest call finds an echo in Me. Don't be afraid of expressing yourself. Put your mouth to My ear. I'm listening.''

While I was digging around the hydrangeas.

''Be one with Me in My toil as a carpenter. It is not what you do that matters, but the way you love Me while you work. And love is oneness. Give Me the spectacle of a soul engulfed in its Savior, and this will be joy, My joy.''

In a country church, seeing that I was making no progress, I said, ''Lord, I've come to the end of looking after myself, so I'm putting myself entirely in Your hands''.

''If you only knew what a joy it is for Me to count for something in a life at last. I can make a new woman of you.''

''When you were little you wanted someone to take your hand when you crossed the street. Ask Me often to take your hand, because you are always little. Don't ever think that you can do anything good without Me.''

March 30 — ''You love our solitude? But I want you to know that if you leave Me for some social duty you please Me just as much. And if you leave Me for a work of love, you find Me. A day will come when you will never leave your Savior and God.''

April 2 — *Before receiving guests.*
''Make everything tidy and attractive remembering that I am the Master of the house.'' (.....)

Visit to the Blessed Sacrament. I said, ''Do I even know that I love You? What a strange love one gives to someone one has never seen.''

''That is the love that pleases Me. What merit would there be in loving Me after you had seen Me? This is the test of life. Pass through it victoriously.''

April 7 — ''Even by your ordinary actions you can make amends for ingratitude and save sinners. I saved sweeping the workshop. Always be one with Me.''

April 9 — ''Don't think that a saint must appear saintly in the eyes of men. He has his outward nature, but it is the inner nature that counts. There is fruit whose rough, even thorny skin gives no inkling of its sweet and juicy taste. That's how it is for My saints: their value is in their hearts.''

April 12 — *The Way of the Cross.*
''I should like you to follow Me without any stress or strain. Just go along My path beside Me very simply, ready to give Me the delicate touches of your tenderness that I'll enjoy 'as if it were all real'.''

April 14 — ''Aren't you going to enter the period of the long trust? Aren't you beginning to understand that the words of your prayers have been shaped like arrows, not to beat the air, but to go straight to the heart of the Father who receives them with love? Every prayer has its arrow. Be certain of receiving an answer. A Father, just think of it! If He doesn't give you the answer you were hoping to get, it will be another — a better one... But you are heard by the One who is enthroned in your very center.''

April 15 — *I was listening to some children playing.*
''I love children. It is I who gave them all these delicate thoughts and feelings: complete trust, docility, a thirst for Jesus, candor and purity, absolute surrender and the forthright glance. You must keep the same sentiments with you right through life. For they come from Me and I so love to find them again in you when you are grown up. So find your child-soul again and give it to Me.''

''Lord, is it possible for everyone in the whole world living in our time to be saved?''

''All things are possible through the merits and the Name of Jesus Christ.''

April 18 — "Ask My dear mother to help you respond to My tenderness with your own. Alone you cannot, you cannot, you cannot."

April 19 — *Before Communion.*
"Consider the height — the greatness of the gift. The depth — God himself. The 'breadth — the gift for everyone' in My Eucharist. And bring others to It."

April 22 — "*Lord, have you advanced this work of holiness in my poor soul that I gave back to You?*"
"Don't let anything shake your faith. Look at Me often. Look at Me always. This is the most direct route — the shortcut. You learn many things in the Cleft of the Rock, My little soul."

May 4 — "Today I ask you to keep your mind in a state of naked simplicity, your thoughts rising pure like candle flames toward My power and majesty and toward My love of Father and Bridegroom.

Even if you don't see the result of your prayers or efforts, don't let this hold you back. Just keep in mind that I know everything, and place yourself once more in the hands of your Redeemer. Remember this: I'll be for you what you want Me to be. If you treat Me as a stranger, I'll be only a judge. If you trust Me, I'll be your Savior. If you live in My love, I'll be your loving Bridegroom, the Being of your being."

May 9 — *Holy Hour.*
"Today you will be the one who speaks to Me. You see, I'm here listening to you with all My heart."
I said, "Pity me, my Savior, as I pity You."
"Don't you think that My pity is greater than yours? *(As though smiling).* But this is only natural...

You come to Me so that I may gift you. You show

your pity for Me by easing My heart, always so eager to give. Oh, My little children, let Me enrich you. Give Me every freedom to sanctify you; can you beautify yourselves… alone? Call Me. Stretch out your hands to Me. Look at Me very simply and trustfully. Think, 'He is great. He can do whatever He wishes, and He is my Father, my Friend'. After that…

Ask the Father to let Me live in people. How could they be said to live if they don't cultivate My life in them? How wonderful it would be if I were there like a guest, the dearest of all guests, the one surrounded with every attention by night and day, knowing that every little act of tenderness touches His tenderness and that His poverty is often so great that the smallest offering pierces Him with love!''

May 10 — *Vigil of Pentecost.*
I was thinking, ''The Holy Spirit must give grace to celebrate His feast.''

''The grace He gives is not just for His feast. It is for always. He doesn't take back what He has given. How could Love ever take away His gifts? Ask Him. He will heap grace upon grace. Simplifying.''

I was thinking of the holiness of the Blessed Virgin, who harmonized with every grace. ''Dear Mother, give me a little.'' And He answered:

''My little girl, all My merits are yours. They are for all My children. You are My heiress, My child, by the communion of saints. But you must believe this and speak to God about it.''

May 11 — *When I had an obsession.*
''You know what that is — just a fly. You brush it away once, several times; in the end it always goes away. Your little spiritual trials are your devotions. Be patient and cheerful.''

At Mass, before the elevation (gently).

"On the way to Calvary, the crowd jostled Me and I fell to the ground. My robe was soiled and although I was not going to wear it much longer, even in the midst of so many other sufferings, I was distressed about it because My mother had given it to Me."

"You see, I'd like to spare you trials because I love you. And yet at the same time I'd like to give them to you because I love you and because I can see the reward."

May 21 — *Battle of Arras. Departure of the Belgians. Battle of Vervins.*
"Comfort all those who are suffering as you would comfort Me."
German invasion. As I was praying for victory.
"Do you want the salvation of the country or that of souls? Look upon the salvation of souls as more important. Renewal comes from humility, and glory from humiliation."

May 25 — "Awaken your trust in My omnipotence. This is what honors Me. It can change the face of the earth when it is matched with the feeling of your nothingness. Remember the centurion."

May 29 — "My grace? Often you do not see it. But it grows like a seed. Only you must make the earth ready for the planting."

May — *On the terrace.*
"Lord, what is love for God made of?"
"The will."

June 2 — "I gave you everything, even My mother."

June 3 — "Love Me in any and all of your doings. Where is the one who will give Me the joy of beginning his heaven on earth? Will you? Love Me unceasingly, that is all."

June 6 — *The Way of the Cross. I was offering it for France.*

"Remember that every event comes by the will of God. See Him in this and it will help you."

June 13 — Holy Hour.

"Have this blessed assurance that the anxieties and toil of the world are not to be compared with the reward. And the reward is your Christ. Just think of it!

So take heart. Bear everything for love in order to win Love. To win paradise, to win the eternal God... there is your work. You have seen how ephemeral everything of time is. But remind yourself of that understanding you had of eternity. It was as though you had always just arrived and the earth seemed so small to you, a mere point, so far away and like a dream. Then since you are still in the midst of earth's battle, accept the loss of everything. You will find everything again, and for always.

Do you believe in My love?"

"Yes, Lord."

"Do you firmly believe in My love?"

"Yes, Lord."

"Do you always believe in My love?"

"Yes, Lord."

"Then give yourself in your wholeness to Me without ever taking yourself back. That means denying your preferences, wanting My joy and My kingdom of love. It means forgetting yourself and remembering Me — My Being — not an exacting tyrant but a Lamb slain for love."

"All of you one: one body, one soul, one prayer. I

choose some only to reach the others. Let us be one, all of us together.''

June 19 — *Escaped providentially in a livestock train as far as Nantes. After that in a good second-class coach with kindly people. Twenty-four hours in the Luçon station. Then in a cheese truck with ten Ursulines fleeing from Beaugency. Put down at Curzon near La Tranche, I was thanking Him for all His care.*

"One would say You had not left me for a single instant.''
"Did you doubt it?''

June 20 — *Curzon. In the beautiful fifteenth-century church. After Communion.*

"All day long remember that My body has lived in your body. Even your gestures will take on gentleness from this. Bring as it were a spring tide of graciousness to this country. The misery of others is Mine. Give comfort with your little cheering words. Don't ever grow weary. You know that I'm there.''

I noticed with distress that the enemy had come quite close.

"But who should utterly abandon themselves to Me if not My most intimate friends, My chosen ones? So practice this abandonment frequently in these hours that have struck for your people and you will please Me so much, My little child.''

German invasion. Taking refuge at C....

"Give Me your trusting thoughts. They honor Me as an incense to My goodness. Haven't I told you that as you have believed so you shall receive? So don't be afraid if the Germans come. It will be I in you who will receive them.''

"Now is the hour of trial. Lose nothing of it.''

In the clearing of a solitary wood where I often came to think of Him, hosts of butterflies crowded around the purple clover.

"You see, even in nature they all need each other. No living creature escapes from the duty of giving itself. Give, My child; My children, give as I Myself gave. The habit of giving — what an armor of power and joy! This is the negation of self. This is My public life after My nights of prayer."

June — "You see, there is a way of ceasing to think of your little anxieties: just think about Mine."

June 26 — "With Me, do everything well: the ordinary things in imitation of My hidden life, and the difficult things in imitation of My public life."

June 28 — *Curzon. Stations of the Cross.*
"Tell Me that it doesn't bother you to go along beside Me. What you do cheerfully for Me pleases Me more."

"I am in the position of one who fears to impose on his friend and so is overjoyed when that friend expresses his ever new happiness to be with him. I am not an exacting Master. I am the fulness of love. So give yourself with open arms. You know how little children leap to be caught and lifted up into the arms of their father."

July 4 — *Return to my home which I found full of German officers. I understood what He had said to Me on June 20:*
"If the Germans come, it will be I who will receive them."

His bust had been uncovered and He was presiding in the living room where the enemy slept.
"Always speak to My goodness since you know it. I am here for you. For your littleness I have My greatness and My power. Make use of your elder Brother. Above all, don't doubt. Seeing in the dark — there is your victory! Being sure, with the assurance of love."

July — *After a cutting word.*

"I permitted that in order to reward you for the humiliation you gaily accepted for My kingdom. My triumph will be made out of such wounds."

"Then give me many others, Lord."

"I make your garment to measure."

July 19 — *Distraction after Communion.*

"That's nothing. Can one stop the leaves from stirring when the wind blows? But take Me back right away into your thoughts, just as though you had never left Me.

I take My rest in people who give themselves to Me; the more work I have to do in them, the more I rest. And while I'm working in you, if you keep your eyes on Me all day long, my work will be more fruitful."

July 25 — "Be just as gracious toward the little ones as toward the great ones. Make an effort particularly when you are with people who seem vulgar to you. Go to everyone with the same gentleness. You are all brothers in Me. Wasn't I everyone's Brother? Don't take your eyes off your model."

August 8 — *Holy Hour.*

"Don't be discouraged. There are many ways of advancing, even by your stumblings. Call out to Me. Don't be afraid to cry if you fall. But let your cry go straight to your matchless Friend. Believe in My power. Didn't I catch hold of Peter when he was sinking beneath the waves? And don't you think I'm more ready to help you than to lose you?

My poor little girl, how little I am known!" (....)

I was thinking of my weaknesses.

"The smaller and weaker a child is, the more closely one holds it to one's heart."

August 21 — *"Lord, since all time is present before You, see my desire right now to offer my death as a perfect sacrifice of love and repentance."*

"Remember... My very little flower that I coaxed into bloom, give Me your breaking like a fragrance."

"Don't be astonished at being fragile; but place your fragility in My strong hands."

August 22 — *Le Fresne.* — *Holy Hour.*

"Lord, before I die, won't I have some inspiration greater than the rest? Won't there be some more heroic effort? Or am I going to vegetate in my usual petty ways?"

"Take power from the power of the saints. From the power of the Holy One. Be one with them. Give Me the joy of helping and transforming you. Surrender everything. Let yourself go. Tell Me often about your great longing. Do you think I would resist? That would be to misunderstand Me. If you are generous, how much more am I! You know the violent wind? the bird of prey? I too carry off. I am the Ravisher. Don't struggle. And because you let yourself be taken captive, I'll bring you into my secret garden among the flowers and fruit. You will wear the wedding ring on your finger. Your step will be in tune with Mine and I'll stoop down to your littleness so that we may talk together easily. How beautiful it will be like that My friend, My little soul. You too will ask Me for pavilions... But we shall make only one. And as you gaze on Me you will understand that the suffering that passes leads to life eternal, and you will say, 'How simple it is!' Because in love, everything is simple. You will say, 'You were nothing but goodness and mercy and I didn't know it.' Then the veil will be rent and you will have the face-to-face vision of all that I suffered for you. Now you are working and fighting in the dark, in the night... But even now you must say, 'Lord, I believe, I adore

You in the mystery of it all. To whom should I go but You'?''

"Then surrender yourself to Me in peace... Oh, may I have the consolation of leading My little girl wherever I wish. Would you like to come with Me, keeping your eyes closed?''

August 26 — ''May the invisible be more present to you than the visible.''

August 27 — *Visit to church.*
"If it wearies You to talk to me, say nothing today.''

"But it rests Me to talk to you, to put a little of My heart into yours, My child... So say to Me often, 'Your little servant is listening'.''

"Lord, set fire to France; set fire to society.''

"They must desire this; they have only to desire Me and I'll wait no longer to come. How long I've waited for them! Pray as best you can. Help them. Help Me. Be the poor little stone that no one notices, the one that lets loose the avalanche that fills the abyss.''

August 29 — *Holy Hour.* — *"Glory be to the Father and to the Son and to the Holy Spirit present in me.''*

"Even if you were to do nothing but repeat this wish for the whole hour, you would not have wasted your time, since not one of your prayers goes unheard. If people only knew how attentive the Father is to the actions and words of His little children; for in fact many of them remind Him of His only Son toiling on earth.

The Holy Trinity is in each one of you, more or less according to the room that you allow It, for, as you know, God never forces anyone. He asks and waits. And when you are faithful, you are sure of the joy — I was going to say the celestial joy — that it gives heaven. Keep this thought always before you: it is when you are living on earth that I enjoy you, My beloved faithful ones. But in heaven it will be you who will enjoy Me.

My little children, consider My simplicity and how easy it is for you to please Me. It means only doing everything that you do as well as you can for My love's sake, in order to grow, to advance, to go higher. Hold out your two weak arms to me. I'll help you. We'll do the work together in unequal shares. It is for the Father to shoulder the heavier end of things. And if the little child fixes his eyes lovingly on the Father's eyes the painful task will seem so little. A look of love... what power for you! what joy for Me! Anyone who loves Me has the right to see Me. Even if you loved Me each day with a heroic love, it would be so little compared with the love you will have for Me throughout all eternity. Then love Me continually. Tell Me about it and live your love-of-Me. I'll receive it day by day, new in your heart and ever new for Me. Do I ever grow weary of you?''

September 12 — *Le Fresne. Holy Hour.*
''Never drink your cup of pleasure to the last drop. Keep a little for Me as a sacrifice — My part — you understand what I mean? since in secret we are together in everything. If you took it all, what would I have? You would be alone with yourself. 'May God be with you!' Otherwise you force Me to stand by and watch you without merging with you. Oh, this desire of My eternal love for oneness. I begin My life on earth again with each one of you — My life wedded to yours — if you want to invite Me. You remember how I walked with the disciples of Emmaus?... I do this for you. I walk along the same path with you, the path that I chose for you from all eternity — in this family, in this country where you live. It is I who placed you there

with a special love. So live there, full of faith, remembering that there is where you will win heaven, where you will win eternal love for this brief moment in time... So pass through this life with the great desire to respond to all My tenderness and with constant impatience to know Me at last — to know Me, your loving Savior. Haven't you always been a thought in My eternal mind? It would be only just for yours to be filled with Me, My poor little children, so often ungrateful.''

"Lord, can we always make amends, even for the faults that we are not aware of, but that Your sensitivity sees?"

''Don't you know that because of My compassion a single act of perfect love atones for a whole lifetime? that one humble and tender look from you pierces My heart with love? that I am sensitive to every cry of your hearts?

Sometimes I stand at the door waiting even before you call Me. Do you remember this or that danger you escaped? And you believed it all happened by itself. Nothing happens by itself. So never lose sight of My watchful, kindly providence. And thank Me for My invisible care. My love loves to plan for you and does everything for your good.

In this hour of agony for your country, see My infinite quest for souls. I am like a hunter who would let himself be wounded to death in order to lure His coveted prey. I am the one who has caught the leprosy from the leper He loves. I have suffered all things, for I have known all things. I have atoned for everything. I, the pure One, by My blood which flowed drop by drop. Then let no one be afraid to come to Me. The greatest sinner will know the joy of being pressed to My wide-open heart. But let him come without any fear; it's easy enough if he keeps his mind on Me rather than on himself... And it will be his path of peace. Go with your prayerfulness and find sinners for Me. Go and seek them.''

September 14 — ''Live in My heart. You've discovered the warm nest of the golden-crested wren, hidden in your acacia tree? It's within reach of any hand, but invisible.

Invite the angels to help you in your upward climb. So great is My longing to have you come nearer. I have so much to say to you, so much to give you... Come. Nearer, always nearer...''

September 19 — *Holy Hour.*

(.....) ''A presence... How much there is in a presence! You do everything — work, prayers, thinking, talking — just as though I were there, and I actually am there. Don't you find this infinitely wonderful? When you wake up, I'm there. When you rest, I'm there. So you can say, 'He never leaves Me alone.' This is what makes your solitude divine.

After the death of your faithful maid, you remember how you hesitated at the thought of being waited on again? I invited you to remain alone; I said, 'Would you love Me enough to do this?' And now you regret nothing, do you? Together we have gone through the years, the evenings of solitude.

You tried to come closer to God and I helped you, for you were able to unite your aloneness with Mine. Have you ever known the desert — the forty days, the nights when I escaped from everyone to pray before My Father? And among the crowds have you known the vast solitude of not being understood, of hostility, of hate, of rejected friendship? It was all for My children — for you, My child. And later there was the solitude of the Garden of Gethsemane. The solitude of churches for My Eucharist, and of the hearts who forget Me after receiving Communion. Oh, may the warm and faithful thoughts of My friends come unceasingly to comfort Me! And I shall comfort them when they fall asleep to awaken in that other Life.

It's a strange thing, isn't it, that a creature can comfort his God. And yet this is a fact. My love reverses the rôles, inventing a new way for people to reach Me, by allowing them to give Me a protecting tenderness. So great is My need of all your ways of loving, all your ways of being tender.''

September 21 — ''To offer a sacrifice doesn't mean that you won't feel the pain of it; on the contrary, the pain will return many times to stir up its bitter waters. But at each new tide of distress, come back again to Me in a spirit of sacrifice, and a rainbow of blessings will light up the earth. So many things are invisible to you. They emanate from your actions like a healing aureole. You know how evil tends to spread and gain ground? Then why should I not give love the blessed and all-victorious wings of light. Who can stop the flight of good from soul to soul right to the very end of the world? Will you ever know the consequence of one or another of these lines read through the lens of My love? Yes, ask Me that everyone may find joy and comfort in them. Can I deprive Myself of giving you anything?''

Holy Hour.

''See how important the sun's rays are for the things of the earth. Will people ever understand that God is their life-giving sun, the great Enchantor of all their days, the unique Goal of their existence?

Keep in mind this prayer, 'Lord, deliver me from anxiety about trifles!' Everything is insignificant apart from God whose life in you you should daily seek to increase. In the next life you will ask yourself, 'How could I ever remain a single instant without loving Him?'

With your merit in mind, I wanted you to seek Me in the darkness and to discover Me again in the half-light. Light untold will be for later on. Didn't I Myself pass through dark hours when My divinity seemed to drift apart from My humanity? How I fraternized with you, taking upon Myself all your weaknesses, My poor little ones. I was indeed 'a man' among men. And even before My passion, I knew what suffering was. I loved it for the love of you, My children. Love it for love of Me. I'll transform it into transformations for others, and into glory for you, since you find everything again in heaven. So take courage for suffering, My little children. There are some people who can't do without suffering so deeply have they experienced how it brings them close to Me. Although I love you unceasingly, I look with special love upon My children who suffer. My look is more tender, more affectionate than that of a mother. Of course... isn't it I who made the heart of a mother?

Then turn your sorrowful eyes upon Me. Show Me your suffering, My dear little ones. You are already in My heart even though you thought you were so far from Me, so far. Day by day try to find Me in you, and there, like very little children, give Me the marks of tenderness that you would give to a mother or a beloved father. How happy you will be when you have acquired this habit. How sweet your life will become!

And I'll bless you, because you will at last have responded to My call... the call of the One who stood at the door listening to the life stirring in the house, and wondered whether it would welcome Him or not. For if He stands outside waiting, it is because He knows that He may be driven away. Sometimes they don't even want Him to wait. They say, 'Never will You come under my roof.' As though He were an evil-doer, He who died for love of them... But when they say, 'Come in, and stay with us,' then this poor, lonely One knows the joy He describes as 'His delight to be with the children of men.'

This is something unknown to you, but God knows it. And you will learn later on how much delight you have given your Savior..."

Visit. I said, "Lord, I love You."

"Say it again, so that it may chime once more on My ear. Prolong its vibration like music. Never shall I grow weary of listening. Tell Me why you love Me and how this love began; tell Me all that you want to do for My love. Of course, I know all about it, but to hear it from you is a joy to Me like a story ever new."

After lunch. In the heat, I lay down for a rest.

"Rest with My moments of rest. If you were not one with Me, it would be better for you to be breaking stones on the Sahara road if such toil would tighten the bonds of our union.

As I often tell you, no matter what you may be doing, it is this love-oneness that you bring to it that alone gives it value."

September 30 — *Visit.*

"Of course you often have to be busy with material things during the day. But do even these common tasks with Me, near Me, because I did them too when I was on earth, and because I am there. I never leave you... (.....)

Give Me everything with your will firmly intent on pleasing Me. How astonished you will be when you discover your treasures. It takes only tiny little stones to make flowers in magnificent mosaic floorings."

October 11 — *Holy Hour.*

"You, who are there, I want to ask that You be loved by everyone. I should be so happy, Lord!"

"Not only ask Me, but offer all that you do for this. Nothing could bring Me more balm, for although it may seem strange to you, there is grace that I cannot give unless you ask Me for it.

This grace is the work of two — your Christ and man. You know how much I love to be one with you. We each have our share, and since I never impose on you, you must invite Me; you must make Me act with you. In this way I live My life again on earth.

That is why I sometimes say to you, 'My little girl, continue Me.' Your life is a gift from me; give it to Me in all your actions. Don't you feel the greatness of it — to make God live. And it's so simple. If you only knew!

Just imagine what it would be like if at this moment all the people on the earth let Me live in them by grace. What a spectacle for heaven! Because you are all performing before the angels and saints *(As though smiling).* You see, you are still on the stage...

If you thought about this how much more effort you would make to do everything perfectly. And if you remembered that I never let you out of my sight — that this is a reality — wouldn't you be more careful? Wouldn't you love Me a little more?

My poor little ones, don't neglect anything that can increase your tenderness. In that alone lies your happiness. As soon as a truth or a thought touches you, keep it in your soul the day long and look at it as though you were seeing Me in a mirror.

Call Me very often. Isn't an earthly father happy when his little one calls him? Sometimes he doesn't answer, so that the child will call again. You remember My seeming refusal of the Canaanite woman? I wanted to lead her to her beautiful answer so full of humility... And so if I seem not to hear you, call Me again and you will give Me joy.

I'm always eager for you — above all for My very little ones, My very poor ones. The weakest are already right inside My heart. Oh, happy unfortunate ones!''

October 17 — *Holy Hour. Feast of St-Margaret Mary.*

(....) ''How grateful I am to those who console Me for the refusal of others and to those who call Me and long for Me. Yearn for Me often, I was going to say always, so eagerly does My heart wait for you. My handmaid Margaret Mary knew this and made Me happy, for it was as though our two hearts were living together. O My Gabrielle, let us have the same home on earth, since we shall have the same one in heaven!

Let us begin heaven. It would be such balm for Me. Do you want to give joy to your Savior-God? Then let your thoughts forever turn to Me.(....)

Hide Me in your heart as though in this way you could save Me from wounding insults. For I receive them, above all in My Holy Eucharist. There, in your heart, thank Me, adore and console Me. Tell Me about yourself as I so often tell you about Myself, My little girl. Be very little; the smaller you are, the more your great Friend will in-dwell you.''

October 20 — *23rd Sunday after Pentecost.*

''Jesus turning around, saw her and said to her, 'Be of good heart'.''

''I turned round for you too, for I had already passed by. And you had not noticed. Now that you have recognized Me, don't let Me ever pass by without taking hold of Me. I do not always turn round.''

October 24 — *Holy Hour.*

"Allow me, Lord, to console You in Your agony as though I had been created for that alone."

"Direct everything in you to this end — all that I have given you, for it is I who gave you everything — your heart, your understanding, your memory. It is I who gave you an imagination capable of stirring your heart. Is it too much to expect that you will use My gifts for Me? When you offer them I forget that I have given them to you. I receive them as though they came from you, and My heart is so touched. If you only knew…! I am like a happy father: 'My little girl did that for Me.' And I am much more than an ordinary father. But only in heaven will you see these delicate touches I've received from my children.

Let this encourage you to live very close to Me, to find life impossible without Me. Let Me share everything. Disappear ceaselessly in My heart. And be sure that I'll replace you. Always act as though you saw Me, for I am really there. And aware of the great yearning, the intense thirst that I have for souls, surrender yourself unceasingly as though it were for the first time. For Me, it will always be like a first joy to receive you.

Don't get the idea that it is the greatest number of prayers that touches your God. It's the way you speak to Him. Be irresistible in love, abandonment and humility. And when you ask Him for bread, He will not give you a stone, but a double portion… When you tidy your house, think that it is Mine and you will make it more beautiful. When you prepare your meals think that it is to honor Me. And when you rest your body, think that it is My body, My friend; and this is the reality, since all that you have is first Mine, isn't it? You will see Me everywhere. I'll be your Host and your Guest, the One who receives and the One received.

The One who has taken your heart and asks the free gift of it. Two lives in one.''

October — *After Communion. Notre-Dame. Nantes.*
''You remember when I called you in C.'s little chapel, how you wished that there were a chapel in every house. You didn't know then that I was in you, that there was no sanctuary more secret than that of your heart. You do not even need to open a door, just a look, a longing, and you are at My feet. There I will tell you, 'Climb higher. Rest on My heart, My friend, My chosen one, and breathe the air of the mountain peaks to take strength for a new upsoaring, My frail little child'.''

November 4 — *Nantes. Recreation time.*
''Do you at last believe with all your heart that I created you in order to make you eternally happy? It was out of pure love that I made you — not for My own interest but for yours: to give you infinite bliss.

O thank Me for your creation. Turn your life toward Me. Never cease to look at My Love enfolding you; and feeling loved, love Me.

You know how much more intensely one loves when one feels loved. It's like an animated conversation. Only in this one there is no need of any words. We love; that's all. And I am so much yours that you don't even feel that I come down or that you rise up, but it seems quite simple to you that we talk to each other on the same level, share as equals, even exchange our two hearts, since for Bridegroom and bride everything is in common, and although you give yourself utterly, you keep your personality and only enhance it the more.''

November 6 — *Holy Hour.*

''Take care in setting down My words so that what springs from My heart will be light and joy, easy to capture. I have so great a desire to give Myself. If you only knew the effort it was for Me — not to give to you, but to refrain from giving... That is why your requests relieve Me. My heart is a fire that suffers when its consuming flame is diminished. Fan it. Fan it. The conquest of the whole world is not too great for My fire. Ask without any fear of exaggerating. Do you feel the warmth of My zeal for you? Who will help Me in this work, if not you, My intimate friends?

We are as though in a secret upper room where our merits, united before the Father, can reach out for this or that people, for this or that nation, before the end of time.

Multiply your sacrifices. Two or three a day are not many, but united with mine — can you imagine what a fortune that would be?... To pray is itself a sacrifice — like the smoke rising toward heaven from the holocaust. You can pray by working and you can take a rest from praying by singing to Me. Then, just look at Me in the silence, in this silence laden with the love that is worth more than whole rosaries that you recite mechanically. Oh, these ways of yours of approaching your Savior and God who is waiting for you... Waiting for you! Then if you didn't come, how could He downflow His grace that is like a burden upon Him. And when your day has been spent so near — within My very aura, so to speak, what a happy day, My Gabrielle... You understand, I am like someone suffering from cold who without a word awaits the tender pity of some passer-by, hoping to receive alms. It isn't so much the gift that will fill Me with joy as the gesture of the heart. You can understand My agony on seeing the indifference and hatred right to the end of the world. My cold sweat... My burning sweat... My sweat of blood...

You are the one who passes by. You pass by in life. Cover Me with your love — all of it. I want to be your now. I want to be you, your breathing, and the beating of your heart right to the very last... And even if after that final heart beat your soul has not yet been liberated from your body, I want your last thought to be for Me.

Try to understand the demands of love. You see, My little girl, I paid for everything on the cross — for everything. I can take as well.''

November 9 — *I was thinking fearfully about suffering.*
''You may be sure that human nature cannot love suffering for itself. My human nature didn't love it either. But supernature uses it as an instrument to serve God, either for His own purposes — and this is most perfect — or for grace that we want to obtain if it is the Father's will to give it.

And always, My little child, you must be one with Me in My sufferings. To quicken your love-will you may choose some of My sufferings — those of My childhood, My adolescence, My public life, those caused by people's words and acts and by the ingratitude of those I loved. And My suffering for the anguish I caused My mother and My friends during the ordeal of My passion.

Don't waste one of your precious sufferings. Steep them in supernatural joy.''

November 11 — *At Benediction with the Reparatrix nuns before the Blessed Sacrament exposed.*
''Begin by closing all the gates of the senses to the outer world. Then place Me before your soul like a sure presence. Finally, enter deeply into Me. (...) You can

imagine, can't you, that there were thousands of good deeds in My human life. Don't grow weary of hailing them, of loving them, since they are yours for the taking. Oh, this oneness with your elder Brother — how it enriches you and how it touches Me. Take everything. It was all lived for you, My dear little ones. I am so happy when you consent to accept them. It astonishes you, doesn't it? — this great generosity of your Savior. Then what will you say when you see Him as He is, when you understand?"

November 14 — *Holy Hour.*
I was trying to be one with Him in His agony.
"The last evening of My life among you — how sweet and solemn it was... I gave Myself not only to the Twelve, but to everyone of you right to the end of the world.

My child, I was already in your hearts by My yearning for you. I had so great a desire that everyone, everyone, might receive the sacrament of My love, since I came to invent it for you. And I saw all the benefits that you would find in it. But in My agony, I also saw desecrations and sacrileges; I saw what I had done with such love become an object of hatred and loss. What an exchange for the infinite delicacy of My love! And I was alone in My suffering."

(....) "You who have the joy of receiving Me every day, ask that this same grace be given to others. Say to Me, 'Choose them — you who know all the secrets of souls — and apply my prayer to them.'

And if you are the means of bringing one or many into frequent fellowship with Me, do you think that I could fail to be grateful, not only for the glory gained by it, but above all for the joy it brings to My heart. I'll let you feel this joy reflected upon you."

November 25 — *I had experienced intense joy.*

"Thank Me as spontaneously as you would thank someone very dear to you. I'm not just a Messenger of suffering as so many imagine. I am also the Giver of joys and I love your thanks, My little children; don't deprive Me of this."

November 28 — *Holy Cross. Holy Hour.*

"I temper the wind to the shorn lamb. There are even people like you who show Me greater signs of their spontaneous love when I send them joys. You often recognize Me in them and you give yourself from your very heart's deeps. And isn't this what I'm seeking in you — real tenderness?

My agony was the most terrible of all the agonies on earth, as much on account of the sufferings that preceded it as the sensitivity of My nature and My deep insight. Come close to Me. Try to enter as best you can into My anguish of soul. Offer this anguish to the Father for all times, for your time. If you could only help Me save everyone in your time..."

December 8 — *I was at the feet of the Blessed Virgin.*

"Here is a way of doing everything well: act as though you had just left the communion table, and you will see how your interior life blossoms out in peaceful communion with your heart."

December 12 — *Holy Hour.* (....)

"Lord, there are still these poor girls in the brothels. I wish so much that they would give up this terrible life. Every Sunday I pass in front of the doors so that You, who are in me, will send grace to someone inside."

"You remember? I told you that when you cannot enter a place yourself, your prayer will enter. There is no sin that I cannot forgive, no soul fallen so low that I cannot heal it. You see in the gospels how some people were scandalized. And I am always the same. My heart always goes to the most unfortunate. (....) Love Me, love intensely. You can never know all that you can obtain and transform with your love on earth. But I know.''

"Lord, I am so poor in love."

Take Mine since you know it is yours, that it belongs to all My children. Offer it to the Father, with full assurance of your power over Him. And then ask, ask, ask!

My little children all down the ages, clothe yourselves with your Jesus as Jacob clothed himself to resemble Esau. Then the Father will give you the heritage of all His treasure. And I'll be full of joy at having paid with My tears, the blows I received, and My blood. Oh, My little children, My very own.''

December 19 — *Holy Hour.*

''Don't grow weary of Me... I go away and I come back to you. And when I go away, you remain close to Me. Don't be like the people who, in a season of dryness, flee from me and abandon Me. They don't know their Savior. It is because I love you that I hide Myself. Must I not test and try My dear flock? Even if everything is dark in your heart, if My voice seems to have vanished forever, think: 'He loves me and He gave Himself for me.'

Gave Himself... if you only knew what this meant for Me... You would need to know all the cruelty of My executioners to understand My courage sustained by My love. Yes, I loved you, each one of you, even to such suffering as that. Then don't ever doubt Me, for I am infinite.''

"Lord, help our faith, help our hope, help our love."

''Have no confidence in yourself; expect nothing

from your little resources. Then I'll help you, for when you are emptied of self I'll be able to fill you. Admit your nothingness.

And I, the All, will act in you and by you. Put your feeble smallness often into My powerful hands. The power of a Father, a Bridegroom — what power, my little girl! How glad you will be that you gave everything back to Me — everything, all I have given you. Give it back to Me with the sole desire of pleasing Me and working better for My glory. Oh, cultivate this desire within you. Let it grow into a passion. Turn all your actions towards this end as some flowers turn toward the sun until they fade and fall. Please Me and increase My glory. Your Christ; never you. And if you forget yourself to this extent to think only of Me, how could I ever resist this charm in My child... I'll give you over and above all your needs, and My glory will shine forth. You know how disproportionate my rewards are to your efforts. What I need is this élan of surrender; you must go out of the door of yourself to enter into Me. And if you do this humbly and joyously, what joy you give Me! I forget the suffering that so many cause Me and I take refuge with all My favors in your heart-center. We are happily at home... And there, within your heart I have a place where I may rest My head.''

December 24 — *I was reading, 'Mary had a faith that no other human being will ever have'.*

''All that a mother has also belongs to her children. Have you ever met a mother who refused to share? She gives you everything if you ask her. Everything! So grow rich through her, for My glory, My poor little girl.''

Christmas — *In my bedroom.*

''Has it ever occurred to you that the love your mother and your sister Clemence had for you — not to mention the love of others who are interested in you — was a little of the love of My mother for you? A little... Thank her warmly for it. And by your tender thoughts for her, show gratitude for the gentle care of her heart.''

December 29 — ''Thank Me for your nature, even with all its faults and failings, for this can be a source of merit for you.''

1941

January 1 — *On awakening.*

''Your keynote for the year: Believe in love. Have faith in My love.''

January 2 — *I was watching Him weep in the Garden of Gethsemane and I asked Him to let His tears fall into my heart.*

''Yes, there were moments when I saw the comfort that My soul-friends would give Me all down the ages. I saw their great desire to suffer in My place, and I sent flowing to them the merits of My fearful agony. For I saw the first man and all the others, right to the very last. What a burden, My child, for One who atones! (....)

You must believe in the love of Christ — once again I ask you for this — for otherwise you will hurt Him. Wouldn't you be offended if a friend said to you, 'Everything is false in your affection.' You would be hurt and you would be on your guard after that. Often you too lack faith in My love and so you put a stop to My gifts, for I'm afraid of adding to the weight of your ingratitude. And I wait... But if you call Me, how present I am to you, how ready to carry you, My poor little children.

Do you remember when you were little how you used to hunt for Me? You would go and hide yourself in the dark room behind your grandmother's kitchen. There, in the corner, was a large doormat rolled up.

You would scramble into it, and when anyone called out, 'Where's Gabrielle?', you would say to yourself, 'I'm with the good God.'

And do you remember how on summer nights at Le Fresne, you would go out alone on the terrace, hunting for Me between the Loire and the stars; and you would say, 'I'm going to think'. You were seeking Me, and I let Myself be caught, but you were not aware of this yet. How I loved you, My little child!''

January 9 — *Holy Hour.*

''Come and watch Me suffer in the Garden, just as though it were that very night. It is always that very night, for God sees all time at a glance. Don't leave Me! I'm like a terrified child who begs not to be left alone. Stay there. Let Me know that you're with Me. A presence is soothing. Hold My hand. I am only a poor man full of distress even though I am God. No one will ever understand the depths of My desolation. I feel the need of being surrounded by all My dear ones, for I see all the powers of evil let loose and I am alone to defend Myself. Pray with Me. Do you have a firmer belief in My love now that you see Me suffer so? Give Me this alms, this faith offering.

How much it means to Me to see faith, hope and love — these three basic attitudes — in the hearts of My children.

Two rungs to climb: faith and hope. From there you reach love. And as you read this morning, love alone counts. You must use every manner and means of reaching it. You must ask Me to make it grow in you, offering little sacrifices to this love that needs to be kept alive. Sometimes you think that you are wasting time, that love in you is feebler, when all the time it is growing. To long to love, why, that's love itself. And all these efforts of yours to love more, only add to the sum of your love in the eyes of the divine compassion.

Advance, advance. Let nothing hinder your trustful steps forward. Trustful — of course — since I am there. And if you count on Me, can you ever imagine that I would fail to help you reach your goal? Learn to desire. And since you have heard this word, 'Be perfect as your Father in Heaven is perfect,' dare to the utmost. Alone you can't do anything. But trusting in Me, leaning on Me, submerged in Me you can do everything. That's why I keep on saying, 'Lose yourself in Me and humbly ask Me to act for you, and I'll act'.''

January 16 — *Holy Hour. Saint-Pierre.*

''Pray with Me. With Me, you understand. I said to them, 'Could you not watch with Me one hour! Watch and pray.' And I say the same to you. Isn't it only natural for brothers to help one another? I am your Brother. I carry the burden of the whole world and it seems to Me that already I am sinking beneath the weight of it. Help Me, My Gabrielle. Help Me by praying. Help Me by loving. Love can work such wonders in a sensitive heart and what heart is more sensitive than Mine? Suppose someone were to ask you, 'What are you doing at this moment?', and you could answer, 'I'm loving My God.' Even if the whole universe were to stand still, it would be a fact of little importance compared with a soul striving to charm Me.

Love Me in all kinds of ways. Love to make amends, to comfort Me, to thank Me, to glorify Me, to obtain, to please Me, and then love just for the sake of loving. That's what the saints in heaven are doing and would you believe it, it is forever the story of My passion that is perpetually renewed. So take all these concerts of praise and all these transports of love and offer them to Me in the Garden in order to veil the assaults of the powers of evil from Me.

Pray for all centuries, all peoples, all sinners. There is infinite treasure in My sweat of blood. What have you to fear? Give My blood to the world — Life ebbing away that it may give Life.

My dear little girl, so full of weakness and poverty, I'm counting on you: help your elder Brother.''

January 22 — *Holy Hour.*
"Do you believe in My powerful love?''
"Yes, Lord, I do believe in Your powerful love.''
"And do you believe that My love is more powerful than all the loves of the earth put together?''
"Yes, Lord. I do believe that.''
"O tell Me that often. It relieves My agony. Unbelievers wound My tenderness, and the confidence of a soul is such balm to Me.

Don't you see that since you let Me act in your place, your joy and our oneness are greater? Don't you see, too, that in this way you will take great strides forward, since it is I who cover the miles? The other day when you had that disappointment *(an important business matter that seemed to have failed,)* I loved the way you offered the whole thing to Me right then and there. I gave it to the Father. Lose yourself in Me always. If you only knew who I am, you would never cease to take refuge in My arms. If you knew the gift of God and who this One is called Jesus Christ!

At least don't check your transports of love any longer. For I am the transport of love, I, your Christ.

Don't even try to find out where I'm leading you. Keep your eyes fixed so steadily on Me that you are not even aware of your surrender. Try to please Me in everything. And see that your soul always wears a smile, because this is what I love and it honors Me. Then I want you to cultivate the habit of multiplying opportunities for helping other people, since you know

104

that they are My brothers. And thirdly, I want you to create opportunities of speaking about Me. It would be so heartwarming for Me and for you.

Can you imagine a single day spent without once pronouncing God's Name, together with a kindly word for those who are listening to you? Perhaps you are shy. Are you afraid of embarrassing? In reality the opposite is true. Make the experiment, and you'll be astonished to see how much people are attracted by these heaven-born words. Just try; I'll do the talking. I beg you, give Me the chance, beginning tomorrow. You know very well that when your Lord speaks, He touches.''

February — *In my bedroom at Nantes.*

''Poverty. Even My words are only just vocal enough for you to hear them. Haven't you noticed how almost imperceptible My voice is? Imitate My poverty.''

In the dark morning, the wet pavement reflected the sky and this helped to guide my steps.

''When grace saturates an attentive soul, that soul reflects God and guides its brother to Him. Who can ever measure the power of influence?''

After a sermon on the Mystical Body of Christ.

''And since you are part of My body, why should you be amazed at the fact that My thinking members hear My thoughts? We are one.''

After Communion.

''Don't be afraid to come back to Me after your distractions. Ask My heart to forgive you and love Me more than ever.

You understand, if you keep smiling before My face, you will always have a smile for others, and it will warm their hearts.''

February 6 — *Holy Hour. Notre-Dame. Nantes. I wasn't*

pleased with my day — so little had counted for Him in it.

"That doesn't make any difference. I take you as you are, with your regrets; so just be sorry. Tell Me that you will be more careful tomorrow. Don't you think that I prefer someone who has fallen and repented to one full of pride in his good deeds? The self-righteous lose all merit. Then always be little, My Gabrielle. Get a true picture of yourself in all your weakness, without even the possibility of being good without Me. But in the distress of your poverty, look at all My riches: they are all yours. Look at My goodness and throw yourself into My arms. Look at My love without ever being afraid; I am your Savior. You know when John said, 'It's the Lord', it meant so much for him. And for you?"

"For me too, it means much."

"For you I must be everything. Everything! You understand? Your life is Mine. (....) Move out of yourself; I'm living in you. Do you grasp what I mean? I take up all the room."

February 20 — *Holy Hour. At the Reparatrix.*

"You are only an instrument. But be that; be always ready to serve Me. Serve Me, not yourself. You're dependent on Me. I'm your Employer. Thank Me for wishing to make use of you. Aren't you happy with your employer? Could you ever say that I don't look after you? You have experienced the delicate little touches of My tenderness and you've seen it also in the details of your life. For nothing is too small for my watchful love. You have learned to recognize Me in circumstances too. And this pleases Me so much. It is really I, your Christ, who comes to meet you so often.

You have the picture: two friends at opposite ends of a road hurrying to meet each other. That's how it is with us. Never leave Me alone on the road, longing in vain for you to come, My very little beloved one.

Serve Me with your whole heart, looking upon everything that is not for Me as nothing at all. And since I am the Host in your heart-center, come there often to visit Me. Pay no attention to the world. Cloister yourself in your inner shrine, and in secret adore your Bridegroom. Talk to Him in your own words and listen to Him.''

February 26 — *My birthday.*
I was consecrating the first hour of my life to Him and asking Him that the last one be full of love.

''Remember this; as one lives, so one dies. If, during these moments that divide you from death, your heart is full of Me; if zeal for My kingdom consumes it; if you are thirsty for My glory, death will find you like that and you will pass on with a thought of love. (....)

To pass on... it's not long, it is just to leave the life on earth to enter into that other life. This is your true birthday; that is what it is to be born to Life everlasting. And I am Life, I, your Christ.''

''Help me to live from now on as I shall live in heaven; I mean, in my soul.''

''But this is the reason why I lived — just in order to be the Life of your life. Always place your life in Mine, doing nothing yourself and everything through Me. Be full of joy when you are misunderstood or overlooked because this makes you just like Me. And when you are alone, think of My forty days of solitude and be one with Me. How happy I'll be, My poor little one, — I who lived only for My children. I wanted a little soul on earth who would live from time to time wholly for Me.'' (....)

Easter — *All along the road to the Cathedral I was saying, ''Hail, my resurrected Christ!''*

"As far as your heart is concerned, may the world be in its tomb. May your Christ alone live!"

At the offertory:

"Through my rising from the dead, offer the resurrection of your own body at the general resurrection. Offer the resurrection of each member of your family, of all those who have passed before you and those who will outlive you, and of all the people you have ever known — all of them. Let them be like a procession around my resurrection for the glory of God the Father."

April 20 — *Le Fresne. Holy Hour.*

"Don't you come to Me with more confidence than to any friend on earth? Aren't you at home in My heart? It should be that way too, since for each soul I am the unique, the incomparable One.

Offer this communion between us to the Father in union with the intercourse between the three divine persons. After you receive the Eucharist, offer Him not only My body, but the perfections of My soul: My power and My tenderness; My virtues, too — the ones you have loved the best — in order to help you to overcome your weaknesses and failures.

You understand — in Me you can find everything: all the love you need to help you. So don't be afraid of making use of the One who loves you so. Unfold your trust like silk to clothe your request, and you will vanquish Me. My heart is easily taken captive by My little children. And you are all My little children. Any humble tenderness disarms Me.

Yes, before you fall asleep, lovingly and humbly confess the day's faults and failings. What gain for you! And what eagerness to restore in the heart of your loving Savior.

You remember, when Mary Magdalene had told Me

of her sins, she stopped to ask, 'After that, can I be forgiven?' I assured her and she went on. But once again she stopped and asked, 'For this too, may I still hope to be forgiven?' 'Yes,' I assured her. Then when all her past had been laid at My feet, she wept from pure love-gratitude, understanding My infinite compassion. Understanding a little, that is. For it is not in you to grasp the infinite.

Love to be blind, since it is I who am leading you if you really want to put your hand in Mine. Don't you think fathers are happy when their little girls leave everything to them in simple tenderness?''

May 1 — ''You thank Me for the springtime with all its flowers and for the birds that sing in your linden trees, for the first butterflies and all My beautiful creations. And you are right, for I am Beauty itself. But the springtimes that I bring to souls by My grace — these are what you should thank Me for most of all. These springtimes full of the elixir of eternity are paid for with the shedding of My blood and create splendors you cannot see. But the angels and the saints gaze on them.

Oh, My dear children — Love that is unloved... how deep a wound, this wound that I bear! Comfort, rest, help Love. Give everything to Love, poor as you are. Lean on My heart, and the burden of you will be My joy; and I'll flow into you as the sap from the root of the vine flows into the branch. And your life will be My life. You are nothing at all by yourself, My poor little girl.''

May 8 — *Holy hour.*
''Perhaps you were in a hurry to say many things to me, and I am late.''

''You know you must give great importance to the

very little things of every passing moment because in My eyes, the eyes of God, only love will give value to what you do. I tell you this often because I don't want you to lose anything. You can be so rich at so little expense and you can enrich others too. So take notice of every little thing. Give everything to Love; and aim at perfection in all your work in order to please Me more and to make up for past flaws. Do you realize that a single one of such moments can make amends for an entire life? Whatever you do, do it well, looking at Me and asking Me for My glory. And God will bless you.

"Lord, help me. You know my nothingness and my bent for doing wrong."

"My grace is sufficient for you. It comes when you ask for it. Often it comes even before you ask. So be very serious about your influence as Christ's bride. Say and do only what your Bridegroom approves. See Him in your place. 'What would He do? How would He answer?' And this will be a new way of pleasing Me, a way of never leaving Me. You see how I'm always seeking for you, for all my children."

May 30 — *I was giving Him a sacrifice and I said: "It's a flower that I'm pinning to your robe."*

"Give Me these flowers often. *(The Voice seemed to smile).* It's as though you added to My beauty. You see, when you become more beautiful, I become more beautiful. Oh, My little girl, how one we are! From the time of your morning Communion, right to your night's sleep, let us be one. And again when you are fast asleep — one. Forever oneness… Would you like that? Then tell Me that you long for it. Keep it always before the eyes of your soul. Remember how all the tapestries in the abbey at Beaune featured a single word — alone — to express the bereavement of the inconsolable widow. Let the tapestries of the temple of your soul be the weaving of a single word — one — to express our undividedness. Child of God, shouldn't you imitate the union of the three divine persons in one?

Ask the Holy Spirit for this when He descends into you tomorrow. Do you think He is inactive on the morning of Pentecost? He makes the earth new and each one of you, too, according to your readiness to receive. He is infinite. Abandon yourself to Him. He is a consuming fire. Abandon yourself. He is the Comforter. Freed from self, ask Him to comfort through you. Just sink out of sight into your nothingness and let God work.''

June 5 — ''Plunge into the infinite ocean of peace, calm as a beautiful sunrise. You remember the tints in the sky at Naples just before the sun rose, when the whole firmament and the whole ocean were bathed in multicolored serenity. Think what the infinite perfections of My heart must be like. Can you realize all their varied beauty? Adore without seeing it. And because you have adored in blind faith, you will be rewarded.

Put your forehead against My forehead. Enter into my thoughts.''

June 19 — *Holy hour.*
''I am the One who makes whole. So give Me your wretchedness. Show it to Me with your two hands like a beggar. I said to the apostles, 'It is I; don't be afraid.' Such gentle, loving words! And I say them over again to you.

You remember how only Moses could approach God on Sinai. If anyone else crossed the borderline at the foot of the mountain he was struck dead. And now that the Son of God has come to die for His brothers,

He says to you, 'Draw near. Come, love Me without fear, for I love you'.''

June 19 — *''Lord, already I wish You the feast of Your heart for tomorrow.''*

''Every day would be My feast if you offered Me the wish, My Gabrielle, for every day is the feast of love, from the time you wake up to the time you go to bed. And it is I who send you sleep. This is another way of loving you. You fall asleep, and yet I never cease to look at you. So ask your angel to offer even the rhythm of your restful breathing for My glory. Love is so simple. Awake, asleep, it goes on and on, like your Loire that never stops flowing by day or night. In heaven you know, there is no pause, for love is pure activity. (…)

You must long for heaven, because this is the same as to long for Me and it glorifies Me. Even when you have such a distorted picture of Me, yearn for Me, for this is a triple act of faith, hope and love.'' (….)

June — *I said, 'My Love, bless this meal.'*

''If only because you said, 'My Love', I will bless it. You know that I am more sensitive than the most sensitive of men and your childlike tender words have great power over My heart. So get to know the paths that lead directly to Me. I yield My secrets to My children.

I am Samson. But he regretted having spoken, whereas I yield myself completely because My love is beyond all your power to imagine. Your belief in this immensity of love that accompanies you is feeble because you judge your God according to man's standards. But you, My child, at least you — surrender to me. Believe without trying to define.

Let Me live in you. If your poverty overwhelms you,

you may be sure that this is the very thing that draws Me to you. You can always take My love if your coldness makes you afraid. I am your Creator, but you are My little girl, and I know all about your emotions as I know every wave of the sea. Even before you speak, I hear you, since I live in you. Do you want Me to walk in your 'garden enclosed'?"

"Rest Lord, pick flowers and fruit."

"I'll sow the seeds. You'll do the cultivating. And you will give me back the whole harvest, since I am the Master of the garden."

July 26 — *In the country.*

I said to Him, "Let us stroll down Your avenue of linden trees." Correcting me:

"Our linden trees. What would it be to Me without you? Try to understand my desire for oneness."

July 30 — *Visit.*

I said, "Loving You is forever new, my Jesus." And He replied:

"Loving you is forever new, My Gabrielle."

I continued and He answered. It reminded me of the little birds that twitter sotto voce in their nests.

August 19 — *In the empty church. He said:*

"Tell Me if you are pleased with your day."

"I hurt someone without wanting to, and I am so distressed."

"Remember what I told you? 'When there is nothing you can do about a situation, give it to Me, full of trust that I'll put things right for you. I'll give you an opportunity to make up for it with an act of kindness'." (...)

August 21 — *Our Lord called me by the name I was given in the Third Order — Sister Mary of the Heart of Christ.*

"The Heart of Christ, Mary, belongs wholly to each one of My children. You remember I said, 'Who is My mother? Who are My brothers? Those who do the will of My Father who sent Me.' Isn't it consoling to know that you can be one of My family, the most loving of all families — My rest and My refuge?"

"Lord, I want to meet you everywhere. Yesterday, I kissed You on every rose."

"Let your eyes, your ears, and all your senses look for Me everywhere in nature, the vast garden where your Beloved walks, perhaps in the hope of meeting you. So many things can come from a meeting. Be with Me, little chosen one — with me, your Savior and God."

August 24 — *Going into church. "Dear God, it is I."*
"But you were already here."
Raising my eyes I saw my hydrangeas on the altar.

August 28 — *I was thanking Him for all His blessings.*
"Even when your faith is no bigger than a mustard seed you must strive to make it grow. Look upon these special blessings of today as My love, attentive to every detail of your life; and at every step of your way, you will find Me watching, going ahead of you. Have you ever gone anywhere that I have not been waiting for you? You often ask Me to take care of your precious belongings. But for Me, aren't you more precious than all?

Entrust yourself to Me constantly. And always give Me each moment as it passes. Isn't it better in My hands? Doesn't it say in the gospel, 'He laid His hands on them and healed them.' I'll take out of this present moment of yours whatever clings too much to the earth — the selfishness that sullies your intention.

Always trust. Trust more and more — even to the

point of expecting a miracle. Don't stop half way or you will set limits to My love. When you have unfolded your confidence you will unfold it still more without ever being able to exceed what I expect of you.

Always count on Me, never on yourself. And you will advance; you will soar with wings like the eagle, My very little girl."

September — *From the monstrance.*
"Rest on My heart, eat and drink. You must take life from this food that is beyond your power to understand.

Dare as only love knows how to dare. Stay on My heart and be sure always to wake up there. Do this for the sake of all humanity, as though it were in your power to give Me every living person in a single instant. Learn to desire this. Desire is a beautiful fruit; you can quench My thirst with it. Go now and take Me with you."

October 1 — *In the country.*
"If this oneness between the soul and Me has begun on earth, can you imagine that there will be any interruption when the soul leaves the body?"

"Lord, is it at that moment only that we shall understand Your love?"

"Yes, not until then will you begin to understand My love — only to continue throughout all eternity."

"I'd like to be now as I shall be when my soul leaves my body — enfolded in Your presence and wholly lost in You."

"Offer Me this desire to see Me and Me only in everything. And I'll take it as a gift from you. Let nothing else count for you any more apart from what grieves or what pleases Me. Sacrifice yourself in My sight to the point of not even noticing your sacrifice. And suffer with the greatest simplicity, since it is all for Me, your Christ, who suffered for you. What is life when one possesses eternity? You remember what you said about eternity: 'It's as though one were always just arriving, and the earth — no more than the far-away, fleeting dream of a moment.' Take courage from this thought. And never suffer outside of My love, but let your suffering be like new accents of love for Me that say, 'You know that I love You, that I am as incense burning before Your face with the utmost desire to please You, My Friend'." (....)

Christmas — *At the Cathedral.*

"Since I came down to you, just think of My immense power put at your service by My love. Don't ever doubt that through Me your work of transmission can reach the very ends of the earth.

Ask again that My kingdom may come.

Ask!"

1942

January 1 — *"My keynote for the year Lord?"*

"Submerge yourself in Me in life, and you will be engulfed in Me in death." (....)

February 12 — "When you pray, keep your eyes on Me. Enter into my eternal thoughts, otherwise you will find your own thoughts wandering.

Keep in mind that you are all dependent on one another, so that if one of you does something perfectly, it adds to the treasury of the whole Church.

My little child, don't miss a single chance of enriching both yourself and others. Take a long look at your model — My life — just as you studied your notebooks when you were a wee girl. And set to work to write on these last pages of your life more with the desire of pleasing Me than with any thought of winning a prize. And I who am always there watching you will lovingly accept this desire to please Me.

Do you grasp what I'm saying? Don't have a thought for yourself. With your whole being enfolded in Mine, think of Me. And then, scatter sunshine on everyone. It will be My sunshine, not yours."

"Lord, I promise, I desire. But in reality, what do I do?"

"My compassionate heart is happy to accept promises and desires. Little by little they become acts. Promises and desires are acts in the bud.

Never be discouraged. Remind yourself often that I am with you. Can I be with you and not help you?

Isn't the creature infinitely precious to the Creator? If you only knew!

Let your ear always be on the alert to listen to Me. You will hear. When John leaned on My heart, he heard its secrets. If he had not shown me this gesture of tenderness, would he ever have heard? I am like the shy person — I have to wait for you to make the first move.''

March 1 — *After Communion.*

''It's always possible to pray, no matter what you are doing. When I was covered with wounds and bruises, I recited psalms. And staggering up the hill to Calvary in the midst of the yelling mobs, and on the cross, My poor cross. And yet you find it difficult to pray while doing your comfortable little tasks. Oh! merge with Me.''

March 24 — ''To give pleasure is to do good. Don't be miserly with anyone, especially those who have been unkind to you. Merge with Me by saying:

It is You who pray in me.

It is You doing the work as I work.

It is You speaking when I speak.

And do everything with the utmost tenderness, My little girl.''

April 5 — *Easter.*

''I rose from the dead for you. Not for My glory, but so that you might believe and live in the hope of your own resurrection.

Never count on yourself, always count on Me, at every moment of your life. Allow Me to live in you at last, to take your place. Step outside of yourself. Be a completely new person — a soul gone bankrupt and then made rich.

Look at My wounds as they are now — glorified. You have so often pictured blood flowing from them. After suffering, glory. Rejoice with all the heavenly hosts.''

April 11 — ''Don't you understand that I prefer someone who has fallen many times but who despises himself at My feet, to the self-righteous person who thinks he is without fault. My little girl, tell Me every day how sorry you are for any way you have pained Me. Take a steady look at your failures and stains, and offer them to Me so that I may wash them away. Tell Me how weak you are and how often you fail. Say: 'My great Friend, help me. You know only too well how helpless I am, but with You I can do anything.' And then go on your way again, trusting in Me day by day. You understand? Even if you see no progress at all, be more patient than ever. Be ready to persevere to the very end. Didn't I need that kind of courage as I climbed up the hill to Calvary?'' (....)

April 16 — ''Here's something for you to say: May my understanding have true faith, my memory true hope, and my will true love.''
In the garden I said to Him, 'I'm weeding so that You may come and walk on the terrace.' And in the little narrow street — 'That's like Your town, Nazareth.' And I felt Him beside me and remembered what He had said: ''So little hinders you from seeing Me.''
''At-onement, do you understand what this means? This is life, all of it. Nothing else counts. Your Christ, the life of your soul, what a beautiful thought! Often My children are not aware of My action. But you, child, believe with all your heart. Offer yourself unceasingly to our oneness, and My action will be even greater. You too will often be unaware of it, but try to stay always closely united to Me in love. Even if this were

your only way of praying, your life would show no ordinary mark but one that is altogether supernatural and precious in the Father's sight. Respond to My tender care for you by your own tender thoughts and gestures.

Act toward Me as though I were shy; you take the first step. Try. How often I wait for My children and they don't come. You remember that time when you got everything ready to receive someone you loved and that person said, 'Oh, I forgot.' You felt so hurt. But what are your human loves compared with Mine?

Yes, ask My pardon for the meetings you have missed. My compassion will make Me forget. My darling child, I am always ready to forgive, to press you against My heart so that you'll find courage there. Even when you are doing the most ordinary little things, be one with Me. There is never a single moment when you cease to be My little girl.

Today, this week, this month — they are all filled with My love just like the other months and years. I'm loving you even when you are not thinking of loving Me, and I'm preparing blessings you never think to ask for. A look, a gesture for Me, and I give you everything, little child of My heart.''

April 23 — ''Even though you don't always feel Me beside you, I never leave you. Sometimes I come nearer, as I did yesterday in the garden when you said, 'Good morning, my darling God.' It seemed to you almost as though I answered you, didn't it? I hide behind a veil so that you may learn to walk by faith, and earn by learning. You are astonished by My love. There is only one explanation: God's extravagance. So just believe in all simplicity in this love of an all-powerful Being, a Being totally different from you. And give yourself up to His infinitely delicate and tender omnipotence. Be taken captive by love, and ask for grace. Love Me with My love and be full of trust. (....)

Be like an exile lost along the roads of life. Think only of heaven, where I am waiting for you to celebrate our wedding day. Tell Me of your impatience and submission, your eagerness under My control, your intense desire yielded to My will; and your humility will wash you ever more clean, will purify you. And your last days will pass by — everything passes... And you will come.''

May 21 — *Le Fresne. In my bedroom.*
''Lord, when it comes to the extravagance of love, isn't it foolish on my part to love You even without seeing You?''

''Can love's folly in one of God's children ever equal that of God Himself? Don't be afraid of going too far. Seek Me. Call Me. You'll find Me. I'll answer. (....)

Don't ever grow weary of Me, My friend. Fall in love with Me over and over again, and let your way of loving Me always be new. Don't worry if you don't hear My voice. Don't begin to think I am far from you. I'm in the very center of your being with the Father and the Holy Spirit. Give yourself to Us. Surrender by getting rid of your self-love and even your self-awareness. Never mind if you don't understand very well.

Everything you have is a gift from Me. You are absolutely nothing. Be sure that nothing is all Mine. I respect the human will — you know that. I wait.

Later on when you understand My love, you will be ready to return to earth for the sole purpose of yearning for Me even for a single instant. Ready to suffer, too, to the very end of time. Don't refuse Me anything. Say: 'My Beloved, just as you wish.' This will make Me happy, and the thought of My happiness will help you. Do your very utmost to be one with Me.

Come closer, always closer. Give up everything that separates us — the lack of confidence and hope. It is a great thing to hope. Hope for holiness. Would I ask every soul to be holy if it were not possible? Very well then, believe in My help. Call Me often, still more often. Don't be afraid of being too insistent. Don't you repeat the same prayer many times in the rosary? You must persevere in your asking, poor finite one in the presence of the Infinite. And unite your words with the words I said to My Father in those nights spent on My knees in His presence. Let it be said of you, 'She is a friend of Christ.' The honor will be Mine and you will add to My glory.

You forget what you do for Me and what you say to Me; you leave it in the past. But all these things are eternally present for Me, and you will find them again one day exactly as you gave them to Me. Always stay very near to Me. This will be a token of your love.''

June 7 — *At Mass.*

"Forget all thoughts of the daily round. Enter deeper into Me. What are you waiting for to do better? to respond better?

Haven't you noticed the song of the birds in the nesting season? They haven't the same voices. And you — as you receive grace upon grace, won't there be some change in your song of love? Won't you discover more piercing and poignant notes? Tell me about it. Prove it to Me.''

June 19 — *"Lord, shine through your little girl and leave a trail of Your light and goodness for everyone along her path.''*

"Let Me come in and take over everything. Give yourself to Me. Don't let anything in you hinder Me from working through you. I act through those who put their entire selves at My disposal. Give Me your voice, your look, and go on your way with the firm resolution to let Me do whatever I want, since I'm living in you. Think about this often.

Make all the preparations for a new life within you. Didn't I give you your life? Then give it back to Me as a charming gift from you. When you were taking lessons in painting, sometimes the teacher gave your work an expert touch and made it more beautiful. This is what I do on the canvas of your souls when you yield them to Me. But you must give them to Me without trusting in any of your own little talents. Oh, the masterpiece taking shape in My loving hands! Am I not eager for your perfection?

For love I take you. Give yourself for love. My little girl, every one of your actions should begin and end in love as all Mine did. My life was a hymn of love. You didn't hear it. But My Father does and so do all the saints in heaven. Adore each one of my loving impulses in Galilee, in Judea, on those roads you yourself have traveled. Never mind if you don't understand very well.

Already I loved you; I loved everyone without exception. Love Me for all of them — or at least offer Me your desire to do so." (....)

June 20 — *In the country.*
Climbing an old flight of stairs and offering each step. "Lord, how can You accept such tiny things?"

"You call them tiny, yet you use your memory, your understanding, and your will; in other words, your entire being. No matter where you give yourself to Me, I take you. Do you understand?"

June 25 — *Le Fresne church. Visit.*
"If you could only see My splendor in the taberna-

cle... My power and My tenderness and the guard of honor formed by My hosts of angels burning with zeal. What reverence, what a sense of nothingness you would feel! (....) You would see the utter unimportance of everything that is not love. You would realize too, that nothing could possibly give you more joy than to give Me joy. And you could no longer cease to gaze on Me and on Me alone. For I am all attractiveness. I am Charm and the Charmer. I am Heaven itself.

Heaven is inside the tabernacle. Adore with all the heavenly hosts. Love with them. Sing. Praise. Never can you overdo it, since all you have is what I have given you and all My merits are yours for the taking.

Do you know about My merits? Only the Father knows them all. And do you realize that if it were necessary I would begin all over again? Find a new way of praising Me every day. Keep on exploring My hidden treasures. You can never come to the end of them. Discover, discover, until fires undreamed of are kindled within you, and you will say, 'It was you, Lord. How blind I was! The best of me is always You.'

And while you are talking to Me, I'll continue to heap blessings upon you, for My heart is filled with them, and to give eases it of its burden. It takes a mere nothing from you to make it overflow. If you only knew! My poor little ones, wake up to your power over Me. Get to know Me a little better. Stammer out your words of love. I'll complete them. You've seen the great sun dancing in tiny mirrors? Who can bear its dazzling brilliance? But what is a mirror without the sun?''

June 30 — *After Communion.*
''Why not decide for the highest perfection? No need to make any vow; it might be a source of anxiety to you. Just make up your mind not merely to do things well, but as perfectly as you can. It would add to My

glory. Sinners too would have their share of the benefit. Don't be afraid; be daring. We're together, you and I.''

July 2 — ''Yes, go to the train to meet her. Never miss a chance to be kind, and give pleasure as though it were I who gave and not you. A thoughtful gesture can do so much good. It can be the beginning of a miracle. It takes only a little kindness to melt a heart, you know.''

July 10 — (....) ''Begin afresh every day as though it were the very first. You are forever at the beginning. Don't be afraid, for I am with you, and I know. Is there anything I don't know? All the same, I like you to tell Me where you have failed and to explain yourself to Me. It brings out your confidence in Me. And what else would you speak to Me about if not your poverty. It's the case of the beggar at the rich man's door. If only you had seen the joy of those I healed on the roads of Judea. They left Me singing praises to God. Sing every day in your heart and make Me known to others through joy. You want to make Me known, don't you? Satan uses others to act for him. Why not I? And since I live in you, don't you see how simple it would be to express Myself through you? Your life is Mine.''

July 16 — *Visit.*
''Come to Me. Show Me your poor soul. Do as the sick folk in Judea did as I passed by; talk to Me, beg Me. The gospel says, 'He healed them all.' Quicken your faith and confidence. Speak to My extravagance of love and long to respond with your own. Think of St. Francis of Assisi, the saintly missionaries and martyrs. Didn't they seem ridiculous in the eyes of the world? They were so engulfed in the love of their

Savior that all things seemed as nothing to them. So don't be afraid. Take great strides toward Me. You will be richly rewarded. I could never bear to be outdone in generosity, even though I owe you nothing. Oh, My dear little girl, moment by moment keep in tune with Me. Do everything for My watchful love, as though it were impossible for you to let your thoughts wander away from Me, your Beloved.

Speak in your own words; make up songs and prayers for Me as they come to your mind. Be My little companion; I am yours. I have never left you since you were born, and even before you ever came into the world, I thought of you with such tenderness. Thank your God for all that came from His heart for you, My little girl, and show your gratitude by asking Me to help you.''

July 23 — ''Here I am. I was waiting for you. When My children receive Communion in the morning, I wait during the day for their little visit of thanks. Haven't I deserved it? Just think what it means to receive Communion. How heartless not to say thank you! I gave all of Myself to My little children. Whoever wants Me may take Me. And those who receive, receive all heaven, for heaven is your Christ. But don't ever take such an immense favor for granted. Think of each Communion as a first Communion.

You were wondering how to use those moments when you wake up in the night. Speak to Me of love, longing for your next Communion. Stretch out the arms of your heart to Me. Call Me by the gentlest names, even when you are half asleep. Be stirred to your heart's deeps as you yearn for My Host-Presence prepared for you since the Last Supper. Today's Communion is different from yesterday's and tomorrow's; the grace I give is always unique. God's love is infinite and creative. Give Me your unworthiness. Does your poverty make you sad? You are like a poor woman who, having shown her ugly dress to the king, received a beautiful new one from Him. Would He have given it to her if she had not humbled herself to show him her poverty? God is full of compassion. He does not even wait for the appeal for help to be put into words, so great is His thoughtfulness. Hasn't He often made you feel this? Remember, you had scarcely taken a step when everything came to you in such abundance that you thought, 'It is He.'

Practice the presence of My love. I am everywhere. Put your head on My heart. Of course, since this pleases Me. If you only understood the gift of God and who it is speaking to you... Come to Me then, and bring others in your heart. Can't I heal at a distance? Just name them to Me. You know there are certain healers who don't have to see the one who is ill, but when you talk to Me about them I see them, and am I not the great Healer?

Yes, you too — I want to heal you of your weak faith, of your life lived apart from Me rather than in Me, of your short-sighted and rare view of My actual Presence. Think, 'My great Friend, My Beloved is not absent. I cannot see Him or touch Him, but He is there with His extravagance of love.' And then you will take My love and offer it to Me as though it were your own. Do you want this? Tonight... Right away... Ceaselessly?"

August 6 — *"Be transfigured, Lord. Be transfigured for my poor soul."*

"Look at Me more often. Gaze more often, loving Me more and more. You will see Me in an endless variety of new ways, loving you always, My poor little child. Above all, believe. Get used to making frequent acts of faith — in My presence, in My power, above all in My poor, tender love, so misunderstood. O try to please this love; you have so many chances, and I accept your little tokens with such tenderness. Since I am the Father, the Bridegroom, neglect nothing. Take care of My heart. What a mission, My Gabrielle, to take care of My heart!''

August 18 — ''Of course. I always forgive if you tell Me of your neglect and feel truly sorry for it. I'm not one of those who spy on faults and failings, ready to be severe. I am all goodness. See how easily little children come to Me. Then keep your heart childlike and come. Try to understand My love better and give yourself to it wholly. You know how one decorates an altar with flowers and lighted candles. Make an altar to My love. Say, 'My great Friend, here is a sacrifice, a silence, a smile for love of You.' Let everything you do celebrate love. That will console Me for many others who pass Me by. Love alone can comfort love.''

August 27 — *On the island of Mélet, I offered Him a flower for His robe.*
    ''Yes, adore Me. Think of Me everywhere, for I am in every place and your thought is sweet to Me. Aren't you always before My face? You could never take Me by surprise, for I am there, waiting for you. What a happy meeting!'' (....)

August 30 — *After a shower of rain.*
    ''You see all these tiny pools of water mirroring the sky? Look thoughtfully and tranquilly at God. He alone is worthy of your contemplation. See Him only, and you will reflect Him.''

After Communion. As the Host came to my heart, I was thinking of the clothes strewn on the Savior's path, and tried to lay down my understanding, my memory, and my will at His feet.

"Give all your loving attention to each little moment. Think of this all your life through. Nothing of the past. Nothing of the future. Only the present moment of love."

September 10 — *Ingrandes Church.*

"Why should you begrudge the help you give your neighbours. Don't forget that in serving them you are serving Me. That should give you courage, and you'll need great courage to become holy. Never lose sight of the goal — holiness; that means to be always in readiness for Me, to belong to Me utterly. It's so very simple; believe Me. Would I ever ask anything that was too difficult for you? Just live in My love — holy, one moment at a time. Drive out all worries, all idle dreaming. Don't complicate things. Give Me your soul simply. I am all simplicity. Wasn't I very simple in My prayer in the Garden of Gethsemane? And in the hands of the men who put Me to death; even on My cross? Did I seem like a God? In the same way, My children, your only greatness is the love in the secret tabernacle of your heart. Nothing need be seen. You may always remain in My heart without anyone knowing, but this is the Father's glory. (....)

Don't fail to supernaturalize everything, night and day. It is My life that is living in you now, not yours. Adore. Give thanks. And when I ask you to be simple, I mean above all in your relations with Me. Don't get the idea that I need any special words or gestures; just be yourself. Who is closer to you than God?"

September 24 — *Fainted in church.*

"More and more loosen your hold on the things of the world. Isn't the Meeting day drawing near for you and Me? Little signs like this are like the three taps before the curtain rises. Make eager and joyful preparations to appear on that other stage beyond. Practice the rôle of the impatient lover about to possess the object of her dream — the most beautiful of all dreams — sure that it will surpass all that you have ever imagined. (....)

From now on, ask Me in your Communion to atone for any way in which you have grieved Me in your past life. When you receive Me like this, I penetrate every part of you, each one of your faculties, your blood — and I restore you according to your wish. I continue to be your Brother-Savior because My love never ceases. And since I am Action itself, I never come to you without acting. So thank Me for what I do in you and give yourself up to Me, wishing with all your heart that nothing in you espace My close embrace. Leaning on My heart say, 'Beloved Lover, give me one sinner a day so that I may give him to You'.''

September 17 — *Le Fresne.*

(....) ''I never remember your faults when I have forgiven you. You are hidden beneath My white robe.''

September 30 — *Ingrandes church.*

''In the Host My heart is beating as it did on earth, as it does in heaven. There are not many hearts of Christ. There is only one. Believe without the shadow of a doubt in My Presence here before you and comfort Me by bringing your heart close to Mine. Look how alone I am and this empty church. I knew it would be like this. And yet I instituted My Eucharist. I would feed even a single soul. Speak with the Host as with your most gentle and intimate friend. The Host is listening to you, and you may be sure that you are most dearly loved. Breathe freely. Relax. Leave the earth.

Enter the realm of Spirit. Let yourself be carried away. Do you want to come? Tell Me about your impatience to join Me and your faithfulness to Me. You are Mine. How could you keep yourself to yourself?''

Absent-minded. — ''You see my Jesus, how my thoughts go skipping about.''

''Tell Me about it. Humble yourself. You are in My heart. Oh, if you only knew the power of humility!'' (....)

And I asked His pardon for always saying the same things.

''What does that matter, since it's all about love?''

October 8 — *Le Fresne church.*

I said, ''We are here all by ourselves, as though we were locked in.''

''All the month of the rosary, call My mother 'Our Lady of Love' and say, 'Our Lady of Love, give me love.'

How can you make progress all by yourself? Let yourself be carried in stronger arms, just as you did when you were little. Don't be ashamed of being weak and imperfect. Be smaller still; I'll only love you the more. Don't lose sight of the path of spiritual childhood. Cultivate your confidence; let it blossom as a flower. You can trust Me, can't you? Look back... don't you find that I'm worthy of it? My friend, don't put any limits to your feelings for Me. I put none to Mine for you. Come to Me, little by little, your heart on fire at the moment of death. Find a sweeter name for death. Call it 'The Meeting' and even now, even though you can scarcely see Me in the twilight of time, you will stretch out your arms to Me. Oh, the charm of an impatient heart longing to be enfolded in Mine!''

''Lord, my little words for You are so poor. Get one of your angels to put them into poetry.''

''My love listening to them makes them sublime.''

October 20 — *Ingrandes church.*

''Your home is also Mine. Put it in order; make it beautiful for both of us. Think of Me as always with you — even your dress, your gestures will show it. 'Jesus is there' — only say this to yourself and you will be still, listening. Do it with love, not fear. You know one of the names Jesus gives Himself: a lamb, a poor Lamb of God. Don't you like that name? It speaks of the gentleness of My heart, you remember? Gentle and humble. And since you should be like Me in the Father's sight, practice these two qualities. Try again and again. Say to yourself, 'I must go higher.' Climbing is hard work, but you know I always help when you count on Me and not on yourself. Never alone. Work with Me, your Friend, your Brother, your Bridegroom. O My Gabrielle, don't lose a single minute of love; you will find it again eternalized.''

October 22 — *Ingrandes church.*

(....) ''This morning you discovered how a sacrifice joyously made is no longer a sacrifice. It is only what one refuses that is costly — what one does half-heartedly. So up with your cross on your shoulder, and on your way! Near Me, always nearer to Me. Each thought for Me; it's like your gaze lost in Mine. Give Me a look of tender confidence. I have confidence in you, and yet, how little you are! So you may well put your trust in Me, the Infinite, the All Powerful. Remember that I can give you everything. But I like My children to ask Me; I love to feel your heart-beats because you are My little, My most beloved children.'' (....)

November 12 — ''My little girl, you may be sure of this, that even though I am no longer on earth, your neighbour is there. And your desire to love Me, to receive

Me, to serve Me, and to give Me rest, as in the home of Martha and Mary, may be realized in what you do for others. How ready you would be to smile at everyone if you could only see your Jesus in them. So remember this and don't economize your kindness. It is I Myself who will receive it all. I have a thousand ways of responding to those who try to please Me.

Don't be astonished at your slowness to reach Me, but just keep asking for help from on high. On high — that's where your heart should be. It should be always trying to take off, to wing its way upward. Don't deprive it of its flights. Isn't your life on earth drawing to a close? And don't you need to warm your heart more often in the secret place of the Most High? When someone is about to make a last voyage to a particular country, doesn't he live through it all in anticipation, holding the far horizons to his heart?

Look forward to the departure then, since it is to take you to your Beloved. Say to Him, 'It's time we saw one another. When will you unveil the sweetness of your face for me? Haven't I been traveling long enough in the desert? May I not leave this cold and barren earth to throw myself into your arms? Quicken my longing. Hasten my steps. No longer can any earthly tie hold me back. Let my soul escape from its body as a bird from its cage, so that the breath you have given me may be lost in Your divine Being.'

I'll listen to your voice, for I too am at work in you, preparing for our meeting. 'Where is my Beloved?' you will ask, not yet seeing Me. But I'll be there all the time, since I am everywhere.

My child, wait upon Me in the silence. Offer yourself to the Father enfolded in My merits. Implore the Spirit of Love to give you love, and abandon yourself forever as I did at Golgotha.''

November 19 — ''Appeal often to My sensitivity. I am the sensitive One, though most people think I am aloof and indifferent. I'm nearer to you than you are, and every tender word My children say to Me delights and charms My Heart. Don't ever doubt it. More often you will come to Me lovingly without seeing Me. And this blind faith in Me is great gain both for you and for others.

It's so easy for you to speak to Me, as to the matchless One in your heart. A glance, an inward smile... Such simple things for you, and yet they mean so much to Me.

Give. I'm like a beggar, am I not? My Love devises all sorts of ways of winning you. Give to this beggar who is waiting and whom you love. Later on the rôles will be reversed: it will be I who give and you will find all your gifts again in Mine. What an exchange!''

December 3 — *Le Fresne.*
As I greeted Jesus in the Host.
''Think of this: I was already a Host in the Garden of Gethsemane. Be one with Me there. Say, 'My poor Love, I'm close beside you.' And I'll take you into My Heart. We'll offer ourselves to the Father. I need you so much in the garden. I was so lonely in My terrible anguish. Oh, My child, there, right inside My heart, pray for sinners and know that you save them, because My merits are infinite.'' (....)

December 16 — *Le Fresne church.*
''Don't worry. Since you can't do anything about these things, you don't need to bother about them; they're My concern. Just put them in My hands, and that's all that matters. Don't you need practice in trusting Me? You know how I love your child-like confidence in Me. These are moments to show how little

you are and give Me a chance to take care of you as a husband takes care of his wife, who is weak and needs love and a strong arm to lean on.

No, it's not an illusion. You're not in error, only in the shadowland. Just feeling your way by faith. I planned it this way. So throw yourself into My arms. Say that you believe, that you hope, that you love — and commit your entire being to Me.'' (....)

1943

January 1 — *In the evening, in my bedroom.*
"The keynote for 1943? In each other's hearts. You will keep yours in Mine and I'll be in yours."

January 7 — *Ingrandes church.*
"Give Me your heartfelt adoration with the Wise Men. You know how people say to each other, 'I adore you.' But for you, it is your God, — your incomparable One, your End. So adore Him with every fibre of your being. And since you are nothing, yield yourself to the All.

You grow greater when you humble yourself before Me. I enfold you. Nothing in you escapes Me and I watch over you. Aren't you sometimes amazed to see that so many things work out well for you? That's because I am there, in My little girl who has put her trust in Me. Make this your fixed rule; it is the purchase price of My blessings. Make efforts to belittle yourself before others. What good practice! Try again and again. Never let a chance to humble yourself slip by. It is the evening of your life on earth. Make haste before night falls. But take refuge often in My heart. You'll find that you make more progress there. Try."

January 14 — (....) "Could any work be more beautiful in this last part of your life on earth than to help Me save sinners? There are so very many. Wasn't that what made Me suffer most in Gethsemane?"

136

January 30 — *In my bedroom.*

"Why should My people offer Me only their trials? Don't you think your joys would please Me just as much — that is, if you give them with as much love: your smallest joys with your greatest love."

February 11 — *Le Fresne church.*

(….) "They say that God is all kindness, and He is. You be the same with Me. What a beautiful exchange! And how welcome each little thoughtful gesture will be… You'll understand later on.

Get used to walking in the dark like the blind. Trusting My hand to guide you. You couldn't insult My heart more than to doubt it. My dear child, so little and frail, say to yourself again and again, 'Where would I be without my great Friend? He is everything and I am nothing.'

Just humble yourself when you stumble and fall. Remember how I paid the price, stumbling and falling Myself on the terrible road to Calvary. Let that encourage you in love. Haven't we said that love alone matters, that the only tragedy in life is not to love God? Hope to help His cause with all your feeble resources. Make it your wish never to work for your own ends. Lose sight of yourself altogether, even of your inner self, wishing to remember nothing unless it be your infidelities so that you may regret them.

And wherever you are, practice the presence of God. It will help you to love Him, to have heart-to-heart talks with Him. Since I am there, throw yourself joyously into My arms. Oh, this joy of yours… don't forget it; it enhances your love."

February 13 — *After Communion.*

"What you can't manage yourself — the control of your words, or the thought of My Presence — you will find easier with the help of My mother. Ask her to help you. I confided Mary Magdalene and the holy women to her. Be like them: don't leave her.''

Holy Thursday — *''Lord, may I invite You to live in my lovely gardens for your comfort?''*
''You are the soul of the gardens and My blossoms are your soul-thoughts. I forget My agony in the Garden of Gethsemane when I feel your warmth for sinners. And when you give Me the Love of your hearts, I forget Judas' hatred and greed.'' (....)
I was thinking how I had made a visit to the Blessed Sacrament twice this morning and twice in the afternoon, and that I was going to return for another visit in the evening.
''A whole day for Me, once a year. You think this is a great deal? My Eucharistic Presence is there every day, every night, among you. I'm there full of tenderness, rich with blessings for the taking. Tell Me then that one of your days is not too much. Remember the feast of My heart.''

Holy Saturday — *Le Fresne church.*
''Rise from the dead. Rise with Me to a new life, a better one, to a life nearer to Me. Always nearer to Me. Beg Me to help you, and be sure that I shall.''

Easter — *Le Fresne church.*
During the Benediction I said, ''My poor Love, risen from the dead''.
''My love has never died. At every moment I have loved you.''

May 20 — *Ingrandes church.*
''Fan the flames of your love. Fan the flames. Don't stand still. Never cease to go forward. Enter ever deeper and deeper into My heart. Reading about My passion

is not enough. Make it part of your very self. Wherever you are, take My sufferings. Sufferings desired, willed, expected... They are My love for My children — for you. When one has suffered so, what can one refuse? Ask Me to give you the grace to respond to this love of your God and I'll light new fires in you that will amaze you. You will realize that it is not of your doing. 'It is from Him', you will say, and this will be the truth. You know how utterly weak you are. Tell Me about it so that I can help you. If you saw an invalid content to be ill, you wouldn't try to heal him, would you? But if he cried out to you to help him, you would do your best for him. And if he thanked you, you would hold him to your heart.

Open the secret tabernacle of your heart to Me so that we may speak together of our new love. The words may be the same, but what an added weight of love! You will wonder how a single moment could ever pass by without Me. Where your treasure is, there is your heart. How long My desire has kept watch for you! Ask that I be all in all to you... and that you be wholly Mine. You remember how at Corte you told Me that you wanted it to be like that? Now is the time to translate your wish into your daily living for Me. If you have nothing to say to me, come and look at Me in the secret tabernacle of your heart. You will never have to wait, for I shall already be there. You will come with your hunger, and I'll read this need-look of yours and satisfy it. Over and above all that you ask or think. If you don't know what to say, just remain at My feet like Mary Magdalene and I'll read your silence. I'm keeping such sweet joys for you, so be waiting in your secret shrine. I haven't many shrines like this on earth.'' (....)

July 7 — ''Oneness. I come back to this thought again

and again. Why do you live all alone when you can be in Me at every moment? In Me: that's heaven itself without the face to face vision and the rapture. Then practice this at-onement. Practice adoration and tenderness. If you could only see Me as I really am, what would you not do! You would throw yourself at My feet. You would hold Me to your heart, thanking Me for My sufferings and My blessings. You would ask My forgiveness for your wilful faults and tell Me again of your love.

Act just as though you could see Me. It's such good practice for your faith. And faith brings hope and love.'' (....)

July 15 — ''Picture Me as a living Being, loving you more than you could ever imagine even in your deepest longing. And keep before you the thought that this living Being who gave His life for you is waiting with infinite yearning for the moment of our Meeting. Wouldn't you show Him your impatience too? And your joy?

Picture Me often this way, as a real person, not just someone near you, but actually in you. One whose presence never leaves you. A presence... what a fountain of joys! And a beloved Presence too, as precious as life itself. No one is more beautiful than I, for I am Beauty. No one more intelligent, for I am Eternal Mind. Do you really realize how gentle and compassionate I am, for all I am so great? And that My face is full of charm and inexpressible sweetness? Ask Me to soon unveil its creative beauty for you. Love will stream from every feature. Tell Me how sorry you are for having grieved Me. Be aware of the fact that very little keeps you from seeing Me. Let your heart be stirred to its innermost depths as My eyes rest upon you. Don't you have something to say to Me? Won't you give Me the balm of your love? How the bridegroom smiles at the bride as she gets ready to lavish all her tenderness upon him; and if she finds words to express her love, I am the One who inspires them, for I am Love and I am in her words. At least praise Me by your love-will, and long to please Me. Long to be My beloved companion, my attentive bride. And since I no longer have a mother on earth, be My mother too. Take the place of John and Mary Magdalene. And at the same time, be yourself. You, whom I wanted in this century, this period, this little moment of time on earth, My poor little bride.''

July 22 — *''Lord, I should so much like to take Mary Magdalene's place on earth, because I know how sweet her love was for You.''*

''Offer it to Me, Mary Magdalene's love. It is yours by the communion of saints, for all time is present to Me. You find it difficult to believe in this treasure that your God devised for you. But just lay hold of it in all its magnificence, even though it is beyond your understanding. Above all, believe it. All that I have thought out for My children is for their good, not for Mine. Humble yourself in faith and love as Mary Magdalene did. Tell Me often in secret of all the ways in which you have grieved My heart. Be deeply sorry. You know how My heart listens. And if your heart is moved as you confess, what do you think Mine must feel?

Oh, My child, may love lift you above your usual ways. Like Mary Magdalene, learn to be a new woman, even to giving up your all. (....)

The sacrifice most pleasing to God is a cleft and contrite heart. What deeper pain could you have than to have little love? So take all the love of the saints and give it to Me as though for the first time. Ask Mary

Magdalene to help you — she who loved so much.''
(....)

July 29 — *Le Fresne church.*

''My child, can't you understand that the trials I send you are all made to measure, exactly fitted to your power to bear, favors that draw you nearer to your Beloved. Thank Me for a little trial as though it were a flower placed with new tenderness on your heart by your Fiancé. Doesn't He find you more beautiful when you suffer with gentle patience united with His patience? Doesn't your soul take on, as it were, a new expression full of love for Him? Be flexible and docile in My hand. Always humble yourself as though you had deserved to suffer. I am all innocence, yet I suffered everything imaginable. Wouldn't you like to suffer everything too, so that we might be more one than ever? Do you think we're close enough now? Wouldn't you love to come closer? Has your love said its last word? Lose yourself and gain by coming into Me. There are many kinds of houses; the home where one lives in intimacy with the Bridegroom is the dearest of all, isn't it? And if you have understood this, why not make it your permanent residence? What could ever touch you there? You are in the arms of the incomparable One to whom you have entrusted everything — your honor, your belongings, your heart. He will use everything for your sanctification. This is one great end: to love God and to please Him. What else matters, My poor little girl!

God... When you see Him, how you will want to have served Him, to have loved Him, to have glorified Him without counting the cost, and with all your heart! Don't be afraid of trials. They only help you to go higher. They make you love Me more. And there I am, waiting for you at the bend in the road. 'How will she overcome this difficulty? Will she ask Me to help her? Will she give Me her whole confidence at last in a child-like outburst of tenderness?' Oh, the serenity of the one who has yielded everything to Me.''

August 20 — *Joué-sur-Erdre.*

''Wherever you are, you are in Me. You are all Mine. Nothing but sin could ever separate us. You can't possibly escape My love! It is all-encompassing. Serve it. Wait upon Me. How often I have served you in the outpouring of My tenderness! What have I not done for you, My dear little child? If you suffer, suffer with Me. All these discomforts caused by the weather — I bore them all, like you, on the open roads. Always be one with Me in everything that happens to you. How I love this attitude — being ready to merge. Isn't that love itself? A longing for at-onement?

I garner up your faith, rewarding it with grace. And if you give yourself to grace, I respond by giving you a greater grace. And so, step by step you will soon rise to heights you never suspected. For there is no end to My gifts and it is My joy to commune with you unceasingly.''

August 26 — ''I gave you all you have. Am I not able to double My gifts? Am I less rich? Or do I love you less?

I can sanctify you in an instant. But I love your long and patient work; it keeps you humble. Acquire loving humility — it will exalt you. Discouragement never elevates anyone.

Keep going. Don't stop. I kept going on the road to Calvary and in spite of such agony, I got there. Look at Me and you will find new courage. And honor Me by calling Me to help you.''

September 16 — ''Say often, 'My Creator, fulfil Yourself in me. There's only one thing that I want — that You may reign in me as You reign in heaven.' And I shall lay hold of you more avidly than a bird of prey. You have seen a devouring flame? Let yourself be taken swiftly. Instead of running away, throw yourself into My arms and lose your bearings. I'll love you like that — blind, letting Me lead you.

I am the Good Shepherd; My shoulders can carry more, so take your place.'' (....)

September 30 — *Le Fresne.*

After the bombing of Nantes, I regretted not having a truck to save my belongings.

''Why are you anxious? Am I not there to keep watch? Don't I know what you need? and what is best for you? Put everything in My hands, and trust. Have you ceased to be My child? Have I ceased to be your Father? My love knows no seasons. I am the changeless One. Just as I gave Myself to you, so I remain.''

I was thinking of the strangers who had taken refuge in my home.

''Don't ever think that chance brought them to you. I chose these people. Do everything in your power to help them, with the tact of an apostle bent on accomplishing his task. Put them in My care. Pray for them. Suffer for them. Didn't I suffer for everyone? Try to be like the Beloved. Let them see My face in your face. The Father will be charmed and will reward you richly. What will you not be able to obtain?

Why do you ask so little? Come to Us, My child, and ease our longing to show compassion. Don't ever forget that the people around you are there in order that you may plead for them. You don't take a single step without Me. How could you ever think that you are alone? I'm guiding every detail of your life. Let yourself be taken captive by My heart.''

October 7 — *Montrelais church.*

I was thanking Him for having spared me the bombing.

"Always thank Me. I give you so much. If I were to give you a trial would you thank Me? You should. I do everything for the good of souls. Never doubt this, and believe in My love. Hope in My love. Love My love. If you love my love you will welcome everything that comes from me and you will act everywhere for Me. If you hope in My love, you will no longer count on yourself. You will expect My help in every difficult situation. You will think, 'I can't do anything, but there is nothing the Beloved can't do.' And full of trust and peace you will take up your task of love again, happy to toil day and night to console Me.

'If only I were sure that I consoled Him,' you say. But keep in mind that I am man as well as God, and you may comfort Me as one comforts a man. Don't be surprised at setbacks; you were made for rest in heaven not on earth. So get used to living for eternity, for nothing has the slightest importance in time that does not count for eternity. Judge everything in Me and by Me. My judgments are not always yours. Let the compassion of My heart flow through you to all who come near you. Let them see it in your smile, in your way of welcoming them. Oh, these contacts with others... how much good can come from them. But implant My Name in your heart like a banner."

October 15 — *Ingrandes church.*

"My child, don't lose a single minute. Time is short for saving so many souls. It is not merely by praying that they are saved, you know, but through the actions of even the most ordinary lives lived for God. Offer Me everything. Absolutely everything, united to My life on earth. What wealth! Give it to poor sinners, most of them are just ignorant. You have known and received so much. Take pains to help them. You will comfort this heart of Mine so full of tenderness, and you will satisfy justice. Offer Me all the crosses of the world. There are so many just now and few think of offering them to Me in expiation for sins. You who do know, help, so that nothing may be lost. Give Me hearts. Give Me souls. I am thirsty. Always.''

"Lord, I want to die for the salvation of souls."

''Oh! resemble Me as much as possible. Say to yourself, 'I'll do this or that like Him.' And in this way you will grow and come closer to Me. You know, on earth the tenderness between My mother and Me was so great that we had only one heart. Try to be like her by making your will one with Mine, your great Friend. Be ever ready to help others right to the very limit of your strength. You remember with what love I gave myself. In My public life, in the midst of so many people all crowding around through self-interest. Seldom did I meet with love. They came to Me through selfishness, yet My tenderness reached out to each one of them. Imitate Me. Don't bargain with Me. Don't complain. Go gaily. For My sake — isn't that a good reason for being full of joy? The only reason. Of course you can't think of it all the time, but in the morning say, 'Everything will be for you, my great Friend.' Then from time to time during the day, a little word such as, 'This is for You.' It will warm your heart and bring balm to Mine.''

November 3 — ''You are worried about this holy hour. You think you won't use it well. But since we're together, count on Me to make up for what you lack. Isn't that natural between friends? Wouldn't you do just the same for someone you love? Then I, your God, your Savior... just think of it! (....)

Be sure that no matter what you are doing I can help

you, and I long to do so in the very depths of My heart, aflame with love. How concerned I am for your perfection! You are My members. May My Body be perfect... Keep your will closely knit with Mine. Be My dream of you.'' (....)

November 11 — *Le Fresne church.*

(....) ''If you have failed in something, you say, 'My dear All, I could have been more faithful today. Forgive me.' You humble yourself most sincerely. And without your knowing it, I press you to My heart burning with love. That is what you call grace, and My grace is sufficient for you. Do you believe that?

This should be your one fixed desire: To live only for Me. Your life will be filled to the brim with good things. I've been waiting so long for the joy of giving you more. Help Me. Ask Me to do so. Stretch out your two empty hands to Me. Give Me a big place in your life. Give Me all of it. Do you realize that you are in exile, waiting for the return of the Beloved? Listen from afar. Say to Him, 'Breathe on this breath of mine which is yours. Your home shall be My home. I could no longer live without Your step in mine and Your voice in my voice.'

Don't people pray, 'Open Thou my lips'? That's so that the Spirit will speak in you, children of God.''

November 18 — *Le Fresne church.*

''Yes, ask Me to be your good will. Since you know that without Me you can do nothing. You can't even pronounce My name with love without My help, my poor little child.

If you only knew the Love that suffered and died a shameful death for you... If you knew its power and tenderness! I carry you even more than a mother her child. I lead you in the right paths, making plans for you to become holy. To be holy means to be always ready for Me, keeping close to Me, like other Christs. Oh, My dear little brothers, think of your Model, your elder Brother, who lived in utter simplicity so that it might be possible for you to become like Him. I was so simple that I passed unnoticed except for those three years when I had a feeble little following of twelve disciples. What a short life Mine was, My child, for the salvation of all the ages! My love for My Father guided all My actions. Enrich yours in the same way and stay close to Me. All that is Mine is yours; you know that. But you must come and take. It is such a joy for Me to give. I only gained to lose, for there is nothing I want to keep for Myself.

You remember when you were little how tenderly you asked your mother for what you wanted. Won't you have still more love when you talk to Me? Find a heartfelt élan for Me quite unlike any you give to others. Ask Me to give it to you. Let it be deeper, more intimate, more full of trust; and be generous enough to be ready to die for Me. Oh, if only wave upon wave of love could bring you to the shores of death! What a direct preparation, My little girl!''

November 25 — *Ingrandes church.*

''Offer even the rhythm of your breathing to Me. Not just that of the body, but the stream of your soul-thoughts. This may seem nothing to you, but it is your entire life, and all of it belongs to Me, for Love has all the rights of conquest. What sadness for both of us if you were to keep something of yourself from Me. From Me! Oh, My little child, day by day tighten the bonds that unite us. Be My joyous captive. Some have found such sheer delight in My sweet bondage that they could say, 'My heart overflows with joy even in the midst of trouble.' For I faithfully accompany My faithful ones

148

and give strength and comfort to those who want so much to suffer for Me. What they endure for Me I endured before them, for I have suffered all things in the sufferings of My friends. Don't you suffer when you see someone you love suffer? Am I not the most tender of friends? Oh, believe Me, for this is a reality, and it will encourage you to love Me more. A little more each day — ever so gently, without taxing your soul. More frequent holy desires. A little upsoaring of your heart to Me, an affectionate glance. Less time spent far from any remembrance of Me; a sunnier loyalty, a silence of humility; a kindness for My sake. And never cease to thank Me. I do so much for you, My beloved little girl. Don't you see that? And there are all the other blessings you never see. Oh, don't ever doubt. *(In a tone touched with emotion)* Don't doubt Me.''

December 3 — *Le Fresne church.*

(...) ''It takes so little from you to give Me intense pleasure. If you had a more perfect knowledge of God you would understand this. Often you judge God according to human qualities. Remember that you are nothing, that you are unworthy of My favors. Let your heart be filled with love as you ponder over all that I have given you this year — filled with the desire to come closer to My holiness. Your desires please Me. Don't put any trust in what you can achieve by your own efforts but ask Me to help you. And even in the spiritual domain, leave your own will behind. You will be in the high-way of truth, the rapid route. I was God and yet I did only the will of My Father who sent Me. Of course it's a mystery. But believe it. Little by little you will find your happiness in running away from the very thing you wanted if it is against My will. If you wish to be perfect you will live in My home and you are on earth for that alone.'' (....)

December 9 — *Le Fresne church.*

''Never leave your Immaculate Mother. She won't leave you either. She loves you even more than your own dear mother. She suffered more to give birth to you, for she bore My death. Queen of Martyrs! If suffering increases love, just imagine the tenderness she feels for you. Nothing could ever quench it, not even your ingratitude. Thank her. Love her. Above all, speak to her about your love, and this will draw you nearer to Me. Where else would she lead you if not to Me? She is much too humble to take for herself what belongs to Me, she who lived for God alone. Ask her to teach you to live for Me. Put all your trust in her. She will help you on your uphill climb; it is strenuous work climbing the mountain of perfection. Just when you think you're going up, you find that you are slipping back. Who will purify you? Who will put light into your mind, if not those who possess it — the saints and the Queen of all saints? See that you are very child-like with her. She was only a woman, but the Woman. The other Eve was called the first woman, but My mother is the woman who crushed the head of the serpent. Live simply with us as at Nazareth. Nothing in our intimate life will be kept from you. I give everything I have, even the love of My mother. When you feel weak or alone, come to us. You don't need any introduction. We've known you for a long time and better than you know yourself. Our poor little child, humble yourself before our great love for you. Love, to comfort us for those who do not.''

December 24 — *Le Fresne church.*

I said, ''Lord, move about in my thoughts night and day.''

''Yes, let yourself be saturated like a sponge filled

with water. Keep yourself before Me. Would you be afraid to leave yourself to be filled with Me? Be sure of this, that when you lose yourself, you gain, and when you seek yourself, you lose. Reach up closer and closer to your Maker. He created you. He knows all about you and how best you can serve Him. And what your share is in the sanctification of the world; for each one of you has some special contribution to make. What sorrow for you if you were to fail! If you didn't respond to the call! The bride takes her share in the work of the Beloved, and the more love she brings to it, the less heavy it seems.

For this work of love, offer everything you do and think, acting as best you know how to please Me, to be with Me, not to leave Me alone, for on earth I am often alone. How willingly would I take refuge in a faithful heart so as to live there with My Father. And I would transform this heart, filling it with such sweetness and happy simplicity. So grow accustomed to living in Me. Try over and over again. Unceasingly. What delicate work and what help we give those who give Us their love-will. My poor little children, when you have given Us your trust, you are never alone. With what tenderness we carry you... Infinite tenderness. Unnumbered delicate touches that would astonish and might even scandalize you if you could see them. A God! to love His creatures so much... Yes, and even more. Love — that is our treasure. Believe with all your heart in this holy extravagance and give yourself up to it unceasingly, unceasingly, for God's love is forever flowing to you, My little girl...''

December 30 — *Le Fresne church.*

''Never alone; you know that. Then let it be a source of strength to you. Strength to speak to Me, since I

151

am there. Strength to act, since I can help you, particularly when you speak to others. Ask Me to speak through you.

Never alone! What a joy for you! Could you ever thank Me enough?'' (...)

1944

January 1 — *After Communion.*
"The keynote for this year: 'Hope in Me'."

January 13 — *Le Fresne church.*
I said, "Truth, I adore You."
"Yes, I am Truth. Sin is falsehood, error, darkness. Every form of goodness is truth: the desire for good, work for justice... You will see later that only one thing matters and that is truth, for God alone matters. Attach no importance whatsoever to anything apart from Me, however pleasing it may be. Happiness is found in Me alone.

When I created man I placed deep within him a sense of goodness and truth, for I created him in My image. When he sins against his conscience, he no longer resembles Me but becomes ignominious, whereas when he tries to draw nearer to Me through sacrifice and effort, he takes on a new likeness to Me. There are some who have so faithfully imitated the gentle Christ that they have appeared in heaven like other Christs. What glory they bring with them!

Each one of your thoughts and feelings and actions has its repercussion for good or evil.

These are great truths. Ponder them on My heart. Picture yourself always before My watchful eyes, My little girl; I follow you because I love you."

January 20 — *Le Fresne church.*
(....) "Don't be afraid of being too tender. Or of

saying too much to your Beloved. Complain about yourself. Say to Him, 'When will You heal me, My great Friend, of this or that?' So many things in you are unworthy of Me. Humble yourself as you think of this. Hide all your ugliness in My heart. It's a hospital, you know, and doesn't one sometimes come out of a hospital cured? Trust in Me with all your heart since I am your great Friend. You remember the keynote for the year, 'Hope in Me'. My help never comes to an end, and I never cease to watch over you. I am infinite and I am Love. So lose yourself in Me, trusting Me to guide you. Be the little blind child who skips joyously because he is holding someone's hand. Oh, learn to be joyous since you are Mine and open your heart to fulness of peace. Keep your glance ever ready for Mine. Don't let anything preoccupy you unless it be your work for My kingdom.''

''Lord, what can one do to bring all people to You like a flock of doves?''

''Pray; speak to Me and don't be ashamed to mention My Name. Don't you know that blessings downflow at the mere mention of My Name? So many words said in one day in the world, and so rarely the word 'God' is heard... Yet all live and have their being in Me and I have saved everyone. Wouldn't it be only natural for them to think of Me? You, My beloved child, make up for this. When you were little and someone hurt your good Jenny, how you found ways of comforting her! Am I not more to you than she? Isn't there in the secret innermost part of your being a language unknown to others, reserved for Me alone? No words are necessary. Let there be outpourings of gentleness, love, gratitude; let your spirit soar and sing. Let Me feel your impatient eagerness to meet Me, your submission, your desire for My glory, your rejoicing in My joy to be at rest with My Father. Forget everything.

154

Think of Me, of Me alone. Anything else, anyone else, how could they ever upset you? I am. Be Mine.''

February 3 — *Le Fresne church.*
(....) "I lived My last hour as you will. Get ready now to unite your death with Mine. Close together, you and I, above all at the final moment. In times of danger, you know how the members of a family throw themselves into each other's arms. You will keep yourself still closer to Me when the last hour is drawing near. This will be the perfect leap, the sacrifice of everything around you for love of My heart on which you will lean. My poor little girl, how short this life on earth is! It is always an unfinished symphony. Do you realize that your home is elsewhere? Why continue to cling to the things of the earth? The other life is tomorrow. Aren't you longing to see Me? To know Me better? Ask Me for this desire. I can give you everything you lack. You don't ask. Above all, don't be afraid of wearying or annoying Me. You are My little child. Nothing that concerns you ever tires Me.

The other day you saw that young mother who said to you, 'When my child is in my arms I forget the whole world.' What is mother-love compared with Mine? Her love is My gift to her. The love I have for you is God-Love. We spoke of the divine extravagance, didn't we? Don't be afraid then. Just ask. Yearn... and thank Love. Call yourself 'God's little child'; it will give you a new feeling.''

February 17 — *Le Fresne church.*
I was thinking of all His blessings: ''Lord, what good things you have lavished upon me! What can I ever do to thank you?''
''Keep Me company more and more. You can never

know what it means to Me to be treated as an intimate friend. It is so rare. I delight in this as a human being. Don't you love someone who finds rest in your company and who wants to confide his secrets to you? And I, the sensitive One! Seek Me and don't ever let Me go away. Keep Me faithful and joyous company.

This morning after Communion you were thinking of My tortured limbs. You hailed My indescribable sufferings. You called Me 'King of Martyrs'. You kept near Me, in Me. Do the same all through the day. Take Me in any moment of My life on earth and be there, very near Me. Time doesn't exist for Me; do you believe that? So you see, you shall have been there just as the apostles were. And I shall be so happy. In this way My life can go on and on in the hearts of others, right to the end of the world.

My little child, do you really want to lend Me your heart?''

"Lord, take out of it everything that displeases You."

"You will never be perfect. There will be deviations, shortcomings — so many chances to humble yourself. But love atones for everything. Practice it often. Begin again and again; persevere; make it bloom. Who has ever talked to Me too much of love? Who has ever regretted having loved Me greatly?

Get used to spending hours in love, walking with love, resting for love. And at last, you will come to death and it will be for love that you will die. Prove your love for Me by the help you give your neighbor, keeping in mind that your neighbor is Myself and that your neighbor takes up more than half of life.

My darling child, try at last to understand love a little better.''

February 24 — *Ingrandes church.*
I said, "How can I come to comprehend love?"

"Try to see Me in every happening, big and little. I say 'little' because it is in the daily round and taking all things from My hand that you will understand the divine care. How sweet and loving it will seem to you! But you will see it only superficially. Then go higher — go to the very heart of your God. Think of His immeasurable sufferings, known to Him beforehand, suffered every one of them beforehand. Ponder this deeply. Don't you think that it will rekindle the feeble flame of your love? Entrust it to Me. They brought Me the sick and crippled. Isn't your love for Me both sick and crippled? Didn't I know how to raise the dead? If you only believed in My power, you would have the greatest hope. You, My child, believe in My love and that will be enough. Of course I'll help you; ask Me to do so. You see I'm telling you what to do. I'm the prompter for your rôle. Appear without fear on the stage of love. I'll give you your cue."

March 6 — *After Communion.*

(....) "Your body belongs to Me. Take care of it because it is Mine. Do your work because it is My work. Rest, to rest Me. And when you speak to your neighbor, that is My public life."

March 9 — *Le Fresne church.*

"Don't have a care in the world unless it be the fear of offending Me. Everything is in My hand and I am All-Power. Don't be afraid of focusing all your attention on Me and what concerns Me. Call back your wandering thoughts so that they follow My way only. Learn to control your mind, and center everything in Me. Take My strength for this, the strength I had in the wilderness to ward off hunger. (....)

Oh, My dear little girl, you can do so much for God's glory in the time left to you before eternity. Offer yourself often to Him as a docile instrument. Tell Him you want His will to be done in you. Tell Him of your impatience for His kingdom to come. Children's wishes are so dear. Be very sincere. Bring your thoughts homing to Him. Doesn't this make you happy? What could you lack when you live in His friendship?... Oh, the unchanging serenity of God's love!''

March 16 — *Le Fresne church.*

(....) ''The all-important thing is that you mean to imitate Me. You see you must continually purify your intention. Hold it up to Me like a little sanctuary lamp. Oh, this love-will to always please Me, to keep Me company, to comfort Me!

Just now you offered Me one of the first violets saying, 'Perhaps no one has thought of giving you any today.' It was just a trifle, yet it was much to Me, for I am kept in the background on earth. I, the King of Heaven!

Faith!... how simple it is, and how glorious. Thank Me for having given it to you. Try to increase it; it will be as though you made Me grow in you.''

March 30 — *Le Fresne.*

''You sometimes thank Me more for My temporal blessings than for My spiritual favors. I am always in both of them. But aren't the spiritual ones more choice? Isn't it as though I invited an intimate friend into My home to show her more kindness and share some of the secrets of My heart with her? You love to pour out your heart to someone who loves you truly. And because I am God, shouldn't I have the joy of a heart-to-heart talk?

Take a rest in Me sometimes, and this will be My feast of love, for you will belong to Me and I shall take hold of you, and the hour will be brief.''

"My Beloved, may every day be your feast of love."

"Stay with Me. You remember Saint John the Baptist? He lacked nothing and was never anxious about anything except My kingdom. His one and only thought was for Me, for the glory of God and His kingdom. Imitate the purity of his intention, the purity of his life, his unique love. You can imagine, can't you, what a rich return I gave him in heaven and how his self-denial has been rewarded. I know how to reward for I know how to love. Tell Me you are sure of this. Ask Me for My science of love. Try to love more with My help. Above all, never grow weary. The spiritual life is a never-ending beginning, you know." (....)

May 5 — *Le Fresne church.*
I felt overwhelmed by my faults and neglectfulness.

"You remember what I said: 'If I go away I shall send Him to you.' So call the Holy Spirit often. Holiness is His kingdom. Ask frequently. Why should you be ashamed? Aren't you all made to be saints, and can you be filled with light without divine help? What a joy it would be for Me if all people became holy.

If you love to please Me, then why not aim at holiness? Seek the help of the Holy Spirit often for this. Let Him possess you; ask Him to do so in My Name.

Do everything out of love for your ever-present God. Think of your neighbor's welfare. Seize every opportunity of doing good, for this is the same as to lay hold of Me. (....)

Oh, this work of purification! Begin. Begin. Make use of My merits since they are yours. Take them and offer them to the Father. They are your adorning jewels. They are your beauty." (....)

June 8 — *Le Fresne church. Holy hour.*
"My dear Lord, I should have been so happy to work in

your vineyard for Your glory. You remember when I was little how I said to You, 'Send me to your vineyard'.''

''You increase My glory and hasten My kingdom by doing any action more perfectly. Think of this often and you will live on a higher plane. Even if no one ever sees or hears you, you will increase My glory. Haven't you read that the more perfect and hidden an action the more excellent it is, because it is for Me alone? Did you know that there are deep forests, unfathomable oceans, and mountain peaks unknown to man where secret blossomings are for My extravagance of glory? So it is with the hidden life of a soul. No human being ever suspects it; but I offer it to Myself and it is there that I delight to be with the children of men. Oh, My little girl, let us always live together in the valley of tears and I'll lead you to my heavenly home, the New Jerusalem. There no one will ever take us from one another. There it will be the eternal now.''

June 22 — (....) ''If you knew what the love of God is, it would be impossible for you not to abandon everything to Him and let yourself be lost in Him. You would not dream of not counting on Him in life and death. Even on earth you prefer to love a superior person, don't you? Aren't you attracted by intelligence? warmth? kindness? Multiply by infinity all the gifts that you look for in those you love; God is more. For there are depths of tenderness in Me that you have never known. And this very God wants to possess you...! You, little nothing, loved by the All!

Don't let your thoughts wander from Him. You are enfolded in His Presence. Breathe in Him, move in Him. Above all, don't be afraid, for this would sadden Him. Your trust and joy honour Him. Expect everything from Him and everything will come to you.'' (....)

July 27 — *Le Fresne church, bombed the previous evening. Holy Hour.*

''Fear? Of course, My little girl, it counts for expiation, for your host-life, for the co-redemption. I Myself was afraid in Gethsemane. And what fear! There again we are together, since I wanted to share all your sufferings. Joyously consent to share Mine. This means so much to Me. Do you see My part in your life — supreme love desiring only at-onement with you? It is for this end that I arrange the events of your life.

Don't ever think that anything comes by chance; it is always I, Love itself, in everything. Don't you always recognize My step? How quickly a practiced tenderness should recognize it. It is quite unlike any other. Wait for it. How much sweeter than chance it will be to you; less cold too. Your great Friend directing your life! Just think of it. Your daily cross, your nightly cross — hold it close to your heart, for it comes from Me. It's not just any cross; it is yours, the one I wanted you to have. Kiss the hand that gives it to you and go patiently on your way with it. With Me.'' (...)

August 3 — *Le Fresne church. Holy Hour.*

While I was doing a hundred and one things I was thinking, ''But I must look after my Beloved.''

''Your Beloved does so much for you. When you are absorbed in other things He is there. When you are putting forth great efforts because your faith is dim, He is there. When you no longer feel His presence, He is with you. And when you think you are deserted He is right in your very center-alive, watchful, loving. Knowing this, how could your tenderness not go out to Him? To Him of whose Being you have only a shadowy conception.

Say to Him, again and again, 'I realize that I know nothing about You. But with faith and confidence I give

161

myself lovingly and without reserve in life and death, for You are more and more present, more and more loving and more and more mine.'

But above all, think this. Go deep into the meaning of those words by going deep into My wounds. Make this your permanent home, especially the wound in My heart. It will refuse you nothing. When people are under the same roof, don't they love to share everything?

Live in My heart. Would you like to try, — since you are invited? What could hinder you? It isn't shyness, nor indifference? nor fear? Then it's just a question of making a first effort. But you know that I always help. Try. Once the threshold is crossed, you will notice that you are more at home than in your own home. You will know the sweetness of the secret life and of silent and heart-searching intimacies. What a joy for Me! Should I thank you now? Are you ready?''

September 1 — *''Lord, after all this war with one another, won't there be a period of love and goodwill among men?''*

''That would be the Kingdom of God. Ask more often that My kingdom come. The hour of the Father's kingdom can be hastened if His children only plead with Him more earnestly, just as the birth of Christ was hastened by the yearning of the Virgin of Nazareth.

Pray, work, do everything to bring about this beautiful kingdom. I put this request in the Our Father so that it might be answered. Take courage, since I am helping you, and kindle your desires. Desires are prayers. They are swift arrows. Take aim and may the mark be struck with power.''

September 14 — *Le Fresne church. Holy Hour.*
''Take My heart and press the blood upon France,

upon the world, so that its purifying power may change the face of the earth. Everything can work together for good, you know, even evil. And I can make even those who seek disorder and violence contribute to My glory. But you must pray. You see how I am always asking you to work with Me. There again, don't leave Me alone. Don't you love to help Me? Try. You will discover that I'm helping you to help Me. Of course, I always help, My poor little girl, only you don't notice it. I am the Friend who does good in the home and who sometimes slips away before being recognized and thanked.'' (....)

September 21 — *Nantes. Chapel of the Recollects. Holy Hour. I was wondering whether I really exercised faith in my daily living.*

''Faith — this embryo implanted by the Holy Spirit, must be given every care if it is to keep on growing. Faith needs frequent practice. You must pray for it, too. If you say to Me, 'My Friend, I believe in You; help me to believe still more so that I may love You more,' how could I fail to answer you? You will believe just as if you had seen and heard Me. Sometimes you envy the people who lived in My day. And yet, apart from the apostles, they didn't have Communion as frequently as you; they didn't have My Eucharist every morning in the depths of their hearts.'' (....)

September 28 — *Nantes. Recollects. Holy Hour.*

''If you suffer, I am there to suffer with you. And this is My cross again — this suffering in your suffering. Share it with Me, for everything depends on oneness. And if you believe in My love, suffering will be sweet to you. It will seem like a little return for what I have given you. Oh, this loving exchange of hearts that vie with one another. I should like to be vanquished by you if this were possible. But you are very little to vanquish your God. And self-love, always besetting man's path, is an obstacle to many things. Tell Me in a heartfelt way that everything in you is for Me.''

October 3 — *Nantes. Chapel of the Immaculate.*
On a day when I was busy with a hundred and one tasks.

''You may be very sure that to do your duty is one way of loving Me. In this way you can love Me all day long. You don't notice this, but I do. Your offering in the morning has told Me. And are you ever so busy that you haven't even a moment to glance at Me? It would enrich Me, for I am poor when it comes to the thoughts of My children. So very poor — I who never leave you.

Try to understand My yearning for you, for all My children. I called the little ones to Me. I call souls. Who will recognize My voice, this tender, gentle voice that you know? You would be sorry if you could no longer hear it, wouldn't you? It's like a rest that is food and drink to you. It holds you up when you must be steadfast. You feel that, don't you? Then be My voice for others. It isn't enough to be good; you must be My goodness. You understand the difference? It's all the difference between you and Me. So forget that you are you. Be your Christ — the One who loves you at all times. Try to imitate Me.

I enfold you. Go gallantly.''

November 6 — *During the Elevation.*
''By dint of carrying your cross you will find that your cross is carrying you.''

November 23 — *Holy Hour.*
''My darling Father, I want only to do Your will and every-

thing for Your will, but most often I do mine and I live for myself.''

"No one succeeds immediately in getting completely rid of self. A glance at Me is sufficient to purify your intention — one of your smiling glances.

Don't forget to look at Me through your days and nights. Don't grow weary. How could you grow weary of so tender a friend?

When tempted against the faith, say a little word to Him, and the temptation will go away.

Don't you understand? You can't get away from Me; you're too weak. But when you come as close as possible to your great Friend by tender and constant contemplation, you may be sure of warmer and more prompt assistance. Why do you doubt? How can you ever doubt?

I am like a master who gives his instructions behind a curtain in order to hide his great love for his pupils. I am like a player who slips quickly away in order to excite and prolong the chase.

Don't I use every means of increasing your merits, My dearly beloved little children? Don't be afraid of Me. Be afraid to be afraid. And with great simplicity make My heart your home.''

November 29 — *Holy Hour.*
"Since the second commandment is as great as the first, have no regret in leaving Me to go to your neighbor. Didn't I bring him into your life — this particular person and not another? Then it's because there is a work for you to do for him; there is your influence. Keep careful watch over your influence.

In Palestine the people around Me were so happy that they brought others, you remember? I created an atmosphere. You create one too — an atmosphere of joy and peace. Not yours, My poor child, but Mine.

I'll act in you, speak in you, think in you. Ask Me for this, so that we may be one, and this will be a sweetness for others as the sun shining through the rain. Can I be anywhere and not bring joy? It is one of the facets of the prism of My love.'' (....)

''Think of Me when you speak to others, so that by leaving yourself behind you have more balm to give, like a fragrance that gives itself unaware.''

December — *On a train I was thinking:*
''I've written His words so often! Is that enough? Or should I go on?''

''Are you tired of Me? Would you want to make it impossible for Me to speak to you? Don't I find comfort in ceaselessly pouring out My heart into your heart? I say 'ceaselessly', so great is My need to be your inner knowing. I in you! My child, this is My delight. So don't be afraid of wearying Me, or of wearying others either; it is through you that I am speaking to this one and that one to bring them cheer and encourage them to come close to Me and talk to Me about themselves. I should so love to have their confidence. Never mind if they don't know how to speak to Me these poor people — I want them to come without any fear and just say to Me: 'I don't know how... it's the first time...' Even if they don't know what to call Me, let them tell Me of their tenderness without giving Me any name. (...)

Pray for those who are afraid. How can they be? How could anyone be afraid of such a good Shepherd? Even the very little lambs climb on His knees and rest there. And this is the Shepherd's joy. (....)

You who yearn for My kingdom, pray. For My sake, offer the Father little sacrifices full of joy — a pyramid bouquet of them — all the colours of love. The patient sacrifices, the violent and the gentle ones, the gracious ones full of the most humble love — very humble, you understand. Be even ready to thank the person to whom you gave for allowing you this chance to be generous to Jesus Christ. Sacrifices of pride, too; consider yourself to be the least of anybody, and be one in this way with My mother's humility. Would you like this?" (....)

December 13 — *Holy Hour.*

(....) "Practice your faith. When you were learning to walk, you leaped forward at a venture, and little by little you became surefooted. Do the same in your inner life. Take a flying leap toward the Trinity, toward My mother, in upsoarings hitherto unknown to you, more direct, more sincere, impelled from the very center of your being. This will become habit and it will exalt you. Do you grasp what I mean? You will exalt others too, since each one of your thoughts and feelings reverberates for good or evil. Didn't you tell Me that you wanted to help Me in the work of redemption? Then do all that you do to this end. This was the motive for all My actions, and we should always be together, My little girl. Do Me the honor of believing that I yearn for this."

"Lord, I am all Yours."

"At this moment, yes, but don't drift away from Me. You know those other moments when you feel nothing but boredom, when your faith is shrouded in mist. You call and I don't seem to be there. O you of little, little faith!

Seek truth with all your heart. In spite of everything, yes, in spite of yourself, call, call out to Me. Say, 'I know all the same that you are mine, that I am You. What do all contrary appearances matter? I'm sure of You.'

And there I am, waiting for you right in the midst

of the battle. In the very place where I want your love: beyond and above all things. Above all things — that is where I am.

Rise to meet Me.

Always.''

PART TWO

"Ask that through this little book
I may come as I once came,
healing, drawing people to Me.
What a triumphal entry
into the silence of hearts!"

He and I

Introduction

"An utterly extraordinary and beautiful story" wrote Daniel Rops of Lui et moi *(He and I), this book alleged to contain the words of Our Lord to a French lay woman called Gabrielle Bossis.*

As I begin this introduction for Part Two, it is Ascension Day, when we are reminded more than ever of the fact that the mysteries of the sacred Body of Christ Jesus are, like His merits, for us. That not only is the incarnation applicable to us and the resurrection our lively hope, but the mystery of the ascension is engraved in the very atomic structure of our bodies awaiting its unfoldment through our union with Him by whom and of whom we are made. So that as man divests himself of his small self to clothe himself in Christ — as he brings Christ forth — then he can truly say with the poet and without any flight into fancy, "I know that I am august".

Far from destroying faith as some have imagined, science only gives it wings. Faith alone gives rise to hope, but faith enlivened and enlightened by science reveals to us the stupendous truth that we are *of the very "substance of things hoped for". "True science and true faith", says Jean Daniélou, "meet in a common knowledge of reality".*

Reality? For the theologian it is that "untraveled world whose margin fades forever and forever as we move". For the authentic mystic it is the Promised Land, and by joyous at-onement with Christ — center and circumference of all things from the farthest star to the tiniest atom of our bodies — he enters into that land and possesses it. It is the eternal kingdom eternally present within him. It is that "realm of the mirror of peace" to which the Voice refers.

As pilgrims *en route* to that Promised Land, readers of "He and I" gradually become aware of the fact that there is unction in these words. To work among them is to be submerged in a sea of light. This book is a song of love, of God-love, an air with variations of the same joyous and liberating theme: At-one with the All and so at-one with all; our true self-expression — the expression of Himself through us.

In Part One the song is more tremulous. There are moments of hesitation, of doubt. The voices of the two that are one seem to be singing separately. The pauses between the notes are more frequent. In this second and last part, there are more and more of those passages to which Daniel Rops refers, where the mystic, having "surmounted the first obstacles and come closer to God, sounds a note of simple and joyous plenitude, of serenity in love" as her soul finds its full fine flowering in the Uncreated Light.

As we listen to the notes and the grace notes, to the tones and overtones, we realize that this is much more than a dialogue between a soul and its God. It is the great Christ-hymn of praise — deep calling unto deep, or "Myself to Myself", as the Voice says. It mingles with the paeans of praise in this Christward movement, this second pentecost that is sweeping over our planet; with the glad hosannas of the triumphal entry into Jerusalem — the New Jerusalem of hearts — of a risen and glorified Christ who has returned, who is returning and who will return again.

No rumors of evil, no menacing discords of our age can ever drown it out. For "as birds flying, so will the Lord of hosts defend Jerusalem; defending also he will deliver it; and passing over he will preserve it".[1]

The story is told of a monk who went out one exceptionally fine spring morning to hear the meadowlark sing, and when he returned all his friends had died; three hundred years had gone by. To go out in the springtime of our spiritual youth, to listen to the Voice, is to pass beyond time. It is to experience however fleetingly what Etienne Gilson describes as "man's supreme bliss": a foretaste of "the face-to-face vision of motionless eternity".

What I said of Part One I say again of this second Part. This is a book of many doors.

"May the peace of great doors be for you".[2]

---

1. Isaiah 31:5.

2. *For You* by Carl Sandburg.

1945

January 1 — *In my bedroom at 3 o'clock in the morning.*
"Happy New Year, my Christ. What is the keynote?"
"Confidence. Flow over into Me."

January 4 — *Holy hour.*
My mind filled with a hundred and one things.
"Tell Me that all of it is for Me. I was for you at every moment of My life. I came for love; for love I saved you. I had you in mind in everything that went to make up My days. So don't do anything outside of Me. Even if you consider that it has nothing to do with Me. Everything has to do with Me. Don't shut Me out; never shut Me out. At every moment I am ready to receive you. If you were not ready for Me, you would lead Me to think that I was not your intimate Friend. Am I no longer that?"

"Oh, yes, You are; You are my great and beautiful Love."

"Then talk to Me in love's simple language. Warm your heart and seek to warm Mine, just as though you were afraid that I was not tender enough and by calling Me gently you would arouse My love. And this would really be to lure Me to My task. Bliss is yours if you believe this.

So go right to the limit of your loving thoughts, your desire to love, your sacrifices for love's sake. Prolong them. And go valiantly since it is for Me, your Christ who loves you — should I say to the point of folly? Because you see 'the folly of the cross' is a reality.

You're not very sure of this, are you? There is always this distance that you put between God and His children, whereas I try to remove all distance. Oh, My beloved friends, come to Me more simply. I always make the comparison of the little child who throws her two arms around her Father's neck. Do you need so much ceremony to love Him, to thank Him? Don't you see that the Father gives more tenderness than He receives?''

January 8 — *I said to the Holy Spirit, "Speak to the Father for me." And our Lord replied,*
   "He is in you, speaking to the Father."
   "Isn't there a little of me?"
   "There is the earnest effort of your good will."

February 1 — *Holy hour.*
   "Don't be astonished at My suggestion that you never cease asking for compassion, humility and gentleness. Aren't these the hallmarks of your Bridegroom's heart and shouldn't you try to resemble Him? Wouldn't you be happier if you had these qualities? And isn't it always your happiness that I'm seeking?... Ask My mother to give them to you and offer sacrifices in exchange. Plant the seed of desire for them. And as always, ask Me to help you.

   How happy a father is when his child who cannot yet walk holds out his arms to him. And if the child is tired, how he holds him to his heart! Who is happier, the father or the child?

   If you only knew what compassion really is — the compassion you must strive to imitate! Overlooking everything to stoop to a heart's needs, paying no attention to any disappointments or ingratitude, being even kinder to those who have hurt you. Just be your Christ for them. If you make this your intention I'll be seen in you. You are so little that you wonder how this could be. You know how grace gives unction to the voice, the look, a gesture? You noticed that yesterday when your relative who had not seen you for three years exclaimed, 'Oh, how I love you!' She was addressing Me in your voice.''

"Lord, I hope people will always find flashes of You in me."

"Then disappear more and more, My little girl. I am your infinite Ocean; flow over into Me. It is so simple for you to lose yourself there. Since I'm waiting for you. One will only — Mine. A single goal — the Father's glory. A single declaration — 'I love You with all the strength of this heart that You gave me.' That's all. And the Father takes us together as a single offering.

One only: I — you.''

February 8 — *Notre Dame. Holy hour.*

"Even if you ceased to love Me, I should always love you. Even if you no longer listened for My voice in the silence, I should still make it possible for you to hear Me. This is how every sinner finds Me waiting. Who could ever weigh My love, or set a price on it, or measure it? And who could ever dream of the immensity of My tenderness? For My love is tender. When you hear Me say, 'I am thirsty', I'm calling your tenderness.'' (...)

February 11 — *After Communion.*

"If I were only sure of comforting You, of giving You pleasure in doing this or that, such a thought would increase my strength tenfold."

"If what My children do for Me or say to Me is the kind of thing that would give joy to an ordinary man, it gives Me far greater joy, for I am the most sensitive, the most loving and the most gentle.

Don't get the idea that you are speaking to a

memory, a past ideal, a remote God. You are speaking to Me, fully alive in you. To your ever-present Presence. And when you speak to Me or My mother, speak with a loving smile. You know that special welcome of yours that people admire? Give it to Me. Come to Me alive with joy, serenity and tenderness. It will transform our relations. It means an effort on your part, but how consoling! Don't you find it so? It's like family life. You see, what I'm always seeking in My people is this life of intimacy with Me.''

February 15 — *Holy hour. (gently)*

''It doesn't bother you too much, does it — this hour that you give Me? I've been waiting for it as for a festive occasion. When you are invited to a banquet, don't you enjoy it in anticipation? The invitations from My children are all the more dear because they are so rare.

Have you noticed how some people are overlooked on the list of invitations? Out of sight, they hear only far-off sounds of the banquet. Perhaps it's a stranger, or somebody not popular enough to be invited. It often seems to Me that I am one of those. So when in the midst of your activities you stop on the way to your friends, I feel like thanking you and saying, 'I too, may I come?' ''

''O Lord, my home is always Yours.''

''You must tell Me that often. It is heartwarming for Me. Give this joy to your Lord God, little child of His. Tell Me all about your desire for Me and I'll make it grow. Even if you don't desire Me, tell Me so and I'll give you the desire. And I'll make it increase to the point where you will long to leave the earth to meet Me. Tell Me that you want to possess Me and to be possessed by Me. Quicken your love; this is your daily work. Then take courage to renew your courage every day. You know that I'm helping you. Tell Me that you know it. These little 'acts' of faith and trust are My joy. I like you to be able to recognize Me even though you are blindfolded. What happiness it gives Me when you say, 'It is He!'

There is your work on earth. Teach it to others and you will make Me loved. Do you understand? You will ask them... I seldom ask; I wait. You be My apostle and bring them to Me — all of them. If they will just take a few steps, I'll go all the rest of the way.''

March 1 — *Le Fresne. Holy hour.*
''To know that you love me so much could make me die of joy, couldn't it?''

''It's not enough to know about this love; above all you must have faith in it. How much comfort people would find and what happiness even in the midst of trials, if they only believed that everything that happens to them comes from My desire to do them good and that all is fitted to the measure of each one. Instead of that some think I am spiteful toward them, and they plot vengeance against their God. It would be so simple and so heartwarming for them to contemplate My immense love. But they no longer recall My passion. And wasn't it the proof of this other passion, this love I have for you all?

Little soul, let it be very simple for you to believe that I love you more than you have ever been loved. Come to this wellspring of My love; come, draw living waters of constant union and levitating joy.

Ponder these words: He and I. Live them. I and you: I in you. So often you imprison Me in your hearts by the two bars of the sign of the cross, and in the tabernacle in the Eucharist. Where else would I prolong My life on earth if not in the hearts of men, at least in the hearts of those who open them to Me. They called Me.

They called Me night and day. And I came. And I made My home with them.''

"*Lord, my heart will always be your home. I should like to engrave on it, 'Home of Rest for Him'.*"

"In My Father's House you will discover the answer: 'Home of Joy for My Gabrielle'. Oh, practice believing it over and over again, and be overwhelmed with happiness as you think, 'I am loved'. You know, don't you, that as you have believed so you shall receive. And from these feelings born of your confidence new favors will come to help you rise higher. Rise to union? Higher, still higher: to unity.''

March 15 — *Holy hour.*

"*Lord, yesterday I was tempted to skip my daily visit of thanksgiving for the Host I received in the morning.*"

"Why? Did I love you less that day? Didn't I give all of Myself as usual? Was I less rich in compassion? Or perhaps you don't realize what joy My children's little visits give Me? Especially when they come to see Me and not the architecture or the beauties of the church. When they speak to Me as to a friend, not in recited prayers. When they humble themselves before Me and in their own eyes.

And you, My little instrument, may you never get the idea that you merit My favors!''

"*Lord, let me rejoice in them, above all if these favors can help bring about Your kingdom. I think of myself as being the pitcher of water in the arms of that man in Jerusalem. It was a sign to the apostles, showing the way to Your beautiful 'Upper Room' where You instituted the Holy Eucharist.*"

"I have filled your little soul to overflowing.''

"*Lord, let the blessings shower upon others. May not one word be lost. Just to think... a word of Yours!*"

"You will see the effects of My tender love. Don't

you know that I give far more than you expect. Haven't you noticed this spiritually, materially? Then be sure to look upon Me as the companion of all your moments. Just now in the garden you said, 'Are you there?'

I am always there, ready for any little word of your heart, ready for a wish, a smile.

You wanted to praise My soul, and this was fitting. For My soul suffered most among the souls of men and that is why I have the highest glory in heaven. Do you know why I suffered the most? Because I had the greatest capacity for love.

Will you at last believe in My love? Very simply, every moment, no matter what happens? And with the greatest joy?''

"How I should like to, Lord! What is there in my brain that keeps me from being absolutely certain?"

''Call Me by the tenderest names. Names like wings beating upward, and you too will mount upward.''

In the street I smiled at a passer-by who returned my smile.

''It's like that when your heart smiles at Me. I smile back.''

March 22 — *Holy hour.*

''You have just been to see a very sick friend and you were full of pity for him. What will you say to your great Friend when you see His sufferings? Look carefully at them because they were for you. They are yours. Be humble enough to hide yourself in them. Say to Me, 'Have pity on me. I am nothing but a poor sinner.' Believe it, and I'll be moved to pity.

Consider your nothingness. If you could see it, you would be terrified if you didn't know My tender mercy. Try to grasp the poverty of your soul, its destitution. The you in you is nothing. This vision of yourself as you are would be terrible for you if you couldn't count

179

on My merits. Make this your consolation at this time of My passion. Look upon Me and discover My obedient death, accepted with the sweetness of My entire Being.

My little children, if you could have read My soul! Some day you will understand better. Love now as though you already knew. Try. Give Me your child-like readiness.''

April 12 — *In the station at Angers. Coming from Paris I had a seat in spite of the dense crowd.*

''You see what great care I take of My own. Even in the tumult I draw them into solitude where the heart is on the alert to hear the Beloved.

Didn't I say to them in the past, 'When I sent you out without purse or staff did you lack anything?' And they answered, 'Nothing'.''

''*Lord, it is often I who am lacking.*''

''For these omissions humble yourself, and don't be astonished by them. Wish to be cured of this lack of carefulness in My service. Take frequent stock not only of the value of your actions, but above all, of the value of your motive in doing them — the forthrightness of your will to glorify Me.

Perhaps if you paid attention more often to what you do for Me, you would intensify your fervor and tenderness. You would be more faithful in the details — these precious details that can earn so much. They are the specks of goodness that fill life... You get the picture — the invisible grains of sand that make up the immense Sahara. Take great care in the very little things, My Gabrielle. Say to yourself, 'They are made to the measure of my little nature'. And this thought will keep you humble.

Have you noticed how often the work of the humble has to be done again? Put all your heart into it, knowing that you please Me. And since you want to live for Me, since you want to see everything in relation to Me, and pattern your life after Me, then consider how short the time is that remains for you on earth. You can give Me glory in that time. Give it to Me unstintingly.''

April 20 — *Le Fresne. At church.*
I had seen flowers of all kinds at the edge of a ditch.
''You see how insurgent the spring is! Let a spring-tide of love in your soul blossom out in good deeds of every color. I shall look lovingly at them just as you looked at the flowers in the underbrush. Tell yourself that love alone can make fresh wonders spring forth.

Then give yourself to Love so that Love may possess you. Don't divide yourself into two — one part for you and the other for Me — since I long to have all of you and cherish this hope. Your love quenches My thirst. I am most demanding: you see I want My children to be wholly and utterly Mine at every moment. So don't withhold a thing. Don't take anything of yourselves away. You would steal from Me if you did, because everything is Mine.

If I require this of you it is because My yearning for you is a consuming fire. And My yearning is born of My love. Do you understand? Do you at last believe? Do you acknowledge My power to love? And if Mine is a love beyond all others, then how could you fail to go beyond your usual ways of loving to make your home in the higher realms — the realms where all is simplicity in our oneness. Above all when you know that it is there that I'm waiting for you and that great is My need to meet you.

Meditate on this need of Mine and you will call to mind that it is in your power to give Me this alms. Then remember the value of a free gift — the gift of oneself

— when offered out of tenderness. What inexpressible joy will be His who receives it. He will multiply His blessings so that the one that receives them will be lost in wonder and gratitude. 'What have I done to deserve the kindness of my God?' he will ask. And I shall reply, 'You loved Him with all your strivings and you let Him love you'."

April 26 — *"Lord, Your poor little girl, Your poor image, is here before you, yearning for You with all the strength of her being."*

"Have you noticed how people talk among themselves, discussing all their personal affairs? They spend so much time this way and it does them so little good. Don't you think that if they gave themselves to Me, their Friend, I should rejoice to have My place in their thoughts and I should know how to reward their confidence munificently? Don't you think that it would create a moment-to-moment intimacy between them and Me, and this would be a joy for them, because close to Me their lives would lose their tension.

You understand? It would be life together with Me — I carrying the heavy end of things. So again I say, speak with Me, My little ones. Speak with Me. And our hearts will merge. Isn't this the aim of My Christians? Isn't that why you want to die? Then begin by living this heart-oneness. Seize upon every opportunity. Find every pretext. You aren't bold enough. For some of you it is because you are indifferent.

But My close friends, why, why don't they call louder to Me from their heart's depths? If only their belief were less like unbelief! If their hope were fixed upon My help... And if, in all simplicity, their love loved Me more. I should be there looking after everything in their day, and when night fell, their eyes would close again on My face.

You know what it is to sleep that way — within My embrace? Would you like to learn better? Remember, it's a question of beginning over and over again. Of trying to grow. Of taking great care not to be satisfied with yourself. But ponder often on your poverty. Tell Me about it and My heart will be all eagerness to help you since you are so little, so weak. And when you call Me, be sure to give Me the most tender names. I'll recognize the voice.''

May 3 — *''My beloved Jesus, I come to receive Your word and above all Your love — Thursday, this day dearest to my heart of all the days of the week.''*

''Enter into my courts. Ask the help of My mother. Go farther, still farther. Leave material things behind. Go right into the most secret shrine. There, where there is silence, the freedom of inner knowing, the flame that burns to burn more brightly.

Then ask the Spirit to brood over you as He brooded over the waters before the end of Creation.

By yourself you are chaos. Do you fully realize this? Do you try to keep it in mind? Have you humbled yourself today in thought or deed? Not to cause you distress nor diminish your strength, but to tighten your hold on the power of your God, who is only waiting for your call.

And now, possessed by the Spirit, what else could inspire your words but Love? Tell Him, the Spirit of Love, to speak for you. Don't you think that it will be in the simplest, most delicate way? For the Spirit also adopts the language of the little ones. Wasn't My very humble mother overshadowed by Him when she answered the angel, 'Behold the handmaid of the Lord'?''

May 10 — *Ascension. After Vespers in the empty church.*

"Lord, I rejoice for those in heaven. But the Ascension is sad for our planet."

"Make a fervent novena for Pentecost together with My mother and the holy women in the Upper Room. Not so much to be comforted by the Comforter, but so that He will teach you how to comfort Me. Earnestly desire to know how to console Me. Make use of this most gentle way of loving, as though you offered Me a new home with rare flowers and perfumes where a wealthy friend waited for frequent meetings and confidences.

It is your heart that wants the hearts of all men to be Mine. It is your heart that wants to find warmth close to Mine. Then if you have a clear understanding of the Ascension, you will try to follow your Beloved and live less for the things of your planet than for His home in heaven. So don't fail to begin doing now what you will do tomorrow: join in the praises of the All-joyous ones, your brothers of tomorrow.

You remember that in spite of the fact that I rose from the Mount of Olives, I remained in the midst of My apostles, hidden in the Eucharist, in the heart of My holy mother. Could I have deserted My poor children completely? You, My child, seek Me always in the Eucharist. It is there for you, for everyone. Don't be reticent. Come simply. Give thanks with joy in your heart. Love simply. Everything is so simple with Me. Don't you notice this when I speak to you? Leave behind your old way of imagining. Enter into the way of Love's clear vision."

May 24 — "Endure the daily thorns for love of Me. This prepares your soul for acts of heroism.

You realize, don't you, that union with God is nothing more or less than doing His will. Every human being is called upon sooner or later to rise to some act of heroic goodness, and grace for such moments is won by loving acceptance of the daily burdens. So you see how valuable the little routine tasks are to one who gives himself to them in loving obedience to Me. Haven't I told you that in My eyes nothing is small? It's the love woven into each task that counts.''

June 7 — ''As I am never at an end of My words for you, I hope you will never give up listening to Me. The hidden fountains of the heart's deeps are given drop by drop; each one is of the greatest value and not one can replace another. And because I give you My secrets, I wait for yours. Yes, I know what you want most to confide: 'Lord, I don't love you as I want to. Make it possible for me to love You more.'

This suffering of not loving Me enough — offer it to Me in pure reverence, straight from your heart. Offer it often. Don't grow weary. I'll heal this poor suffering of yours. Perhaps by sending one greater still, one that brings with it a piercing ecstasy such as you have never known. 'O precious wound!' is the cry of those who have felt it. Haven't you often asked for this Seraphim's dart?''

''Lord, may I not die before it pierces me!''

''Humble yourself to obtain it. Sacrifice yourself. Keep looking at Me. Do your utmost to tune in to My thoughts. Approach love, and love will take hold of you.''

June 28 — *Holy hour.*

(....) ''Avoid the little faults. Ask Me to help you to see them more clearly, in their true light, like a window in sunshine. You will not dare to repeat them; you will be on the watch not to hurt Me. And when you notice that you have done wrong, you will ask Me to forgive you. My heart has seen everything and is ready to forget because it listens to your words of distress and humility.

Oh, the power of repentance! The sacrifice that pleases Me is a cleft and contrite heart. Such a heart I do not despise. So be My very little one.''

July 2 — *"Lord, may each of my visits bring joy and peace to others. But am I pure enough?''*

''Who is pure? There are only sinners or those who have been purified. Woe to people who pride themselves on not yielding to a temptation that never bothered them.''

July 25 — *Le Pouliguen.*

''My helper? You can be. By accepting events that are the expression of God's will. By sunny submission — your smile adorns your soul; I always look for it in all your dealings with Me. It's like love moved to tenderness, like a caress during an effort of the will. When you smile, your work wears a diadem.

And your way of speaking to Me... Don't you get a feeling of serene beauty when I speak to you? Then let your answer be like the echo of My voice. This will be another chance to imitate Me. Don't miss a single one. It takes so little to make you climb one degree higher. And degree by degree you come to a deeper knowledge of God. You climb for others as well as yourself.

Live graciously in your inner shrine. If you knew that you could always find a very dear friend there, you would not hesitate to go to see him often, would you? Well, you know that I am in you every moment. You don't even have to ask Me, 'Are you there?' So just come often, full of love, and throw yourself at My feet. And I'll take you in My arms.

You must really believe I'm in you. You must get to

know My love and abandon yourself to it. If someone said to you, 'Do what you like with me', wouldn't you take the utmost care of him? And I! What wouldn't I do for those who give Me their whole self?

I want to help you to grow in Me. So leave yourself to Me.''

August 12 — *Le Fresne church.*

''Of course, even in a season of dryness when life seems to have lost its savor for your mind and heart, I take you. Don't resist; just let yourself disappear in Me. You've seen something floating on the vast ocean at the mercy of the waters? I am the Waters. I am the Immensity. Can you see where I'm taking you? What else is there for you to do but to set yourself adrift on Me. Hope that your course may bring Me the greatest glory. Hope to be balm for My heart. Haven't I the right to privileges, to your favors? To be the chosen One, the most beloved of all?

When you say to Me, 'Beloved Jesus I give you my entire life', do you realize that at the same time I've given you more, since even what you are giving Me is what I've given you? Admit that everything you have comes from Me. It's all a gift from Me, not to display My power, not chosen at random, but by My most attentive love — chosen especially for you, My children — for your path in life, in order to help you to reach the goal that is yours.

You have everything you need to perfect the Gabrielle I dreamed of in creating you. Did you watch Me creating you? You see you can have no idea of the tenderness that I pledged to your soul so long ago — from all eternity. Then I ask you not to consider Me exacting if I say to you, as I do so often 'Give Me everything'.''

August 19 — *Lourdes. Rosary chapel.*

(....) ''How much I need you to be sure of Me. Do you feel My warmth? Quicken the fire of your love with Mine. Ask for everything through My mother. She is so good, so attentive in caring for your souls. If only you knew! You don't know her well enough. Give yourself to her without reserve, like her little Jesus. And think of your rôle: to be as one alone among the crowds. Alone with Me. Nothing exists but your Christ. Look upon the distractions of the passers-by as no more than the branches of trees swaying in the breeze.

Come to Me directly. Isn't that the shortest way? I am so eager to have you. Your influence will be transformed. And how could you be indifferent to this influence which is like the aura of your soul? Didn't I have Mine? And My apostles? St. Peter's shadow had healing in it. If you could only heal the wounds of those who come near you! Ask Me for this. Ask My mother.

My little girl, so dear, so dear, will you let Me live again on earth in you?''

August 21 — *Departure from Lourdes.*

''Why should you be afraid of losing Lourdes in leaving it? Am I not always with you, helping you, arranging circumstances so that you may keep your resolutions? (...)

Don't let your eyes wander from Mine. Now that you understand better, don't stray from My loving look. Do you know what this is: God looking at you — you looking at God with His eyes? In this way you will make amends for so many other glances — yours and those of others. And how can one ever express the love in a look? Your poor love looking at the poor Lamb of God, who is all humility, tenderness and compassion. Weigh these words. Live them. Love them. These words that I give you on your last evening in Lourdes.''

August 30 — *''Lord, I should like to take care of You as You take care of me.''*
''My child, to love Me is to take care of Me. I don't seem to need anything else. But great is My thirst for you. Perhaps you think that I say this often. But My longing is ever new. Love never repeats, you know. It finds in itself the eternal notes of its music. Take care then to comfort Me, very simply: a glance, an inward smile, even a movement of pity for My sufferings, or a prayer for sinners.

Child, give Me your life.''
''Lord, you already have it.''
''I want it unceasingly, like a fountain springing upward, like a symphony that never ends. Every effort for Me. When you hold back a word, when you put on gentle manners, when you do something against your own will, when you humble yourself, when you forget a discourtesy, when you sacrifice a pleasure to help your neighbor. Everything for Me. What true happiness, My beloved little girl! There will be only one music — we'll turn around on My record, you melodious with Me, I in notes flowing from you.''

September 6 — *Holy hour.*
''Take and read. Take from My heart and read love. Do you know how to read Love? With the eyes of ardent desire and the most loving simplicity enlightened by the remembrance of what I said through the prophets, the gospels and My intimate friends.

Read love and read the call, for love always calls. A call is like arms outstretched to enfold. Wouldn't you give Me the joy of letting yourself be enfolded? And what do I want if not you in all your wholeness — your entire being. You understand?

Then you mustn't refuse Me. No, not anything. Try to be the one I desire, the one who keeps Me company in her heart joyously and leaves Me only to find Me again in her daily duties.

I am everywhere for the one who seeks Me. He lives with My life all the time he is living for Me. I possess him so that he may possess Me. How could he get along all alone? Haven't you recognized My help at certain moments? Isn't your way through life more joyous and safe when God possesses you?

O come close, come purely to the All-Pure.''

''Lord, I never cease to long for You, and yet I never cease to be indifferent.''

''And it will always be like that, My poor little girl. The weakness of your nature causes you to fall, and it's the humble effort you make to get up and go on, the effort to please Me that charms your Beloved. And this is a joy, a joy for God. Isn't that strange? Later on you will see. Later on you will understand.

Believe in that 'later on'.''

''How can I believe, Lord?''

''With your heart. For if I am often a joy for you, be sure that you are very much more of a joy for Me. Think of this; it will help you to drop anchor in My boundless compassion, and it will give you more assurance of the goodness of your God — His perfect goodness, which never ceases to flow to you.''

''Lord, make me like this for my neighbor.''

''I'll be your Self-Expression.''

September 12 — *Holy hour.*

''Don't you think that if you were to spend this entire hour of adoration repeating the words, 'Your will be done on earth as it is in heaven', you would not be wasting your time? For My will is all love. It is out of love that you ask Me for it, and when the sum of all the love on earth is greater than the sum of hate, that will be a step forward. Hate is not from heaven. Hate is the very breath of hell.

Love, My dear little girl, not only those who are kind, but those who would snub you. Try to counterbalance the fearful weight of opposition to My desire for kindness and love. Very few are My truly loving friends — those who love Me for the sake of My love.

During these days of family reunion you understood how tenderness leads to joy, to happy understanding. Let your mind reach out in the same way to the whole human race, which should be just one big family, and see the peace that will come from this, while on the contrary...''

''*Lord, I should so much like to get this peace for the whole world.*''

''Pray. Show an example of heartwarming love. You remember how good My mother and St. Joseph were to all those who received them during their travels. Long afterward people remembered their visit. They left a wake of blessings all along their way.

And haven't you received wave upon wave of light?''

September 20 — *Le Fresne church. Feeling utterly empty, I was a little frightened at the thought of what I was going to write.*

''Why be worried, since I am the one who is dictating? Do you think you would have been able to put down anything all by yourself? My poor little child, you must be sure of Me in you. Perhaps you do not seek often enough to live within My aura — the aura of the Lover, the Mighty One. Yes, that's what I am: this joy.''

Friends had come a long way to enjoy the moonlight as they dined on the terrace.

"During these two hours of poetry that seemed to pass so quickly, it was I who led your conversation to the life beyond time.

Don't ever be afraid of pronouncing My Name. Am I not the greatest of friends? You call Me your most beautiful Love, and you are right. Then let Me look after everything in your short life. It will not go on forever, since the end does come. So cherish Me as a miser does his gold. How this would increase your charm, and through that very charm, your influence. It is I who go from you to others. I love to find channels."

"Lord, make me a faithful and ready channel."

"Examine yourself often. See if you play the part I have assigned to you with regard to others. I mean, the rôle of giving Me to others."

"Lord, it is always very imperfect."

"But you don't know. You don't know what goes on inside the one to whom you are talking. Can you see a soul? Can you see My grace? Oh, don't stop in your working-drive for Me. One day you will see the result. Be the faithful little servant who works all the better because she has secret converse with her most loving Master. His is not a love like any on earth. It's a love of flame and of fire. Then don't be amazed to feel your faculties alight, and to find that after this converse you have risen to a higher plane of consciousness by the route of the joyous ascension."

September 27 — "Do you understand the appalling ingratitude of flying from Him who loves you so dearly?

Find your happiness in serving Me, even in the very smallest details. Nothing that is for love is little."

"Lord, how can You be touched by such weak things from Your weak creatures?"

"Haven't I been your Brother? Don't I know human nature and the life of man on earth? You are so used to picturing Me as the God in heaven that you forget how I toiled, suffered from cold, heat, hunger, just as you do. But I was always more afflicted than you.

When the last day comes and you look for Him who on earth was the poorest and most tortured of men you will recognize the Son of Man and you will understand why He received the greatest weight of glory."

October 4 — *I had just finished a delicate piece of embroidery only to find I had made a mistake and had to begin all over again.*

"Didn't you say to Me as you were sewing, 'This work or another, what does it matter to me, since everything is for You?' Show Me that you meant it and that you can take it all out and do it again for love of Me.

Show Me that you are remaining flexible in My hand and that even if the foundation on which you are building falls apart, you are not less happy in Me. You see, you must never consider yourself, but only Me and My loving will, which is sometimes to test those I love.

Do you fully realize that you need trials in the spiritual life, our life together. Life on earth is not yet the life of heaven. It's only love's beginning. Love grows in trial — even in the very little ones, but it doesn't notice this; its hunger is never satisfied. What joy it gives Me to help you!...

Come along with Me then, keeping close, and we'll talk together. You will hear Me, and humbly you will translate My words into daily living. I know how to take a soul captive. I don't speak in vain. So just work together with Me since I'm leading you to the Father.

My little girl will grow, not by herself but by Me. I go on creating you. In our intimacy this evening before you go to sleep, when your heart is close to Mine won't you give Me its most tender thanks?"

October 6 — *I had repeated the gold embroidery work on the Benediction veil, and I thought of showing it to friends, a little out of vainglory.*
"Isn't it enough that My eyes see it?"

October 18 — "Come before My face. Now unfold your soul. Stretch it out like a fabric remembering your stains. Yesterday's and today's. You show them to Me without saying a word, and yet this is a prayer. You are humble before the display of your wretchedness and this is the most eloquent of prayers. The voice of the just rises day and night and how can his cry be anything but humble? You see that even your short-comings can bring you closer to Me. Use them; you can transform them into the love that makes amends, the love of contrition. Everything should lead to love. In this way you will meet Me. And won't I have gone more than half way along the road?"

November 22 — *Thursday.*
"I am like a child who has been waiting all week for this day to come. You come to me and you love Me. For an hour we are all in all to one another, forgetting created things to such an extent that if an angel announced the end of the world, the message would make no impression on your mind and you would remain at rest on My heart.

You too, do Me the honor of waiting for Thursday as for a festive occasion — the celebration of My heart. Summon up all your powers to love, to hope and to believe. Tell Me how helpless you are and I'll fill the

194

emptiness so that as you live, you will give the impression that it is I living in you.

I love to live My life again on earth through My children. If you knew how few allow Me to do this!''

''Lord, my body and my soul are your home. May all my powers be used for Your glory.''

''Then do something to atone for your self-love and the self-love of others. To make amends should be joyous, you know, since it heals and since it is for love. It is sin that is sad — the continual tendency to self-love that often makes you forget your God.

O try to exchange self-love for God-love. No longer think of yourself at all. How this would lighten you! And what a new entry into Me! For I am eternally new. I am the infinite One, and it is for the Infinite that you have been created.''

November 28 — *Holy hour.*

''Why do you doubt, you of little faith? Am I less great than yesterday? Could My love ever fail? Do I love you for what you are worth? Or as always, for your poverty? Does love seek its own interests? The love of a God! Haven't I taken you as you are, with all that you know of your weaknesses? Then why, after so many free gifts, should you doubt My merciful goodness? Haven't I told you that justice is for later on?

Close the eyes of this fear that paralyzes you and throw yourself into My arms. I am the very gentle Shepherd; you know that I'll give you rest on My heart. What matters most of all is the fusion of our two wills — 'on earth, as in heaven'. No refusal then. Perfect acceptance, not forced, but with tenderness and from the desire to be more than ever united to Me. Don't you think this would help you to win your daily sinner more easily? Because you see, the more you are one with Me, the smaller you are in yourself and the greater you are in Me.

Come close to your heaven. Heaven is our oneness — your mind in My mind. Begin, My child, my very own.''

December 13 — *Holy hour.*

''Say this: 'Right now I offer You all my power to believe, to hope and to love' and I'll take it. By dint of saying this to Me, you will make your heart an altar of reconciliation both for yourself and for the world. And in My sight it will be like Noah's rainbow that joined earth and heaven on its two buttresses — man and the Man-God forming only one figure.

You feel very small and very much alone. Noah too, was very small and alone on the earth and yet God allowed him to save the human race. One little lonely soul, lost among the people of the earth but united to the Son of God in the fulness of His blessed will may, through His compassionate heart, become an instrument for the uplifting of others.

Then gather up all the powers that I have given you. Bind them together and surrender them to Me. I'll use them as My own.

What are you but a heap of good intentions? And to whom should you reach out if not to your Source? Do you know anyone greater than God? Have you another friend like Christ? And after so many proofs, how far have you advanced? What is your response? When will your love begin? Don't you feel how flickering and feeble it is? When will you quicken it to a luminous, steady flame? Don't you think that in your place someone else might have held the torch better?''

''*Yes, Lord, I have never deserved any of Your favors. Change me.*''

''Change yourself, by patiently beginning over and

over again. Watch and pray. You do pray, yes, but pray in another way, seeing everything through Me, full of confidence, with a sense of your poverty. Then I'll help you, My poor crippled little girl, paralyzed by so many weaknesses from birth, and you will travel along new paths. You will leave behind your old slavish attachments, for My yoke is gentle. You will no longer be the one you serve; Christ will be the One you serve. What a difference! And because you will serve Him and not another, weaving Him into the very warp and woof of your day, He will call you His bride, He who was your servant.''

December 27 — ''If you have to make sacrifices to reach Me, don't worry about them. I'm in you. I'll shoulder their weight. If you find no words to express your love, keep silent and I in you will speak to Myself. If you can't keep your thoughts on Me, come back to Me as soon as you notice this, gently, without bitterness against yourself. Since I can put up with you, you can surely put up with yourself. Transmute this into an opportunity of being humble. Oh, never miss one of such blessed opportunities. My little girl humble… What a joy for Me!

You understand, I see all that's going on inside you. I can fathom you. Don't parents see right through their little child? And I… Shouldn't that hearten you? Shouldn't it help your inner life? I'm at rest in your soul.

At the beginning of Creation, God walked in the Garden of Eden and talked with your first parents. There was God and there was man. Now it is the God-Man, and He is in you, still nearer, since He took on human nature. What oneness, My child! Think of it. If you understood better, your heart would melt with love.''

''*Lord, give me the grace to understand better.*''

"Ask St. John to help you. It's his feastday today. Although I left him on the day of My ascension, he went on living with Me right to the end of his life on earth. Ask him for the tender faithfulness that won so much light for him. And trust."

1946

January 1 — "The keynote? Faithfulness, with the thought of comforting the heart of your Christ."

January 2 — *On my way home from Mass I bought a loaf of bread.*

"You see the difference? Bread for the body and the Living Bread."

January 3 — *Le Fresne.*

I thought of the way I had been spoiled by everyone at Nantes and of all the good things awaiting me here, with the magnificent panorama of the Loire river gilded by the intense cold, and I said, "How beautiful and good You are everywhere, Lord!"

"Then why do you have such difficulty in believing in My love? This scenery that you find so enchanting is My love. And that sunset that calls to your mind a bleeding Host... All the kindness you received during your eight days in Nantes and that unexpected opportunity you had of being really helpful — isn't it perfectly clear to you now that My love arranged all this for you? Then why didn't this thought occur to you without My having to remind you? You always think that these things just happen. Nothing just happens. I am in everything. And I am all Love. Be imbued with this thought."

"How can I?"

"Look at it often in your heart. By trying, by trying again and again you will become sure. You will live with love. You will never leave love. And when you call Me, you will no longer say, 'My God' but, 'My

Love'. And this will be the reality. And your heart will be flooded with tenderness as the soil by a torrent.

But think, dwell upon love, since this pleases Me. I so yearn for you to believe. What a poor idea you have of Me! Remember that man is made in the image of God. Does a child understand his father? Aren't there mysterious bonds between them? And isn't it love that gives life to the heart?

Why are you on the defensive? Why do you run away? Come!''

January 10 — *Flu: feverish, dazed, coughing.*

"Lord, shall I be able to take down Your dear words today?"

"Haven't I always taken your inability into account? Even when you were traveling and when we were not always alone? Has anything changed in our heart-to-heart communion? Don't you find in this the adaptability of a Presence, the Presence of your God?

Then don't worry about anything. Come as a little girl who has to be taken by the hand. Humble yourself always as someone utterly useless.

You remember the joy you felt this week during your illness? 'Perhaps I'm going to the Father's home', you thought. And your soul was flooded with peace and longing. Never think that this comes from you. Even the thought could not occur to you if the Spirit didn't inspire it. I want you always to keep in mind your constant poverty. It honors Me for you to do so, and it is the true picture of yourself. You were conscious of it when you felt an astonishing force, and with it came the thought, 'What is the use of staying in a beautiful home when one is about to die?' So many opinions change, don't they, when one is on the threshold of the eternal home?

Be grateful when you are surprised by a sudden illumination. Welcome this light; make it your own. Follow its beam as far as it shines. It is a blessing from God. You are discovering His love. And how often in a single day! Then is it too much to offer Him everything in that same day? Isn't it as though you said to Him, 'The soul You gave me returns lovingly to You with all that You have given it'.''

January 17 — *Holy hour.*

''Don't you see that faith should permeate everything you do? Faith in My actual Presence in you. Faith in the love that is leading. When you are very sure of the love living in you, what a change in your life, My child!

You know the difference between a solitary voyage and one with a companion — two dear friends, or a man and his wife? There is no comparison, is there? Well, when you have given Me the joy and honor of sharing everything with My all-loving Presence, your being will be as it were enfolded in another Being — Mine. So try to form the habit of seeing everything with the eyes of faith. You can practice this many times during the day. You don't like to run out of wool or thread for your spinning wheel, do you? And you find it easy to make provision for all these earthly things. Then how could you go through this life, so brief in reality yet so seemingly long, without this spirit of faith so necessary for holiness? Faith — the living spring of the fountain of love.

And do you realize that love is the one and only goal and that everything should serve to lead you to it? A very little thing becomes big if it takes you to love. And an important work is absolutely nothing if it fails to lead to love. O humility... contrition — if love enlivens you what power is yours close to the heart of the Man-God! And how could you love if you did not believe in the Love living in your heart? My home is there.''

March 21 — *Holy hour.*

"All night long I waited for you in My Eucharist — waited to give Myself to you in the morning. Why should this astonish you? You believe in My presence in the tabernacle, don't you? You believe in My immense love? Then put the two together. And when you wake up during the night, look at the One who is already longing for the dawn to bring you to Him. This will quicken your love and give you confidence in My power."

"Your power, Lord, is greater than all atomic energy, isn't it?"

"All power comes forth from My power and is nothing compared with it. Even My tenderness is invested with My power, for there is no tenderness like Mine.

Do you ever think of adoring each of my qualities? This would be a tribute to My glory.

Let Me profit by the days of your life; they are not many. Prolong Me in them as much as you can. Don't let a day go by without doing something for Me, for there is not a single day when I am not at work in you for your own happiness. Do you believe Me?"

"Yes, Lord."

"Then humble yourself for not having responded better to all the lovingkindness of your Creator.

You know how I love to forgive? You know how your confidence attracts My compassion? Your trust can win anything from My heart. Count on Me. Call Me. Don't you love your name? I love to hear Mine on your lips. Don't deprive Me."

March 28 — *Holy hour.*

"Why be so anxious about the opinion of others? Isn't Mine enough? If you are with Me, let them talk. Take your place on My shoulder and forget everything.

You're walking in My footsteps; you're seeking to please Me, aren't you? You may judge yourself on this desire to please Me at all times. And you may be sure that this does not come from you but from the Spirit who is in you — in your inner temple when you are in grace. Then could you find cause for anything else but humility?

Seize upon every opportunity of keeping silent and give Me this silence just as though you were picking a flower for Me. Oh, this beautiful silence full of peace, humility, serenity and intimacy with God! How much you can obtain in these blessed moments!

And then there is the silencing of your thoughts and memories.''

''This inner silence is not easy.''

''Try. If you don't succeed one way, find another. You remember the branch of the tree that you couldn't cut down in your garden until you tried cutting from another direction? It fell by itself then. But it takes patience. Never think you have fully succeeded.

Aim to the best of your ability. Isn't it for God? Why should you give up? My very little girl, you must begin to be happy to suffer for Me. You know that I was happy to suffer for you. Don't two friends seek to give one another things? Would you be content just to receive?

Take the initiative in love. Above all, don't lose your smile. Give it to Me so that I may bless it.''

April 4 — *Holy hour.*

They had forgotten to put back the altar covering. In thought I made a mantle for Him with my arms.

''If you cover Me like that this evening you may be sure that in heaven where the evenings are eternal mornings, I shall offer you this same mantle, and its folds will shelter our secret conversations. Do you think that My gifts come to an end with your life on earth? Don't you expect to receive new ones, still more powerful ones? Then long for them and increase your faith by looking forward to them.''

''Lord, I think You give me all I need for my salvation.''

''And suppose I wish to overflow you, to overflow Myself? If, relying on My power, you expect more than you ask or think, could anyone restrain My generosity? Don't you believe rather that My infinite heart loves to give infinitely? That's the divine principle, isn't it?

Prepare your soul as you prepare your garden. You turn over the soil and bury the weeds. Come the sun and the rain, the new flowers — the ones you weren't expecting, the ones you hadn't thought of. That's how it will be for your soul. And once again you will say, 'There is nothing of me. Everything comes from Him.' For everything always comes from Me. Just look back over your life; don't you see My face in this or that event? And that other one, that took you to a place where you had not thought of going, wasn't that also to your measure? It was heavy, I know, but you could bear the weight.

Don't be afraid of anything. Death? Of course not. You will receive the grace to clothe yourself in death. You will enter into it as you enter into a task received from Me, I helping you as always. You know what actual grace is — what you call 'grace for the moment?' I am grace. When you are with Me, are you afraid? Didn't I always say to My apostles after the resurrection, 'Don't be afraid!' My little girl, if you were afraid I should be hurt.''

April 11 — ''Have faith. Everything becomes simple then. It will be simple to love Me, simple to serve Me, simple to be happy to suffer for Me. Believing is almost the same as seeing. To see Me!... What progress, what riches to exploit, when you speak to Me, when you tell Me that you love Me.

The proof of your love for God is the affectionate care you take of your neighbor. Be sure that you see Me in him, that you charm Me when you charm him. This will keep you humble beside him. Always be the smallest. Think of the size of the Host. Begin today to do your best to speak to Me when you speak to your neighbor. I expect this of you this afternoon when you get together with your friends. You would not want to refuse Me anything this week of My passion, would you? Begin. I'll continue. When you were very little, your mother would say, 'Three stitches on the canvas', and that was all you did; she finished the row. Look at Me. Am I not still more tender than your mother? How happy you will be when you believe in Love as it is, as I give it to you now and as I want to give it to you in eternity.

Hunt for Me everywhere. I'll let Myself be captured with such joy. How could you expect to find Me if you didn't search? And when you have found Me, give Me to others. There are people I'm waiting to reach only through you. This is the mission foreseen for you from all eternity. Don't be unfaithful. I was faithful even to torment, even to public disgrace.

Look full in My face and try to understand. Enter into the inner stillness. Everything was for My children. For you, My child — like a love letter written to you with My blood and received by you long afterward. But I am always alive and My love is always the same.''

Holy Thursday — *Alone in the church near the Blessed Sacrament.*

''Tell Me that you are beginning to be more certain of the power of My love, although you know you are unworthy. Tell Me this to comfort Me for the ones who do not believe. You will give Me heart's ease. Let us make an alliance between your poverty and My riches. Never fail to lean on Me. Have no confidence in yourself, not even for a moment. Where would it lead you? Does one call upon nothingness to help nothingness? Who better than a father can understand his child? My eleven children in the Upper Room knew that, and they were so deeply touched during their thanksgiving that some were in tears. And what about My own emotion! Adore it. It comes from My tenderness. The next day at the same hour will I not already have died for them? For you... Aren't the last moments of a man sentenced to death lived more intensely?''

April 26 — *Holy hour. In the empty church.*
''Empty... but filled with Me. You don't think often enough that I am everywhere, that nothing exists where I am not present. Think of this. It will help you to reach Me. One thing only I ask of you: oneness with Me. Since we are united in the morning in My Eucharist, let us not be separated by your indifference; it leads to constant mind-wandering. When people are in love they never stop thinking of the beloved, do they? Then what should I conclude if you don't think of Me? Come to Me directly; I'm waiting for you. Let our life together be vibrant with your life.

Vary your ways of loving. Charm Me. Be at My feet in humility like Mary Magdalene, or on My heart, resting there like John, or taking care of Me like My mother, or glorifying Me, as in heaven, or taking your place with Me beneath the Spirit hovering above our heads.

And when you suffer, suffer with My sufferings. You understand? Oneness. Never separation, not even nascent in the twilight of forgetfulness.

Be alive in Me. I live in you; let Me feel everything

in you. Of course, even your faults. Am I not compassion personified? Haven't I the power to blot out everything? To make crooked things straight?"

"Lord, reform me. I am nothing but pride from morning to night."

"Tell Me about it every day and humble yourself. It is I who unfold each one of your days. There is Jesus in the Holy Eucharist; there is Jesus too in circumstances, in encounters, in happenings. See Me everywhere. Follow Me everywhere. I have been what you are on the earth, except for sin. Be filled with the divine science. Let your heart overflow to those who come near you, just as though you were carrying a vase filled with precious nectar spilling over with every step you take. My poor little girl, enriched by My riches alone, may she be careful never to think she is worth anything by herself. But may she be conscious of her power through My power."

May 9 — *I went into church saying, "Lord, your little nothing is coming in."*

"Who is anything beside the infinitely great God? And you, particularly chosen to be showered with blessings — you are nothing but wretchedness. I feed this wretchedness every morning with My Eucharist because I want to keep you in My friendship, for I am drawn to the weakest and the poorest. Give Me everything that you blame in yourself, since I am the One who transforms even the ugliest, the lowest, the most vile. I transmute everything into the gold of My glory. How can this be done? By love."

"I should so much like to do something for You! Even in giving all of myself, I give nothing. What can I do?"

"Take Me and offer Me to Myself with all the trust I always expect from you. Since I am yours, you are rich. You are only poor when you count on yourselves and expect to act in your own unaided strength. How destitute you are then! But if you lay hold of My merits with humility and hope, what a priceless fortune is yours? And above all, never doubt Me. I won My merits only to give them to you. My poor children. You don't think of this, because you are living in the mists that veil the delicate touches of your divine Friend — the touches full of charm.''

May 16 — *Holy hour.*

''Lend Me your hand to write. Lend Me your voice to teach the little ones the living truth. Lend Me your gestures to love them. And to cheer your pastor in his duties, lend Me your kindness. In this way, through you, I shall be among them, among yours. Your influence will be increased and you will think less of yourself. 'This is not the fruit of my own effort,' you will say. 'Jesus was there with me.' Say it to yourself over and over again; it will keep you humble. And humility is truth.

Lend Me your body too, when you travel, when you toil, when you eat and when you sleep. I did all these things when I lived among men. Make Me live again among them; and they must be aware of Me.

The grace of God — this beautiful, this wondrous grace — is never withheld from those who, through the instrumentality of someone (it could be you if you wish), leave behind their usual indifference and begin to aspire to greater intimacy with their Savior.

As for you, don't bargain with Me, but go joyously to your post when I call you. Say to yourself, 'He wants me there.' And with that, you remain courageous and at peace. You remember what courage it took Me to fulfill My mission to the very end?

Imitate Me. Am I not the elder Brother, who sets an example because the Father has confided His secrets to Him? Confide in Me, My child. Tell Me about your-self quite simply. I understand everything so well. You know that, don't you? And yet, I love to have you explain all your emotions and fears and desires. Would you love Me as much if I were more distant?

I am your center and your end. I am your circumference. Wherever your eyes may turn, they will see Me. In you, all around you. Everywhere.''

May 23 — ''You remember the prophet's advice? 'Go and wash in the river.' And the leper, finding this too easy, wanted to go away. But his servant said to him, (....) 'Something simple can always be tried.'

I ask My children for the most ordinary actions: eating, drinking, sleeping, working, your whole day united with Mine in the past, your actions dipped in My blood and clothed in My merits. There is nothing difficult about this; it heals you of your usual poverty and wraps you in the richest garment. Then, My little child, couldn't you try something so simple? Acquire the habit by gazing at Me as I gaze at you. You love this look of your great Friend? It's like a caress. Always it is power. Like My words. Like My Eucharist. Every-thing about Me is power. Life-Power. Isn't that a joy? Doesn't it give wings to your love in a greater under-standing of the divine Being? If you only knew who God is... And how much He deserves to have you study His unsearchable riches, His generosity, His extreme goodness, His love, and again — yes, and always — His love, for love is the essence of His Being.

When you have entered into the treasure-house of His love, you will stay there. You will make it your home. That's where you belong. And from there, as from a lofty balcony, you will see life, your neighbor, service for God's glory from a new viewpoint that will completely change your usual petty opinions. The saints saw things differently from others and that is why they seemed to lead strange lives. They didn't have the same eyes.

The atmosphere of the world is so false that it is foreign to truth. So go deep into My domain of love and lock yourself in.''

May 30 — *Ascension.*

''Do you believe — do you really believe in My mysteries?''

''Yes, Lord, I do believe, and they are the source of my greatest happiness.''

''But do you believe to the point of merging your thought entirely with Mine? To the point of living for one thing only — to please the ever-living heart of your Bridegroom, to be a faithful comforter for Him? Do you believe enough to find in each Eucharist the food that should strengthen your love? You know that this is all that counts: to make love grow in your heart. When you love Me perfectly and above all things, all beings, all ideas, everything will be fulfilled in you because you will have attained the end for which I created and redeemed you. Don't be afraid to offer yourself to the fulfilment of My dream of you, as though I were waiting to be encouraged by your burning desires. Say, 'Lord, make me what You wanted me to be.' At least form the wish that we never be of two minds and that, seeking to know all My will for you, you take care to respond as faithfully as you can. And this too will comfort Me for the lack of love, the scorn and hatred that I meet, just as I did during My life on earth.

My child, take care of Me. Haven't I taken care of you? Tenderly?''

June 13 — ''Don't you feel full of Me? Don't you see how your physical trials drew Me to you? And your heartbeats that you were able to count tonight — didn't My own heart beat to the same rhythm? 'It's His heart', you thought. And right away your faith was enriched and your soul became like a watered garden. You forgot everything so that you might think only of our oneness.

Of course. You must see everything through Me, as one sees a drawing through the architect's tracing paper. 'That's what it is to be a saint.' Didn't someone tell you that? Keep on trying. It's frequent practice that makes perfect. Practice love in order to love, since I reward every effort with a greater grace with which you must harmonize. For we never remain long on the same plane, My child. We are going to the Father, and this means daily ascension. The Father is waiting for all of you. Have you felt His impatience? Don't keep Love waiting. Yes, Love. You have the blessed assurance that God is Love. Let every one of your thoughts and actions be a trysting place with Him. Poor little helpless one, He will help you. Doesn't He rule the infinite stars in their harmonious course through the nightly heavens if only to respond to your trust? There is always a response even if you don't hear it. If you only knew the heart of God!''

"Lord, don't ever let me be ungrateful. I want to be always on the lookout for Your Will."

"Not by fear but by love; remember that. For it is love that waits upon love."

June 20 — *Corpus Christi.*

"I give my whole self to You today, on this great feast of My Lord."

"You know, often it's the one who is fêted who gives the presents. Haven't I always something to give? You need so many things.

Supposing this evening I offered you the desire for

211

heaven — a yearning for Me? Yearning is thirst. If I gave you this thirst?... You can't have it unless I give it to you."

"*Lord, give me whatever can make me less poor in Your eyes.*"

"It's enough for Me that you show Me your poverty, since that is what always draws Me to you."

June 28 — *Feast of the Sacred Heart.*
"*Love, rest in my heart. Sleep in my heart.*"

(....) "Darling child, rest your head on My heart and listen... You don't listen enough, so how can you hear? And how can we have intimate conversations, not just mouth to mouth, but heart to heart? Without any words, with sighs, with the soul's breath. What beautiful intimacy, what utter purity!

And what joy that one gives Me who shows himself as he is, in the hope that his humility will bring Me the glory and love that the world has weaned away from Me.

You, child, love Me. Love Me for others. Love Me for Me."

July 4 — "*Thank You for wanting to come tomorrow morning to my old house, since my leg hinders me from going to Your house.*"

"You have only to call Me and I come."

July 5 — *He came.*
"Why should you doubt? You were deeply stirred when you saw Me there on your little table. My loving-kindness could go as far as that. Has anyone ever measured the goodness of God?

Won't you praise this goodness by trying to imitate it? Draw power from it often and ever so simply. If only you spoke to Me as often as that blackbird you hear singing from four o'clock in the morning to ten in the evening without a break. Sometimes he warbles sotto voce, but his pure voice never ceases to rise. And he's only a bird... And little children prattle constantly to their parents, don't they? — without any reason, just for the pleasure of feeling near them.

You, child, shouldn't you speak unceasingly to My lovingkindness, if only to be close to it. It would enrich you more than you ever suspect. Talk to it just for the pleasure of greeting it. Never mind if you don't have a reason. Ask Me to make My lovingkindness known to others through you. O don't lose a single opportunity of being the representative of God's goodness, even if it be only by a gesture. Think about this. Ask Me to help you to think about it; ask Me very simply, your lips to My ear.''

July 11 — *Holy hour.*

''All this month is consecrated to My precious blood, and you think so little about it... And yet, there is fruit for your picking. The season of flowers is over. Now we are in the more solemn time of the harvest for the eternal garnering.

Don't be surprised at having to suffer for Me or at being tested and tried for My sake. These are records to be filled out for eternity. You take your place in the sacrifice for which the crown is prepared. You play your part in the unfinished symphony of My passion. Love these last sufferings. They are part of your travel wardrobe. The most ordinary sufferings — heat, insects, unforeseen mishaps, petty annoyances that you offer Me in expiation — are part of the harvest of the autumn of your life in this ever-marvelous springtime of love. Aren't the seasons simultaneous in the bride-soul where the light of love never goes out? This little light illuminates everything in her, but she is so simple that she is not even aware of it. As for Me, I see. You feel far from Me; you're afraid that you have left Me, and there I am in your center.

Just keep your will for Me; that's enough. Your will in Mine — that's everything — for My joy and yours. I want you to be completely joyous. You will be when you have emptied yourself of self. Then you will no longer feel the gravity of life, but the gentle and buoyant breath of uplifting joy. Do you believe what I'm telling you? Live in the home of the beloved ones.''

July 25 — *Holy hour.*
''Don't you find that the inward smiles I've asked for and that you give Me make your life joyous? And don't you think that your neighbor will notice this radiant peace and find comfort in it? A personal grace very rarely fails to brim over to everyone. It's the overflow of My love that always spreads out in freshets in all directions. Accept everything from Me child, as a faithful and docile instrument, ready to echo it all to the whole world with the ardent longing for My glory.

You often ask that My kingdom may come. Aren't you happy if you can contribute to the coming of this kingdom? This is why you need to be holy — to increase My glory. Think about this.

Believe in the effectiveness of your work as part of the universal work of the saints. Think of the 'living stone' that you are adding to the spiritual house — this stone that no one else but you is called upon to place in just this same position. This ought to encourage you to make efforts of every kind. Some of them remain a secret between you and Me, and aren't they the most charming because of this intimacy?

Above all, don't ever grow weary of our intimacy. Vary. Improvise. Perfect. Increase. Call upon the Spirit of Love to help you. Ask My mother to show you —

214

she who never left Me. Even when you feel good for nothing, give Me this nothing. Didn't I create with nothing?

All I ask of you is the will to give yourself to Me at all times, in cloud or sunshine. And I'll take you into the happy Upper Room of My servants and My friends.''

August 17 — *On the altar I recognized two little vases that I had offered and that I had treasured as family souvenirs.*
''They are in My house but they are still yours.''

August 22 — ''Why do you sometimes think of Me as a severe master waiting for a chance to find fault with you? Wouldn't you rather see in Me a very loving Friend, ready to make excuses for you if you fall? The Friend who keeps watch over you. Don't you think I'm like that?

Wake up your tenderness. Live in love's trust. Ask Me for your God's science of love, the love He gives you and the love you owe Him.''

September 11 — *I was weeding in the garden.*
''Of course. Instead of thinking that you are working for yourself, why not think that it is for Me all day long. My meals, My walks, My garden, My room, My mending. Won't that be more tender? Won't it be balm for you?''

September 12 — ''Ask Me for everything you have lost through neglecting to harmonize with My grace. Ask humbly, with confidence, and My compassionate heart will give it to you because with love nothing is impossible and My love is victorious. I'll help you pick up those dropped stitches of your life. You will have light that you have missed and you will find your wedding ring again. Don't ever give way to the distress that keeps you aloof from Me. Be sure that My goodness is infinitely greater than the sinfulness of My children. If you didn't count on Me for help, to whom would you turn? Hope and trust to the utmost in Me, and you will honor Me. And I'll answer every time you call.

I alone know how to answer you. I alone can satisfy you. Haven't you felt My tenderness? Are My attractions new to you? Remember all the times you have hungered for Me. Didn't I come quickly? And although you didn't see My face, didn't you recognize Me? Then make short shrift of your doubts. And although on the earth you are constantly exposed to weaknesses and failure, come back immediately and throw yourself into My arms, for I make whole.

Look often at your Friend, your Savior. This is what I expect of you and what I love in you. It is life together and it is My delight. How I wish you believed Me!''

September 19 — *''Lord, at certain moments I feel full of You, and at others, I feel dry and deserted.''*

''You are always full of Me, for in yourself you are only nothingness. I am life, and you live by Me alone. But sometimes I leave you to your littleness so that you take stock of all that you lack and send Me those secret cries for help with sincere and humble tenderness.''

September 26 — *Holy hour.*

''Try to grasp what I'm saying: I am the one and only End. You are still too little for Me to tell you that the only end is suffering, for suffering, you see, is the surest way of coming close to Me and of being like Me. But when you accept a joy and thank Me for having given it to you, this gives Me both delight and glory. Knowing how weak you are, My providence gave you all these little happy incidents that you noticed this

216

week and for which you thanked Me spontaneously. At each joyous cry of thanks I blessed you. You know how I bless a very beloved friend or bride? I take her on My heart. She doesn't see, but she feels strengthened and ready for greater devotion to her neighbor. Oh, when you help others, let it be for Me and not just for the satisfaction of being kind.

Purify your look at Me. Make it keener. Do everything to assure our intimacy. It's not sure enough, is it? Not constant. It is troubled by strange earthly thoughts.

I only; your only One. Engrave this on your heart. Remember that everything exists by Me alone.

"Lord, I know this. Then how is it that I can forget it as though I never knew?"

"You are always My little girl. But be careful not to wander off. Better to stay closely bound to Me, face to face as it were, so that nothing will be lost. I let Myself overflow. Are you there to receive Me?... And if you are not there, which of us suffers the most?"

October 3 — *Holy hour.*

"Consider yourself to be very little, like the little Sainte Thérèse and you will ravish My heart. Realize that everything comes from Me. The faults in your work — that's all that you should count as yours. Recognize this in all the imperfections of everything you undertake. See yourself as you are — weak, poor, and yet full of self-love. Think of your stream of thought and the few remembrances you offer Me, for Me or for My cause. Get rid of yourself. Adopt Me, your Father, your Center, your Source, the One who helps you hold up your head and make all your movements, the One in whom you breathe. I: Love! And to remain in tune with My thought do everything for My loving will."

October 17 — "Are you near Me?"

"Yes, Lord, I'm listening to You."

"Are you quite ready to understand that joys can serve Me as well as trials if you give them to Me, if you live them for Me? If you recognize them as My special gifts, and if you love Me more because of them? And am I not free to bestow happiness where I wish and as much as I wish? Sometimes you like to prepare a lovely surprise and your whole heart is alight with the joy of it. Can you imagine My joy when you thank Me for making your cup run over? And I never come to the end of all My gifts. Doesn't everything belong to Me?

Merged with Mine, let your heart overflow at the thought of such lovingkindness. You have only a fragmentary idea of it. In your Homeland you will see it in all its fulness. Such love is beyond your power to imagine, although you have already been dazzled by My blessings. Sometimes you are embarrassed by My favors, for no one is worthy of them. You can lay it all to My goodness and never to your own credit, poor child.

Hide yourself under My robe all woven of My virtues. I'm a bigger size than you and can wrap you up entirely in it. The Father will see no one but Me."

October 23 — *After Communion.*

"I am praying to the Father for you."

"Lord, tell Him what You would like me to say."

December 5 — *Holy hour.*

"Come very close to Me in the garden of My agony where My sweat is like drops of blood. You understand? I'll be less alone... The others are sleeping. No one is here. Except My mother, who is thinking about Me. They are sleeping. This is the picture of those whose life is one long sleep where I'm concerned. Indifference. Distraction. Forgetfulness. How sad for them! Even among My friends, a little more fervor would keep them awake.

Ask My forgiveness if you accuse yourself of any omission — not at My feet but on My heart. Remember that if the mighty ones of this world are honored with noisy eulogies and public fanfare, I am honored by the silent and attentive heart, by a delicate sacrifice known to no one, by a secret surrender, a tender inner glance. It is in this way, very simply, that My children console Me.

Try to offer Me something of your own creation, as if every day were My feast. 'What charming thing can I do for Him today? What more tender words shall I say to Him?'

And in the quietest room within your secret inner shrine, dedicate yourself to Me as you dedicate your thread to the distaff. But this will be the thread of your life.

Don't be alarmed when your imagination gallops. It is your will that concerns Me. I died to make your will Mine. Do you want to give it all to Me? Don't just treat Me as the guest of your great moments, but as the Beloved you never leave. You know what 'never' means? As often as you think of yourself you find Me, because you are always before My face.''

December 12 — *As we were going in procession to place a statue of Christ in the theater, I asked Him to transform the country and He said, 'Help Me'.*

Holy hour (later) — ''Yes, even in your thoughts you must aim at perfection. Get a clear picture of their importance. Your acts and words flow from them. They are the fountain-head. Does one stir up the waters of a spring? Let your mind be like a limpid pool upturned to My face, mirroring the desires of My heart. Could you believe that I'm waiting for your efforts to increase My glory? You feel unworthy, and you are right. But you do not know the goodness and tenderness of your God. Adore these attributes. Love them. Crucify yourself for them. And give thanks. For is there at this moment another home as happy as yours? And not because you deserve it in the least. Well then, since there is every good reason to be grateful, let your heart talk. When you speak I listen as one who is in love, My poor little child.''

December 19 — ''Like a poor man I'm waiting at your door for what you want to give Me. Try to find the moment when you pleased Me the most today. Wasn't it when you were little with the little ones — with the greatest simplicity?''

I had a great many rehearsals at the theater and only came to Him late in the evening.

''Don't you find Me the most patient of friends, even though I am the most impatient to have you? You remember the poor man at the church, so humble, eyes lowered, shy and shivering with cold. I am that cold one rejected by the world. Then don't be surprised to know that a faithful heart is a joy for Me and try to imagine Me as I wait My turn. Be altogether Mine in this moment given to us, this moment that will never come back again in the same manner and in the same setting — the winter with all its intimacy.

Don't be afraid to discover how little it takes to touch Me. I am the hypersensitive One and you can never know how your gestures make music in My heart. Be afraid of hurting Me. Always try to give Me joy and above all don't imagine Me to be far off. You realize that I'm in you, don't you? And if you do, why don't you think of it more often? I was going to say 'Always'.

Then My longing for you would be completely satisfied. I am the same for all people. They are all My children. I long for every one of them. So in offering yourself, offer the others too, with My joy in mind.''

December 26 — ''You see, in the manger I am like you, so that you may all become like Me. Try to resemble Me in every way. Keep thinking, 'What would He have done? What would He have said? How would He speak to His Father in this situation?' You understand? Always take your inspiration from Me. Be one with Me and believe that this pleases Me. Didn't I come in order to be one with you — so that we should be only one being? Don't try to shut out this thought. Of course you're not worthy, but it is My desire. And nothing on earth can give you an idea of what this oneness is that I ask of you. It is God's oneness; that means the oneness of a Love above every other love. I alone can help you find it. So think of this and ask Me for it. Above all, don't be afraid of loving Me. Don't you know that the more you love, the happier you are? Because this is your end, the end for which you are created. Don't you feel that you are made to love Me, so much so that outside of Me there is nothing but emptiness?

You remember your desolation one evening? Let Me fill you with joy.''

1947

January 1 — *"The keynote, Lord?"*
"Keep going. Do good."

January 16 — *I was thinking of the 5% discounts and I said to myself, "Will we ever be able to get holiness too more easily?"*
"You can't compute holiness like a column of figures. A single act of love with absolute abandonment and trust can make a saint even at the moment of death. And how this honors Me! I am like Samson; I lose My power as judge when someone tells Me of his faithful love. Not because the love is so great either, but because it is the greatest he has to offer Me. It touches Me to the quick and I am ready to bend to his will and make it My own."

January 30 — *Holy hour.*
"Thank you again, Lord! You seem to go to all lengths to fill my cup to the brim at the end of my life, don't you?"
"Isn't that My special task? You see I am Fulness. Everything exists in Me. And those who possess faith drink deeply. But you must believe and hope. Oh, this great quality of hope! Practice it often so that it will grow in you. Don't you understand that the more you expect, the more you receive? Then expect even the impossible and you will have it. Do you remember that saint who removed a mountain? There are all sorts of mountains and My power is always the same."

"Then, Lord, may I ask You to be My unique 'raison d'être'?"

"Help Me to grant you this. There again, we shall be one — you in the striving, I in the grace. What would be simplest for you would be to incarnate My goodness. In a single day you have so many opportunities to do this by your actions, your gestures, your words. Give birth to Me again. Every evening review your day to see if you have given Me life again by you. I'll add My charm to all you do and there again we'll be one. You can never know how deeply I desire this. Above all you cannot grasp it. You know all about the Redemption and the Passion, but can you understand the love of your God — the feeling of this heart? Its intense desire is beyond your power to comprehend.

Repeat to yourself often, 'I believe in Your love for me, in Your boundless love. I know that you have loved me with an everlasting love.'

Oh, My very little child, who has ever lifted love to such heights!"

February 6 — *Holy hour.*
"I should so love You to be happy in my heart."

"Your desire in itself is a call that pleases Me and gives Me great honor. You make amends for yourself and you make amends for the ingratitude of so many others. Do they think of Me with a little affection even once a year? Do they accept the thought of My love for each one of them? When will they realize that time — the span of earthly life — is too short, that I need all eternity to love them? That this present life of theirs is not their goal, but only a means given to them to earn the other life?

Pray for them. You can do a great deal without seeing the fruit. But I see; I hear. I see that in helping others to arise, you rise yourself. Do you believe Me? Come to Me and bring others with you. I know how to talk to them all — to the ashamed and the timid as well as to the rebellious and the proud. Didn't I say to Saul, 'It's hard for you kicking against the goad'? And immediatly he surrendered his will and asked, 'What must I do?'

Oh, My child, what power there is in My gentleness and in the tenderness of My voice! You know a little about this, don't you? Imitate Me as much as you are able. If you could only bring all the people around you to Me! Try to tell them that I love them and how much I love them. My love is so vehement that I'll forgive them everything from the moment they repent. Bring them to Me and I'll enfold you with them.''

February 13 — *Holy hour.*
I said, 'You made my cup of joy run over last evening. I was lifted right out of myself.' You said to me: 'You realize, don't you, that I'm here?'

''You are never alone. Can you be separated from your breathing, or from the blood that flows in your veins, or from the very essence of your soul?

So few people live for Me and for others. Once in a while perhaps, and then they return to their self-centredness. My child, let our two beings be so closely united that the you in you is no longer noticed and all your thoughts come homing to Me. I am your happiness. I created you this way so that you might make your home in Me and so that I might heap My blessings upon you as I did last evening. And once again, My little girl, once again, this is love.''

February 14 — *In a moment of sadness.*
''Remember... I traveled all your roads.''
During the day.
''If you want to gain strength to make a sacrifice, don't look at the sacrifice. Look at My joy.''

February 16 — ''Now is the time that I veil My holiness and My justice. Do you thoroughly grasp what I'm saying? Now is the time for love, longsuffering, patience, compassion, confidence in what I expect from you: your generosity, your response. That is the true picture of your God now as long as you are on your planet.''

''I implore you, live in My love every single second. I don't force you. I never force, even with regard to My gifts. You are free to take or leave them. How often your freedom has crucified Me! And so, I wait... I wait for centuries. Don't you realize that I've been waiting a long, long time for you? No two souls are alike. None other can give Me what I expect from you.''

February 18 — *Holy hour.*

''I am more present to you than you are to yourself, but there are moments when you feel My overflow like a high tide of love, and then you say, 'It is He.'

How it rejoices My heart to be recognized! What distresses Me is to remain near you like an outsider, almost like someone unwanted.

Not to be wanted... to have to depend on your welcome! I, who would always want to lavish My love on each soul. And how can I, if you keep your door closed to Me? I was going to say, if you look hostile and suspicious.

Some are afraid that I'll ask too much of them. If they only knew how happy they would be in giving Me everything in complete and joyous surrender.

The most beautiful gift you can give Me is your joy in serving Me.'' (....)

February 20 — *Holy hour.*

''Give more importance to the little things. Some are so little that you often neglect to fill them with love.

And yet, in My eyes, God's eyes, do you think there is a big difference between the small actions of your daily duty — your little fugitive moments — and what you call the great events of your life? Then learn the secret of charming Me no matter what you may be doing. This would please Me so much that I should be tempted to thank you. My happiness — isn't that sufficient reason for you? Do you love Me enough for that? Oh, My beloved child, just think of all that I've done for you. Doesn't that quicken your zeal?''

February 26 — *Visiting.*
''Don't speak when you should be silent. And don't keep silence when you should speak.''

February 27 — ''Do you seek Me? Do you often seek Me? How can you find Me if you don't hunt for Me? Don't you look for what you need most? And since without Me you can do nothing, what do you need more than God? As for Me, I love to act for you and through you.

Together, I and you, My little girl, what can we not accomplish? You will say, 'Yours is the glory, Lord. Yours is all the glory. I am nothing.' And this will be the reality. But in offering yourself for My service you will have been a tool in the hand of your God. To be His instrument you must let yourself be used by Him at every moment. Your eagerness will glorify Him.

Just imagine, I am perfectly happy with My Father, yet I can't do without My children, for My love for them is beyond all their power to conceive.

And if they consent to leave behind the things of the world to devote all their faculties to Me, even for only a few minutes a day, to keep silence in order to listen lovingly to Me, they force Me, as it were, to take them in Me so that I may share My secrets with them. And

My secrets give power by strengthening their faith. My secrets have only one purpose: to bring My children closer to Me. Oh, the beautiful secret that completes our oneness!

Little girl, always purify your motive so that I may recognize My face in yours. 'He who has seen Me', I said, 'has seen My Father.' You remember? May it be the same for you.''

March 6 — ''Each soul is the object of My special love. That is why I am so grateful to those who are resourceful in bringing back sinners to Me. Keep this in mind, then. I gave My life for them in the most atrocious torture, for these poor beloved ones. A humble repentance, and they are already on My heart. So speak gently to them. Speak with tenderness. A brusque remark could drive them farther away.''

''I'm going to meet one tomorrow, Lord.''

''I'll give you the necessary tact. As always, I'll be in you. You will look at Me and call Me, and say, 'Speak through me.' I'll be the listening Brother.''

I had just received telegrams and telephone calls for a hundred and one things.

''That's life, unforeseen events, moving from one place to another, variable weather, rough weather. But come what may, remain steadfastly in My heart. Keep your eyes fixed on Me as you ask Me for advice or as you tell Me that you love Me always. Remember that nothing happens without My permission, and be very serene. There is nothing like serenity for convincing people of the Good. This was My response to the craftiness of the Pharisees. So be calm in your soul and happily docile to My will. As you look back over your life, don't you see that My will was always for your good? This is because I love you and it's the same for everyone, since I love each of you individually. I see you all differently; I see every detail about you, you under-stand? My love is not a global love.

I need each one of you as though you were the only person in the world, as though the cosmos had been created for you alone, and My love is greater than the cosmos. So let this thought be a strength to you and your smiling calm.

Let us include My mother in this life of ours. Do you really believe that her love is active on your behalf? Oh, My little girl, have faith in the great things that you can do with us. Without us… but you are already aware of your nothingness.''

March 20 — *Holy hour.*
''You are worried about the passage from this life to the next? But since it is the greatest proof of love that you can give Me, be glad. Offer your death to Me now with complete detachment, ready even for heroism. Say, 'Even if I didn't have to suffer death, I would choose it in order to be more one with Him.' And in this way you will give Me the greatest glory a creature can give his Creator. Oh, precious death of the saints that echoes even in the heavenly courts of the Father's Home!

So don't be afraid of losing your brief life on earth for the eternal Meeting with the Beloved. And since I'll be there with you, what a moment of faith, hope and love! Try to take this approach. And then, as always — simplicity. You are with your Father, your Bridegroom. You belong to God's family. Live, think, love as among your own folk. It will be a sign of love.''

''When you give Me a token of your love, you give Me so much joy. If you could only know! No longer to feel a stranger, the one left out in the cold as I am for most people. Gabrielle, get to know Me better. Talk to Me intimately. I'll place your words like a bouquet of myrrh on My heart.

Adore My love, My need-love for you. Adore the extremely delicate way in which I share My secret thoughts with you and make you aware of My desires; and try to be for Me a little of what I am for you. You see how awkward I am at asking? Your freedom often prevents Me from saying what I should like to say to you. It's as though I were waiting for you to discover by yourself what My heart desires. And what is not My joy when you guess!''

March 27 — *Holy hour.*
I had obtained a very great temporal blessing.
''*Oh, thank You, My dear Friend!*''
(I was almost in tears).

''You know how much I love My little children's thanks. You know too that what is so simple and sincere goes straight to My heart, and during these days preceding 'holy week' I'm trying to bring you closer to your Christ who will be overwhelmed with suffering. I would like you to be with Me there. Would you like to try to remain with Me, like Madeleine, with My mother? I want you to think only of Me, suffering for you, and I want you to seek ways of consoling Me. So sometimes I give you a very keen pleasure in which you recognize Me and this fills your heart with love. You are too small to thank Me for a trial so I treat you like the little ones. You see how thoughtful I am? I stoop down to your level so that you may not be overpowered by My immensity. And then you give yourself to Me joyously. I wouldn't like you to feel compelled to give yourself. Reticence suggests regret. I want you to be cheerful in serving My love. And love is eager to serve. Aren't you happy when you can offer Me something?

Today may I express a desire — you're listening? I should like you to acquire the habit of seeing Me in everyone, in the little daily incidents too. To see Me everywhere would be to think of your Savior always. Make an effort to do this as you commemorate the last fortnight of My life. And do this as tenderly as you can. Your rapports with others will be changed in a way that will charm them. Oh, don't be afraid of having too much unction. This is the way the good touches. Evil seeks to seduce, doesn't it? So charm, Gabrielle. It will be I through you who charm. Since you offer Me your humanity I'll know how to use it. You often attribute something to you when it is I expressing Myself in you. The other day, you remember, you said something to X that touched her so deeply that she hid her tears, and you thought, 'That wasn't from me.' It's clear that we're together, isn't it.''

Holy Thursday — ''Just as wrong desires are the source of all evil, so good desires are the source of all good. So formulate many of these daily: desires for our oneness, for your purification, for contrition, the desire to meet Me at every moment.''

Easter — ''The disciples of Emmaus said eagerly to Me, 'Stay with us.' Now it is I who say to you, 'Stay with Me. Stay with Me, My little child.' *(In a beseeching voice) At vespers.*

''The grace for this Easter: In future you will live by Me and in Me alone.''

April 10 — *Holy hour.*
''I am with You dear Lord, in the Garden of Olives.''

''Your fidelity is precious to Me; it's like a tender tribute. You see My generosity for My children makes it seem simple and as though natural to suffer the pangs of death. But when you are ready to sympathize with Me and to enter into My distress I feel touched to the very heart and I want to make your kindness one with Mine so that when the Father looks at you, He sees you and Me — His Christ.

Will you ever comprehend My sensitivity, and how your every tender and compassionate thought thrills in My heart. But even if you don't understand very well, even if your love never gets beyond the stage of trial, I always take into consideration the earnest effort of your will and this is My delight. Yes, I mean just that — My delight...

You see how simply I talk to you about Myself? Humble yourself at such kindness. Doesn't it spring from Love? Of course, My poor little girl, I love the nothing that you are so much that if you give Me permission, I take up all the room in you.

Lose yourself in Me. Surrender yourself. Fade out of your own thoughts. Enter into My eternal Being. Live and move and have your being in Me.''

April 17 — *Holy hour.*
''I never find you near enough to Me. My Word within you has never spoken enough. I am always thirsty. You are thinking, 'It's difficult to satisfy Him.' But believe that a very little effort, the least gesture of yours, delights Me. It's like the joy of a mother when her little one expresses himself in a new way.

The unfolding of My love in you is My personal happiness; I'm waiting for it. Everything that affects you touches Me personally. My friends, you are part of Me and I, your Christ, am part of you. Then why should I alone desire this close union? Don't you also desire it? You see, it's quite distressing for a friend to have to say, 'Love Me. Think about Me. Serve My cause. Give Me your life.' Don't you think that the one who

loves would prefer to have the other read his sentiments? And when this does happen, he is so deeply
touched that the ardent soul would be filled with joy
could it but comprehend.

You to whom I confide these secrets in the silence
of your heart, be this friend who believes without
seeing, and outreach yourself with the sure knowledge
that you have never done too much. When it comes
to Me, could anything be too much?

Look at Me always and give Me the oblation of yourself, My little child.''

April 25 — *Montmartre.*
*A light bulb was missing in front of the Blessed Sacra-
ment. ''Lord, let my heart burn before You there in its place.''*

''To burn would not be enough. You must be consumed. I mean you must burn right out. This is what
I did for you, for all of you. Don't you feel the desire
to do the same for Me? This is what it means to simplify everything in you to a single principle, a single
élan towards your great Friend. Isn't this restful? Isn't
it your goal? And don't you find that this changes your
entire being? You can see that My call is a blessing,
can't you, and that your response will bring you joy?

O answer! Answer unceasingly. Your strength will
increase and you will give it to others so that it will
go from soul to soul as a torch is passed from hand
to hand. The living spring is your Christ. Drink at the
very fountainhead, for the closer you come to the fountainhead the more your cup will run over.

Oh, My little girl, don't seek Me far from yourself.
You have Me right within you as a candle has its
flame.''

April 27 — ''Tonight when you went to your open window to look at the splendid sky strewn with stars

whose light glinted among the flowering cherry trees, you listened to the nightingale of the island and you felt the joy of having so powerful a Bridegroom. Oh, may this and many other spectacles in nature increase your confidence in Me.''

May 3 — *Rome.*
Chapelle des Ancelles du Saint Sacrement.
''You don't have enough trust. Who will give Me this look of abandonment that I'm waiting for? Keep in mind more often that I give you everything for nothing: all My heaven for your nothingness and for the mere pittance of your earnings. Think of this more often so that your heart may be stirred.''

May 5 — *Catacombs of Saint Domitille. At Mass.*
''I spoke of your look. Now I'm speaking to you about the way you look at Me: confidence, oblation.''
Rocca di Papa, Cable-railway to Notre-Dame del Tufo.
''Reach the degree of intimacy that I've desired for you. Make the break-through. Enter into the realm undreamed of.''

May 22 — *(I was going through a series of anxieties.)*
''Give Me your trials unstintingly. I may be in need of them to save a sinner, don't you think? Later you will see all that came from your suffering both for others and for you.

And now that you accept the sacrifice, don't you feel freed from the earth, as though ready to take off? And don't you see how ephemeral everything of time is.

See everything in Truth. May your whole life speak the language of love, in Me and by Me. And may the moments that remain for you be nothing but goodness and tenderness — the gift of yourself. You remember that evening before My death? Wasn't it as though My entire being had been translated into Love during My last supper?

Be full of indulgence and compassion for everyone. Remember that I called Judas 'My friend...' Imitate your Bridegroom. Desire to be identified with Him; so many others have striven for this, why not you? 'Like Him': this could be your watchword. And it would be full of peace and joy. Wouldn't I help you? You see Love finds it impossible to stop. And when I see the work of a soul of pure intent, I take the heavier end. Tenderly.

Have faith, and love will follow.''

June 15 — *Feast of the Sacred Heart.*

''Enclose yourself in Me. If you knew who I was, you would pray today for all sinners, those that you know and others too, with all the trust one feels in the Infinite.

Shut yourself in never to depart again. Be like My cloistered sister; the cloister, you know, is the image of My heart. There's where you will live — in the midst of others — with such love and tenderness.

Don't be afraid to be transformed. Abandon yourself to the strokes of the chisel; everything is for your good. Isn't My love for you beyond reason. Yes, I love you to the point of doing the good that I want to do to this one and that one by you. You will not always notice this. Sometimes you will wonder, 'Who spoke then — He or I?' You know how I have merged with My faithful child? Wasn't this My desire — to be one with you, with each one of you. Not for just a moment but for your life long.

Which of you will give Me the joy of being invited to your earthly pilgrimage? Who will say to Me at the end of the road, 'I should like to live again because of You and yet I find it sweet to die for You.'

234

I have called you to union. My invitation is for every man, woman and child. Yet few have listened. Very few have responded to the call. Gabrielle, My little girl, consent to this oneness. There is still time. You will console Me and you will make amends for yourself; you will give Me, as it were, a taste for forgiveness.

Oh, My little ones, created by Me, what power is yours! Let your heart overflow with love and gratitude. What would you find to love outside of Me?''

''I love You, always You, yet I scarcely know You.''

June 19 — ''Without Me, what are you? And if you want never to be separated from Me, why don't you try to be more one with Me? What hinders you? You receive Me in your Communion in the morning. What is there to prevent you from giving thanks all day long? You want to love Me in all circumstances, but you are in the world and surrounded by others. Then you can continue to love Me in this one and that one, can't you? What keeps you from doing this?

And when you hold a sweet joy to your heart, welcome Me in it. I hide Myself like that. For you to find Me. That's God's game. Win. And when you win, be sure of this, that I am the real winner, I, the most sensitive.''

I was looking at thousands of flowers like tiny golden stars and I was thinking of the firmament.

''If people contemplated My creation more often than the works of man, how this would draw them nearer to Me. But they think too much of earthly things. Seek every means of coming close to Me, Gabrielle, not just once a day, but at every moment. You understand? May your life be Mine — uninterruptedly Mine. You breathe, don't you? Then there I am in your very breathing. Don't I recreate you? Breathe with My breathing. Always. It's so simple. And this will be power in you.''

June 21 — ''If you offered Me your joys and your moments of recreation, I would send you few trials because it is only your union with Me that I am seeking, and as a rule you come to Me only when you are unhappy. Then come — oh, come always.''

June 26 — ''It's not the lips that should pray, My little girl; your heart should look at Me and speak to Me. Do you understand the great difference both for you when you talk to Me about yourself and for Me as I listen to you? Always begin by placing yourself in My Presence. Why don't you do this? Wouldn't it be balm of Gilead for you? Don't you love Me enough to be happy with Me? It's not fear that keeps you from doing this; it's just the lack of habit, this wonderful habit of remaining in My embrace. Would you like to try right away? Yes, I'll help you. When you give Me your confidence — it's then that I enrich you. Oh, this gracious exchange where the One who receives the least is the happiest!

Haven't I given you a great deal? Offer Me everything that I have given you so that it may all contribute to My glory — to the glory of Love. Everything can be used, even the very tiniest things. It is because I am great that I stoop down to you. It is because I am great that I am avid for you and that I enfold you in your smallest gestures.''

July 10 — *Holy hour.*
''Are you living for Me? Do you love Me enough to desire Me alone? Don't look upon money as an end in itself but as a means of procuring My glory. Try to serve Me no matter what you are doing, just as I served

you by every manner and means in My life on earth.

Why do you grow weary of doing good to others? Am I not in them? Would you ever grow weary of helping Me if I were near you? You would help Me joyously, lovingly. You would say, 'Is there anything else you would like, dear Master? Does that please you?'

Act with Me as if I were near your eyes, near your heart. And am I not? Then be near Me not only in My outward life, but seek Me also in My inward life turned toward My Father: in the perpetual offering of Myself for you all, in all that I did to make amends for you, in My moments of silence imbued with love, in My humble surrender as Man-God before God, My Father.

And as I always say, be one with Me. For your encouragement keep in mind that this gives Me a joy you never suspect. Don't you love to please your friends? Then I, your Christ? Treat Me as a friend. Even this is not enough for My love. Live in Me, for I live in you. Isn't this alone a reason for loving adoration and heartfelt gratitude?

Remain very little, close to your Mighty One.''

July 24 — *Holy hour.*

''Which of us is waiting the more impatiently for the moment of intimacy, you or I? Yes, I know that you are thinking about it and preparing for it, that you are coming out of a sense of duty. But I'm coming from pure love. Ask Me for this love as though I were a merchant.''

''What shall I give you in payment?''

''Your gratitude, which will burn like the flame of your joy. What I give surpasses your poor little means and awakens new feelings in you — feelings you thought to be beyond your power to experience.

This unexplored domain amazes you and proves that

it is I Myself who act in your attentive and docile soul. Oh, be attentive to Me! This is a signal way of reaching Me. To be attentive means to empty yourself of everything except the desire for Me. It is then that I come, and the greater your desire for Me, the greater will be the measure of My grace. When someone is waiting for you, don't you hurry? Don't you like someone to call because he cherishes you? And when someone seeks you out to talk with you, this gives you pleasure, doesn't it? I am still more sensitive because I am always the One who loves first.

Even if you do little, you touch Me deeply. I, a Man-God... what delicate sentiments are Mine! Who will be able to feel the heart-beat of My love? Above all, who will know how to respond? Learn day by day, so that the moment will come at last when you will know.''

July 27 — *During the High Mass.*
''Do you think of yourself as one not yet born? Your real birth is your entrance into the other Life. Prepare for it. Make everything ready. Recall the life of the humble caterpillar crawling on the earth. Then its secret, hidden life within the chrysalis. And at last the butterfly with its magic-colored wings, flying free in the clear blue.

Oh, rejoice at the thought that you will soon be born to fulness of Life.''

July 31 — *Holy hour.*
''Don't interrupt our conversations by irrelevant thoughts that you could easily suppress. Are they worth as much as the minutes that I give you? Enter into the inner stillness. You will always find Me there since you love Me and keep My word. I come to you and I make My home in you. Even if I don't talk to

you, I'm there. Remain at My feet. Get ready to listen to Me. Make your will one with Mine; this too is union. This is how I kept Myself before My Father — 'Your will not Mine be done'.

This is the sign by which I know those who belong to Me: they leave behind even their own desires to follow Me. These give Me to others unawares, for the Spirit possesses them and expresses Himself through them.

Ask often for the Spirit to take possession of you. He breathes where He wishes, you know, and all the more on those who call Him.''

August 10 — *Lourdes.*
At the procession of the Blessed Sacrament, I was thinking of a proud answer I had just given.

(With tender pity) ''How your littleness makes you suffer!'' *And I remembered what He had told me once before from the monstrance in this same place, surrounded by cardinals and archbishops in rich vestments:*

''You see, I am the smallest.'' *(In the monstrance.)*

August 15 — *In the street.*
 ''I love you so!''

September 9 — *Lourdes, at the grotto.*
''Together, all three of us: I, she, and you. I receive lovingly. She conveys My love. You offer yourself to the utmost of your ability. And the Father sees us.''

September 11 — *At the grotto.*
''Break free of yourself. Take note as to whether even here, you are acting for Me or for you. Cease to exist in your own eyes and focalize everything on Me. First and foremost your thoughts, since your actions depend on them. At noon couldn't you take stock of your inner

life in such a way as to tighten the bonds between us? I call you so often. Call Me, so that you may come; it's not I who fail to come. Ask My mother for the grace to live like her, in our company which is more real than all the visible world.

Enter, enter into Me. What really counts is the life of your soul, you understand? Everything should be subservient to it. And the center of it should be I, your Christ. All things uplifted to Me, everything for Me, since we are one as I and My Father are one. Didn't I give the example?

Oh, My little girl, in this hallowed grotto, give yourself wholly and for always.'' (....)

September 18 — *Le Fresne. Holy hour.*
''Have you really understood that you may come and take rest on My heart? And if you have, why do you not come? It is I whom you deprive. I have to wait, to refrain from insisting, since I respect your liberty. I am with you and I yearn for you. And you would not come? I ask you only to think of this more often so that you will come to Me more often. I'll give you My love and My patience for your neighbor; you will have a clearer understanding of the fact that he is I, and you will go to him for love of Me, very simply, always with the thought that you are less worthy, like the least among all souls.''

September 25 — ''Strive for goodness, the goodness that anticipates — plan your kind deed beforehand and add charm to the gift. In this way you will comfort and console.

What immeasurable harm can be done by a bitter word! I alone see the extent of it. So limit your influence to the most exquisite gentleness and you will obtain more. Remember Me in My life on earth: the way I was with children, with sinners, with the woman taken in adultery, with Madeleine, with you. Am I not infinitely patient and gentle? Be your Christ for others. Poor, weak little girl, I'll be in your heart when it speaks. Increase your hope by frequent little words of the utmost simplicity, such as, 'My God, You are my life. You never leave me alone. You are in my pilgrimage right to the end of my dying.'

I am in the one who hopes, the soul that is full of trust. I look after that one as My brother, as My bride. Have I ever disappointed anyone? Have I been unfaithful? Oh, how I know how to care for My own!

Abandon yourself to Me; you'll never regret it. Go out of your depth in the Ocean and let yourself be borne up. For the Ocean is Myself.''

October 2 — *I knew He was very near.*
''Why are you astonished when I come in like a rushing tide? I should like to do this for everyone... What a joy for the Beloved!

Can you imagine what the earth would be like if all men loved Me and did My will? How sweet life would be! Will they ever understand what they lose in hating Me and each other? Oh, scatter goodness and love; above all, scatter it on those who do wrong.

Keep Me in mind. Imitate Me. Reflect Me, more by your actions than your words. Oh, the beautiful silence of those who act! You remember My hidden life, and the life of My parents? And the influence we had on all around us? Yet everything went on in a quiet way.

Act... and more often than not, keep silence. The power for this is in Me; take it. I am ready to give you everything you need if you ask Me. Why should you be afraid of asking when you have first of all praised and loved Me? I love everything about you, and it's the same for everyone. Aren't you all My children that I wanted to save?

If you realize that your praise gives Me glory, you will praise Me better. Know that your love gives joy to My love; it's like two mirrors forever reflecting each other. Aren't you happy to think that you reflect your God? This God, so much yours that He wanted to create you in His image. You see now why I keep on asking you for this unending oneness with Me. Divine longing... how vehement it is! How far beyond thought! At least honor Me by acknowledging it. I am thirsty, do you understand what I mean? I am thirsty for you all. Let Me drink.''

October 9 — ''Tell Me that there are moments when you are sure of Me. This will comfort Me for all the other moments.''

Holy hour.

''If you would know God, be born to Him. Born in your soul's depths, quickened by the Spirit. You remember how an angel came to stir up the pool for the healing of the sick? No one knew when this would happen. That's the way the Spirit comes. So listen for Him, respectfully, lovingly. You know Him, don't you — this Spirit, this Fire with its secret light? This Flame of tender goodness that suddenly sweeps through you? Then wait in the inner stillness; wait attentively for His coming. Be like 'a garden enclosed'.

This birth that takes place in the depth of your being when you are more faithful than usual, will help you to know the Unknowable a little better. Don't you think that it's worth while making preparation for it? Poor, weak little girl, waiting for the mysterious voice of her Father! Even were He not to come, how sweet to yearn for Him!

Be a-quiver with hope. Light the flame of your joy:

He will come. And when at last He comes, let your love and humility melt one within the other like the cloaks cast down along the route over which I passed as I rode into Jerusalem. You will make Me your home then, and everything will be so simple.

So be born to God that you may know Him, and afterward, fully aware, you will recognize Him. Isn't it like that already?''

October 17 — *Paris. Boulevard Raspail.*
I was thinking that it was very monotonous to begin all over again every morning to offer my day.

(Briskly) ''Don't I begin all over again every morning to offer Myself in the Mass? Did I consider that once would be good enough? And is it so difficult for you to give yourself often to Me when I'm always waiting for you? Love multiplies its words without ever repeating.''

October 23 — *''Lord, I am so very little. Even what I have is only what you have given me.''*
''Ask for more. Ask better, and although you are very far from perfection, ask Me for it unceasingly in order to bring you nearer to Me. How many blessings you miss by not asking for them!''

October 30 — *I had a pain in the shoulder and I was thinking of the weight of His cross.*
''Any suffering that you offer Me with love eases My sufferings. You know that I saw everything in advance, right to the end of the world.

Be glad to suffer if you love Me. There again we are one. Let us work together for the conversion of sinners and the growth of My kingdom.

Trust yourself to My eyes; they see what you cannot see. Let your intention be to serve My intentions.

And this will give you the courage to suffer. My little one, ask Me for this courage. It is always a feast day for Me when you ask Me for something — the beautiful feast of giving you My help. This is life you know — our life, Mine and yours.''

November 9 — *At Mass.*
I was watching someone come in.
''Couldn't you sacrifice your eyes for Me? Make them look at Me. Put them inside you. Fear whatever makes your thoughts wander away from Me, and go after whatever brings them back. So many things can come from a glance. So many things flow from a thought. You are right in mistrusting your thoughts more than your will. Do everything to keep Me in mind. Center everything in Me. Be conscious of the fact that I control your entire being, since I am in you and you are in Me — two foreheads touching; no, one inside the other.''

November 13 — ''You are all so ignorant of the power of your God. Are you afraid to know Him, you who seek Him so little. And yet the joy of your souls lies in constant communion with your Creator and Savior in the Christ consciousness.

Abandon yourselves to God no matter what He does. Let His breath blow you along, fanned by your fervor. Come to Him eagerly, My child, since He has the answers to all your needs: of tenderness, rest and intelligence. Your thoughts are short, but at least prolong your desires so that you can reach a higher plane — the new heights where the Spirit is waiting for you to help you to climb even higher.

And season everything with joy. It adds to God's glory. Would the father of a family be happy if his children came to serve him in fear, with long faces? When you approach Me, My little girl, be full of joy like a happy child. You are thinking, 'He's always asking me for inward smiles.' Could you believe that even though I am God I need the smiles of My children, because your happiness is essential to Me? Who can comprehend this? Who can even bear such a thought? But believe. For it is My love that speaks, and you must listen to My voice in a way that you listen to no other.''

November 20 — *Le Fresne. Holy hour.*

''Do you believe in Me? Do you really believe in Me? Are you sure that I am in you, and that I loved you even to the folly of My cross? Do you remember My kindnesses for the universe, and those chosen especially for you? Go over My favors and see if your life will be long enough to thank Me for them. Tell Me that in every one of these minutes that remain for you, you will love Me with your gratitude, and this will be balm to Me. Your tenderness will 'pay Me'.

What then can separate us — the fact that I am God? But I have been man and the law has changed. I came to take away fear and to gather love. Give it to Me. Give for others. If you feel poor, hold out your hand to Me. And it is My heart in your heart that will love.''

November 25 — *After Communion.*

''Your keynote for today: 'For God and against myself'.''

November 27 — *Holy hour.*

I was returning from a tea at the home of Count S.

''Now forget the world and look at Me. I was pleased that you spoke of the prisoners and their fruitful solitude that brought them nearer to God. Did you notice how the conversation remained at a higher level right to the end? In this you were My instrument. Be so again, often. You see, I have few instruments on the earth… Ask the Spirit to guide your mind. Don't talk out of yourself, but out of Me. Speak in My place.

My little girl, do you know when you speak like Me? When you put goodness and charm into your words. When you touch hearts. When you give a gracious answer to an acid remark. When you make excuses for someone. When you serve. When you give. When you calm an angry person. When you comfort. When you keep an even temper in all circumstances. When you remain humble without seeking to shine. When you are grateful for the kindness of others. When you are generous. Who was more generous than I? Who more gentle and humble? All this is yours. You are part of My mystical body.''

December 4 — ''When you have entered into light, you will comprehend. Until then, you will just feel your way in truth: you will be able to take Love only little by little; otherwise your mortal eyes would be wounded. But when the eye of your inner vision looks deep into the infinite, you will discover your poverty and you will be overwhelmed with gratitude to God for having stooped down to your nothingness.''

''Perhaps from now on my only reason for living will be to thank You?''

''The way to thank Me, you know, is to love Me. To be one with Me in every moment of life. Never to imagine that you can be there and I somewhere else. Wherever you are, there I am. Oh, My child, what love Mine is! Make it your work to believe. Is that so difficult? Try often and you will please Me.

Of course. This work can save a sinner the same as any effort to overcome yourself. Let this encourage you.

Think of Me in My human life more often, for in this

246

way you will draw the power to imitate Me. You must take all the means: look at Me, call Me, love Me.''

December 11 — *Holy hour.*
''My child, even if you seemed to lose everything, even if all the affections of your heart were to fade away and you found yourself alone and misunderstood by everyone I should still be your Treasure, your Goal, your incomparable Friend, your Beginning and your End.

So don't be upset by anything. Once and for all, place your heart in Mine, in joy as in distress. If I fill your cup to overflowing, I am your peace. If I put you to the test, I am your companion. Nothing ever ceases to flow from Me to you, if you accept Me. Now do you understand a little better the reason you were born? To be one with Me. Begin, begin right from this very moment. Tighten the bonds of union. Ask the Immaculate One for this grace. Her heart never left Me. And you, child, never leave Me. Never. I'll be tempted to thank you.''

December 21 — ''If I have ful-filled you, it is for the sake of others too. Be ready to pass on to them with love all that you have received. You owe Me this; you also owe it to them. Believe with all your heart that in sharing this overflow of graces you will help many others. A river gives everything to the sea, yet it always swells anew. My little girl, don't you see, one can never give too much. Step outside of your self-center. This will be a new way of coming to Me. Try to see Me more clearly in those around you and your entire association with others will be transformed. You often feel sorry that you were not alive when I was on earth so that you could have been with Me. Be fully aware of Me in those around you, and without stopping to contemplate Me serve Me in them. Later on you will be glad of this.

Remember what is written in the Gospel: 'Lord, when did I take care of You?': 'Every time you took care of your neighbor.' And how true it is that these charitable acts bring you closer to Me. Who can bring you closer to Me, if not Myself hidden in the other person? O wondrous theme of love with all its variations: ever on the alert to please Me.

Ask the Father to give you many more opportunities of pleasing Him. Isn't it a joy to be pleasing to God? He has everything He wants, yet He has your hearts only if you care to offer them to Him. You see, there is always this respect for your freedom.

So go to everyone without partiality. And since it's for Me, give them your whole self. Go to the very outermost limit of your kindness. Why stop half way? Scatter kindness on everyone alike. Am I not unchanging? Don't I scatter My sunshine and rain on the just and the unjust?

Widen your smile as you did yesterday. It glorified Me. My very dear little child, I'm counting on you. I'm waiting for you — already giving you all the grace you need, the grace I want you to make use of so that those who meet you will meet Me.''

December 25 — ''You mustn't be afraid of aiming at perfection, since I am with you and I have lived it, and since it gives Me great joy to look after you. You see you are not alone; you have Me.

You remember how you used to love to see a team of horses harnessed in arrow formation. I'm at the head and you're following, at a little distance — but you are following. The good thief on the cross understood love and cried out his repentant sorrow. A few moments later he was resting in My heart.

Love calls to love. Answer Me, child. I am thirsty for you. What intimidates you? Your repeated neglectfulness? Your deficiencies, your vagueness, your absentmindedness, your distressing memories? I take charge of everything. I collect miseries and make glorious things out of them. So give me everything. Since we are one, could you be bold enough to say that there is something in your life that could not be for Me?''

''Did you understand this Christmas grace? Not to leave My mother — neither her nor Me, no matter what you're doing. We are worthy to go with you everywhere, aren't we? Could you ever be ashamed of us? When you were a little girl you were ashamed to be seen with relatives who were poorly dressed. My little child, understand that we are your wealth, your success, your salvation. Welcome us in whatever you do, as one welcomes power and charm. Do us the honor of placing us above all your friendships and ambitions, and be faithful to the grace that calls you to so close a union.

At Bethlehem do you think that Joseph could forget his two treasures for a single instant? His whole heart was centered on them. Be like him. (...)

Sink down deep into the thought of My humility as a little child. I became humble for your sake.

Would you like to come to the manger every day for lessons? Every day right up to the Purification? I give you a rendez-vous there. Call it a rendez-vous of love. My love wants to bestow on you My adorning jewels. These are My virtues and they are so powerful that even the worldly admire them. But you must let yourself be adorned. You must turn your will to your highest good.''

December 31 — *After Communion.*
  ''The keynote for 1948, Lord?''
  ''Very close.'' (*An invitation to union*)

1948

January 3 — ''Never mind if you haven't kept your word, or if you have fallen lower than yesterday. If you despise yourself and tell Me so in sorrow, you needn't be afraid to believe that you are in My heart. This heart, so great and good, so little like the hearts of men.

I am compassion, not malice. I carried you as a mother when I carried My cross. Then you can imagine what tenderness I feel when I hear you telling Me of your shortcomings, what eagerness to forgive you...

Oh, the tenderness of a Savior — who could ever fathom it? Who could even hear about it without being scandalized? So from time to time, be glad to be counted as nothing; to look at all that you lack, at the good that you failed to do; to see yourself in the faults you didn't want to commit but committed after all. You may be sure you don't see them all. I alone know the number and the weight of them. And yet, I love you. I am Love.

Don't offend Me by being afraid and running away. That's what hurts love. Enter into My immensity like a little child who joyously seeks to drink and sleep on its mother's breast. Rest. Take strength for yourself. Take joy. Everything is in Me. For you.

Renew your trust and come back to your humble path ever nearer to Me. You know that your spiritual house is not firmly built and that its only foundations are in Me. When it topples down, I take the debris and build a new temple more beautiful than the last because you have humbled yourself. Think of this; it will help you to take pleasure in humiliations. Wasn't I Myself intimately acquainted with humiliation during My entire life on earth? I — God. What company, My child!

You see, what pains love is indifference, apathy, stagnation. When it comes to Me, many people act as though I were still dead. But My child, I am alive and I'm near them, in them, waiting for them to talk to Me, to smile at Me. Waiting for their heart to beat a little for Me.

I require so little, am so readily pleased. I only ask to be invited and I look after the banquet.''

January 10 — *Holy hour.*

''Don't you love this hour when we come close to one another in such intimacy that My thoughts seem to be yours? It's as though our souls were one inside the other. And how can My joy be described? The joy of your Christ who yearns so much for oneness with His children that He invented the Eucharist in order to merge with them. Oh, new Spirit, freeing God's people from the old yoke of fear!

Because I came to earth, everything has been changed. Because I died, you have received life. And life is love. There is no other life, my little girl. Simplify everything in love. Let love be the mainspring of all your actions. Believe and hope with your heart. You will comfort Me for all the hatred. And the more you love, the more you will want to love. Set aside a quarter of an hour a day for love, for nothing else but love.

When you were little you did exercises in French. Now that you are big, give yourself to divine exercises, either during the day in the secret of your heart, or at night, if you wake and seek Me. Wake up loving

Me. Hunt for Me, and I'll let Myself be caught. You will win, and we'll begin the game again and again until, tired out, you remain asleep on My heart. It will be another way for Me to keep you 'very close'. You remember the keynote for this year?''

January 19 — *(With tender intimacy.)*
''When the moment of death comes for My friends, you believe, don't you, that I come gently, with all the delicate touches that you know, to take their souls into My kingdom? You would do the same if you were taking someone into one of your beautiful homes. You would want to feel the joy of their surprise, wouldn't you? Then I, God, who love more and own more, how could I fail to be interested in the passing of My friends from time?

Nothing that you may possibly have imagined of the love of My heart comes anywhere near the reality. Remember that I wanted your joy so much that I came down to earth to know suffering. And when I see you suffer, and suffer for Me, I gather each of your sufferings with great love, as though yours were greater than Mine, and had a value that My heart would like to make infinite. And this is why, when you allow Me to do so, I merge your life with Mine.''

January 22 — ''I am the God of every moment of your life, since I am the Soul of your soul.''
Holy hour.
''Would You like us to talk about Your love, Lord?''
''I am like the shy people. I prefer you to discover it yourselves, fearing that by speaking about it I seem to force it upon you. There again, you are free. But what is not My joy when of your own free will you seek ways of multiplying our meetings and deepening our intimacy. I let you be the one to come, to call. I

hide Myself to increase your desire for Me. And when you think you are lost, there I am with all My gifts!

My very feeble children, what you lack is the assurance of faith, this faith that is like a second sight — the strongest — the one that helps you to see the things of the earth with My eyes and evaluate them accordingly.

Do you want to practice faith? Do you understand what an élan this would give to your prayer, your Communion, your every day interior life? Would you like to try? You may be sure that your hope and love would grow in the same proportion. And to grow is to come close to Me.''

January 26 — *Surrounded by people.*

''When you smile at them, you give them the communion of thought.''

January 29 — *Holy hour.*

''Believe that I am happy to spend a whole hour with you. Why don't you believe? Yes, of course, it's your extreme poverty that is like an invitation to Me to stay. I live in you and I make you whiter than snow. Your faculties become filled with Me. Your memory, your understanding are made pure by My direct contact. Your will is placed in Mine. I want to be always at home in you.''

''I should be so happy if You were, Lord. Perhaps you don't get many invitations?''

''And yet you are My creation — My children. Your life should be one continual thanksgiving for all that I have done for you. You should keep your souls like the garden of Eden where I could come down to walk and talk with you as I did with the first man and woman. What a prelude of silence! What joyous awaiting! They were quite sure that I was coming to add the bliss of My presence to all their other happiness. Have the same certainty yourself — now, since I have not changed. Does a God who is All-Love change? Your name is not Eve but you are her daughter. And I love you with the same powerful love of those first mornings. Then don't be afraid to talk to Me about yourself, to blossom in My sight, to let Me look at you just as you are. Even though I know you, I like you to express yourself. It creates new longings and desires in you. You must have secrets to confide in Me. Aren't there always secrets in any intimate friendship?''

February 12 — *"Lord, I want to be always near You. It's only my thoughts that run away."*

''Call them back gently, without getting angry, since I am not angry. I know you, and I love your goodwill. It was for this — the peace that the angels sang when I came to make the world new again.

I am often more indulgent toward you than you are yourself. Believe this and you will give Me joy.''

I had arrived from Paris, and in the solitude of the country I felt Him so close that I did not know how to thank Him.

''Don't be surprised when My presence takes hold of you as though to possess you. Act in faith, My child. My little companion, I ask this of you: get used to My Presence. Your joy is in this, since it is a way of being together always. So lose yourself in Me and feel the wonder of it. Say to yourself, 'He has come. May He live in me since it is He who will carry me off.' You know how the eagle swoops down.

These matters are so great that they astonish the angels, and yet I speak so simply to you about them. You see how I stoop to the level of My children, for Love wants to explain itself and suffers at not being understood. Yet My love draws your attention to itself during the day by the blessings and delicate attentions you notice. And you don't always see them, either... Sometimes one offers a present without a word. Often I think, 'They will guess...' Alas! how many take them and pay no attention to the giver. It is not My honor that suffers but My love. You, My child, who know better, never make love suffer.''

February 19 —

''Humble yourself for your shortcomings.

It is your faults, My children, that make you unhappy. Recognize when you are in the wrong. Let your thought probe to the depths of your misery. Look at your short-sightedness. Your cowardice and laziness in making any effort to improve. Your willingness to stagnate in your usual petty ways. Your negligence in studying the model of My life. Your vain self-satisfaction no matter what your condition may be. The almost contemptuous attitude some of you have toward My sacraments. Do any of you have the loving desire to be made whiter than snow through repentant sorrow? Do you try to quicken your desire for My Eucharist of Love that wants to help you along your way? Don't you live as though you were all going to remain on earth forever? You so seldom give even a furtive glance at the life beyond, at your residence of tomorrow, when your heart should already be there, thanking Me, praising Me, adoring Me every day and in every action of the day...

You, at least you, child, is your soul filled with Me? Do you breathe for Me alone? Do you still put your interests before Mine, or in your earthly pilgrimage do you carry Me before you like a lantern? Have you made My anxieties yours? Have you taken your part in the conversion of the world? Near My martyrs, can you say, 'I was there', even if only in desire?

Who will help Me, if you, My communicants don't keep close?''

February 26 — *I was celebrating my birthday with a group of friends.*

"Lord, You are first among My invited guests.''

"I have the right. I created and redeemed you, and with what love! Who can weigh this love of Mine? Who can comprehend it? When will My poor love, My immense love be recognized by man?

Can't you say on your birthday, 'Everything in me is You, Lord, except sin'? Be full of joy to have been a thought in My mind. Thank Me. Serve Me. Love Me. Remember that you are one of My members and that in placing you on the earth, I have mapped out a path for you alone. Promise Me again to follow it as the one you cherish the most, since I planned it for you and because coming from Me it brings you to Me. This is the beautiful high-way, the direct route. Each one has his own, but few follow it. Many invent paths according to their own whims, paths beset with danger and loss. Simplify your pilgrimage to follow My will alone so as to be sure of fulfilling it faithfully, even to the very smallest details. Fidelity places more value on small opportunities than on big ones. These are the little love-tokens, like the small coins that add up to a fortune.

Since you have recognized the road I have marked out for you, don't turn aside from it. Your birthday made you feel how near you are to the end of it. That's where your great Friend is going to appear. He has hidden so long only to reserve a greater bliss in rest and possession. Do you firmly believe what I say?''

March 5 — "Haven't I prepared everything in your life, in your homes, for a solitude for two? Wouldn't even the nuns envy you? What or who is lacking to help you contemplate Me without interruption? What powers do you not spoil from Me, fortunate little one? You are like another person now. You aren't even aware of yourself — like a shrub that thinks it's holding up its prop.

Never forget that you are nothing without Me. What would you write if I didn't dictate for you.

I must travel the roads of the earth still for I have messages to give. Others speak on the radio. I use a very little soul made in My image and likeness and bound to Me by love. Don't you think that the best way for this soul to give Me to others is to bring Me forth. You know how a fragment of a mirror can reflect the big mirror, and if the little one were conscious, what joy it would have in giving back a perfect reflection of the big one.

My child, all people are invited to bring Me forth. My invitations are sent out at baptism and again in My sacraments. It is for you to respond even though imperfectly. I am there, anxiously wondering what progress you will make from the cradle to the grave, ready to help you at your first cry. Don't ever get the idea that I'm far away, My dear little ones so often exposed to danger. Your humble voice is balm to Me.''

March 11 — *Holy hour.*

''Consider Me. I have so many faces. A man, as you know, has his sadnesses and his joys in the little events on the earth. A Man-God is the same, but His look is longer because it is eternal, and His heart is multiple because it holds all yours within it. And this is not at all figurative, My child. I really carry each soul in Me, enfolding it in such all-encompassing love. You don't see that I'm carrying you, and you don't know that

257

all-encompassing love. Yet the sufferings of my passion are the proof.

Take a long look at My face full of pain. You have the time? You can think about it a little, can't you? This would be like the soft cloth that Veronica held out to Me. With one hand I placed it on My face, leaving the imprint of My features on it. That's what I'll do with your mind when you offer it to Me. I'll print My own upon it so that you may give it to others and in this way all this treasure in you will enrich your brothers too.

The more you give, the more I give you. Every day find new people to inherit the legacy that you receive in the morning. You will then see My joyous face.

When the apostles came back happy, to give Me an account of their mission and said such things as, 'You are the Christ, the Son of the living God,' or 'To whom Lord, should we go?' My joy was great. And when hearts are transformed so that they humble themselves before Me, adore My happy face. During this day, think about the lights and shadows that passed over My features in My own days on earth. Adore them. Keep watch for the feelings of your great Friend.''

March 15 — *Coming back from Mass I was thinking of sinners. It was cold and I was walking barefoot.*

''Perhaps, Lord, You will give me two for my two feet?''
''Two what? Two thousand?''

And He made me remember that He had granted six thousand conversions for one of St. Teresa of Avila's prayers.

March 17 — ''I am thirsty. I have only what one gives Me. I take nothing.''

March 18 — *On the street in the morning among the laborers going to work, I said, ''I too am going to my day's work living for You.''*

"Do you realize how many sinners you can save in a single day? Think of My dazzling power, riches and generosity. Who could hinder Me from giving you souls if I wish to do so?

For the earth, My justice is shackled by My mercy, moved to pity by the prayers of those I love. So count more on My generosity both for you and for all those you commit to Me. Dare to hope more than you have ever hoped before, as you come to believe in the divine open-handedness. We aren't on the same plane: then expect the extraordinary. You have already experienced it. It will strengthen your faith and hope in a way that you don't suspect. For it is I Myself who come and can I come other than as God?

My love is the source of everything. Did you think it was My pity? My pity, yes, but moved by this love of Mine that is greater than all other loves. I can only teach you about it little by little, because you are so fragile. For you would faint like the beloved in the Song of Solomon, if more vehement words from My heart fell upon your ear, and if, as in beautiful books, I added pictures. You're thinking, 'He's talking to me again about Love.' And I'm thinking, 'When can I begin to talk to her about it?'" (....)

April 1 — *Le Fresne*.

"I have risen from the dead. Who could restrain your joy? Won't you honor Me in this new way, in this joy for My joy? And if there is joy in you, how can you stop it from brimming over on others? Do you think I find very much joy in many hearts? People don't think of this perfect way of praising Me and yet it brings Me such balm. Don't I share all your emotions just as all true lovers share? You remember how when you were leaving someone dear to you, you said, 'Promise me you'll be happy!' as though it were your heart's need.

Mine takes delight in your joy. Learn to be joyous for My sake, even in times of trial. Live entirely for Me, My child. What depths of joy! And no one can ever rob you of it. Don't you feel the charm of it? What else can be compared with this?

During the day, tell Me again and again that you are one with Me. But don't let it be a burden to your mind — just a simple happy élan. You used to climb the steps to the verandah often to give your dear mother a hasty kiss in the midst of your little doings. It's simple and yet it's everything. You didn't realize what joy this kiss gave your mother and you don't know My joy either. Even so, don't deny Me, My little girl.''

April 8 — ''Have you thanked Me for all I did for you, for mankind, for the angels, for My mother? What a concert of blessings, My child! Gather them all as though they were yours and join in the symphony of thanksgiving. Sing your part in the choir of number-less voices, and I'll know it from all the others. Are there two voices alike in the whole world? Aren't you struck by the diversity in human creation? In heaven too, each saint differs from the other, and if you are enchanted by the variety of colors in your garden, you may be sure that Paradise flashes with a myriad many-splendored things, all for My glory. There too, I know the voices, for I know you all. My children, I atoned for all of you and I know My redeemed ones.''

''*Lord, who will teach me to thank You and what words should I use?*''

''The most simple — straight from your heart. Say them to Me at Mass. Say them again after your Com-munion when we are only one. Once more it will be I who give them to you. How I love to act for Myself in you. Can you believe that? I feel at home, and I feel you are Mine. Be very much Mine... I was going to say, 'Be your Christ before the Father, before others. Be the gentlest and the smallest'."

April 17 — *"Lord, I should so love to live Your words, and I am always myself, still my old self."*

Is it so difficult to think of your Lord? Is it so difficult to talk with Him and to keep Him company?

When you meet someone in a waiting room, don't you instinctively approach that person and in a kindly way do your best to make the time pass pleasantly for him? And if he were a poet, or a scholar, or someone great in the eyes of the world, wouldn't you go even further and show more joy?

My child, it's a God who is waiting at the door of your heart, a God who is all yours and who is in you. You open to Him when you talk to Him, when you look at Him, when you try to take your thoughts off the things around you so that you may turn them to Him with the utmost tenderness.

Don't think that this is a fable I'm telling you. It is the simple reality. But as it's all happening in the shadowland where everything is imperfection, you find it difficult to believe, and you are slow in acting upon it. That is why I am like that person in the waiting room. If only you could approach Me more often with all your kind charm, you might suspect My long yearnings. You might think, 'He's waiting for the world.' Yes, My little child, for everyone, and for such a long, long time... I came to Bethlehem to seek them and I shall go on seeking them right to the end of the world.

This is the patience of God. This is His love. Then how could you ever understand? Yet it would be very sweet to believe, wouldn't it? So quicken your faith by telling Me about it often. More often. Don't get weary: you will hope more and love more. It's your great God who wants you greatly, My very frail little girl."

April 9 — *Leaving for Paris.*

''One step ahead. One step in your attentive will. One step in your faithfulness. Up until now you have lived for Me, by you. Now, live for Me, by Me. One step forward...''

April 26 — *Returning from Paris, I had the surprise of finding that a family of nightingales with the loveliest song in the world had a nest above a window looking out on the avenue of lime trees.*

''Nothing could make you happier, could it? I too know how to make surprises. Some people don't see them. I'm so glad that you guessed. On earth you always have to guess. I'm always hidden behind the door. Sometimes you haven't seen Me: do you remember?...

See Me in everything, for I am everywhere for all of you... Oh, that look of yours that I love: you understand? It's like a declaration of love from you, as though you gave Me a little of your soul. And I take it right away, carefully watching for a chance to pick you up like a collector of works of art who jealously hides his discoveries so that no one may steal them from him.

Tell Me that you are really and truly Mine from now on. You say, 'You know that, Lord.' But don't deprive Me of the joy of hearing you say it again. Any words at all... you can say them to Me. But with others, get to love silence. I mean by that a silence of goodness. You will find Me there. I shall hear all the words that you don't say. You will keep them for Me, for My sake. You will ask Me for the strength, and these silences will be like cut flowers. I'll offer them to Myself in a bouquet. Right now would you like to begin this silence with others, this silence that will speak so eloquently to My love?

I ask you for this new way of pleasing Me. I need

all your ways. How could I not want your entire being when I know that you are free.''

April 29 — ''You think that you are the richest person in the world because you have a nightingale in your trees and its pure, strong voice enchants your evenings and your nights. But what is this poetic wealth compared with the pure, strong voice that you hear in the secret gardens of your soul? It doesn't command attention like the voice of the bird. It waits for you to try to arouse it so that the words it speaks are like invited guests who enter your heart, where you will welcome them. The voice is never late. It is so eager to speak, knowing the good that will come and having so much love to reveal... But it wants you to be the one to call. Then it comes with more joy.

'As a man speaks, so he is,' you say. What do you think of the sincerity and forthrightness of the words? Don't they express your deepest feelings when you dare to share them with the one dearest of all to you?

My little girl, listen to Me as My love flows to you directly. And may it be an ever new enchantment for you, like those treasures old and ever new spoken of in the gospel. These are the inexhaustible riches that the heart of your Lord wanted for you — a never-ending beginning again of the joy of hearing Him.

And since you are approaching the door leading out of this life, since you want to start leaving behind this world of the senses in order to live more often and more silently in My intimacy, keep on rereading My words. Let them sink deep into your heart. Pray that they may be food to a great many others — to all people.

Then, like a very little worker, her day ended, you will disappear from this life — humble, because everything comes from Me; happy, simply because you have obeyed. You have been a nothingness to whom I have given the desire for My glory.''

April 30 — *After Communion.*
''Keep watch on your thoughts; they control your words and actions. Dwell upon My thoughts, so full of kindness and compassion, and you will do My deeds.''

May 11 — *I invited the angels of the terrace to come and sit before the magnificent panorama of the peaceful Loire and its islands in their Maytime greenness.*
''My child, heaven is not far from the earth when you ask it to come. Live more with the saints. They can all help you to love Me more, now that they know. Oh, this science of love! Are you sure that you delve deeper and deeper into it every day even if only for a quarter of an hour?''
''Lord, be my teacher. What should I do?''
''Look at Me in My gospels. There you will find My history, My life-story. You follow Me; you see Me comfort, heal, suffer, obey My Father for all of you. There you see Me denying Myself, keeping silence and speaking; seeking solitude, followed by the crowds; teaching, contradicted. Full of courage in defending truth, in rebuking the mighty, in taking the part of the little ones. Filled with compassion for the humble, the repentant, the oppressed. Thinking only of My people, not of Me; for you and against Myself...
You remember the other day in Paris when you found yourself in a broadcasting studio filled with noisy, bold people, you thought, 'What am I doing here?'
When I came from heaven to earth, I might have asked Myself the same question if I had not come to

suffer, to prove My love for you all along the path of My life... longer than the road to Calvary.

How could you ever count My sacrifices? The stars witnessed My nightly prayers; the cold, My frozen limbs; the earth, My broken feet.

Who could have guessed at My ardor for My Father, the intensity of My love for you, you of every age and race, right to the very end of time...

You have noticed how sometimes you get others to follow you without saying a word? I wanted to leave all of you My example; it said, 'Follow Me; this will be your response to Love.' Do you think there were many who heard and followed? My sweat of blood in Gethsemane was for that. For that the tears that disfigured My face so much that Peter, James and John had difficulty recognizing Me.

Oh, little flock of My most faithful friends, come to meet Me every day in a passage of the gospels. Look for My heart there and give Me yours.''

May 13 — ''Wasn't that a good idea to ask you to live with My grandeur today? You saw it in My power, and this gave you hope in your matchless Friend who can do everything. How you revelled in the feeling of your littleness, in the poverty of your knowledge, completely abandoned to My knowledge, trusting in My infinite tenderness. You were reminded of the big butterfly holding a flower captive between its wings. My darling child, how short your day seemed to you!

Couldn't you grow to love this habit of placing one of My divine qualities in your thought like a kind companion in your pilgrimage. It would be a new way of watching for Me. Oh, the soul that wants to lay hold upon its Savior, how it varies its ways of running after Him! And He finds a thousand excuses for letting Himself be caught. If you only knew!

All of these things belong to that secret life that you call 'interior' — a life beyond the world's dimensions. These are the trial flights, the first freeings. You remember the little swallow that seemed to dart right up into the sun the very first time it left the nest? Take care of your hidden life. Love it, since I love it…''

As I had just held back an unkind word:

''Offer Me that cut flower.''

May 14 — *After Communion.*

''Don't let your thoughts run wild. Call to mind the uncultivated Sahara and then picture your well raked terrace dotted with roses.''

May 20 — ''Look at Me. Do you trust Me? Do you hope in Me? Unwaveringly, unreservedly? The hope I want you to have transcends death, since I am all in all to you; haven't you told Me that?''

''You look for Me in the beauty of the rose, in the voice of the nightingale on the terrace, in the song of the cuckoo from the island that comes winging its way to you over the Loire, in the brilliant stars of a May night and even in the far-off twittering of birds in the marshlands.

But am I not first of all in souls created in My image? In these human beings whose Brother-Savior I am? And wouldn't this be an incentive for you to reach Me through them? They will not even be aware that you have sighted Me, but they will find consolation by it. And I will add to their consolation.''

May 27 — *Corpus Christi.*

''Lord, I want so much to work for Your desires.''

''Take your place near Me where John is as I invent My Eucharist. Look at My happiness. I seem to forget even My fearful passion that is about to begin, so completely am I engulfed in the love of man. Not just the Eleven, but all the people to come, even to the very last at the end of time. You understand, it's as though I took everyone — all of you — in My body, promising you to be members of it. The thirst for union with you is so great that I want to be consumed by you in order to merge our minds, our beings. I want to be your thinking and your doing.

Such love amazes you, and yet you can guess at only a very faint part of it. Does the flame of a torch give any idea of a conflagration?

There, near Me, in John's place, are you aware of My deep joy at having found a way of remaining among you — all of you who were not there that evening at the Last Supper. You whom I already love so much that I am ready to die a shameful death for you. You whose entire life will be accompanied by My Hosts, and whose death will be the sweeter for them.

And from your place — John's place — see how the apostles have already become new men — gentle and fervent. They believe. They possess Me. I already act in them as I shall act in you.

Can I be present and not make your cup of blessings overflow? Who is as rich as I? Who could desire your highest good more than I? Then help Me to fulfill this desire by asking the Father that all people allow Me to have My own way in them. If only they would consent to let Me come in. They are afraid to be seen. They have no time for anything but business; they have none for Me. They don't believe and they don't think about these things. They are scornful. Others believe, but hate Me and basely persecute all that they can in the ciborium.

You, My faithful friends, surround Me; adorn My tabernacles; comfort Me; respond to Love, in life, in death; wish to remain longer on earth in order to love

Me the longer there. Others will come after you, but who will replace you? For Me each of you has a face, a path.

Keep your face before My face and hasten along your path.''

June 3 — *Holy hour.*
(I had just returned from Paris — from the Rue du Bac where I had admired the chapel full of Vincentian nuns in adoration before the Blessed Sacrament.)

''You saw My doves? It gave you joy to see them surrounding Me with their love. Unite with them, very little as you are. In your desire to be one with Me, join more often with the saints on earth and the saints in heaven. You will be stronger; alone, you are so little. You see, then you are part of the bouquet and I'll be tempted to give the entire reward to you alone.

Remember how I loved oneness: 'When two or three are gathered together in My Name, there am I in the midst of them.' Because union too is love. And I am Love. Don't be afraid to lose your personality; you benefit from all the others. These bouquets, these baskets of flowers around My altars are but faint and far-off images of the people united together to love Me.

In your thought, place those you have commended to My care near My tabernacle, and I'll draw them to Me. How could My heart fail to bless those in your care? Would that be like the measure of My love?

During this octave of Corpus Christi, love with all men, adore with all men, hope with all men, and yearn.''

''When will you come to get me, my dear Love? I am ready to go without any regrets, so that I may be with You.''

''Be united with all those who have called for My kingdom to come and My day to dawn within them. Be spent with loving enthusiasm for My house. Act

268

as though I had entrusted the victory to your littleness. What wouldn't you do to be equal to your task? Let the fire of your zeal consume you. May I not expect this of you? You ask and I fulfill. You see, once again this is oneness?''

In the evening, the nightingale had ceased to sing.

''He has finished his little day. But you, child, will sing to Me throughout all eternity.''

June 9 — *Holy hour.*

''My Love, how many holy hours will I have kept in my life?''

''Don't you think that they have made Me forget a good many other hours of yours? You don't like to be late for your friends, do you; nor to be ungrateful. Then for the One who loved you before you loved Him, for the One who ransomed you... Oh, My child, humble yourself for doing so little, even though all you do for Me gives Me such joy. Keep going. Increase. Hunt for new surprises in these little sacrifices that charm Me. And yet it is the Spirit who inspires you to make them. It's like a proposition where your will consents. It is this act of the will that goes straight to My heart like the stab of ecstacy in the Song of Solomon: 'Oh, exquisite wound!'

That fills you with wonder because you cannot fathom the meaning of the words, 'God is Love'.

In our intercourse don't be afraid of your littleness, for this is what touches My compassionate heart. And don't have any fear of meeting Me too often, since I'd be happy if you never left Me. Try to believe Me if you cannot understand. A child believes its father. A woman believes the one she loves. So won't you believe Me?

You must practice joy in order to open wide your hearts. And yet how easy to be joyous when you know that you are loved boundlessly by a good God. To know that you are happy about it would increase My own happiness. When you see, when you know, you will be ready to come back to earth to complete what you have only just begun. Then don't be afraid to love Me, to tell Me about your love, to wait for Me and to call Me. It's so simple. When one loves, everything is simple, even to die.''

June 24 — *Holy hour.*
 At home, looking at a bust of Christ.
 ''I am the Head. You are My arms raised toward the Father. Let us glorify Him together My child. Put your whole heart into it; I mean your will. And you will be exalted. And your union with Me, the Head of the Body, will give you power undreamed of. All that is good in you is I Myself. So make room for Me.

Long for My consciousness to take over yours. Let yours go as you assume Mine. I don't make as it were official use of My instruments in you at every moment. But at every moment it should be your joyous privilege to have them in readiness for Me.

You remember the story of the little maid whom the King condescended to employ and who charmed him so much by her faithful service that he raised her to the rank of his most intimate friends? So united did they become that her one and only desire was to remain with him forever.

Gabrielle, what name does your love invent for Me?''
 ''Lord, I find no name worthy of You.''
 ''Then just love Me without giving Me a name.''

July 1 — *Nantes. Holy hour.*
 ''Love Me. You see, I ask this of many, of everyone. How few stop to listen to Me. Some hear without wanting to understand.

You know what is My enemy? Money. People think only of money. They live for it and nothing else. And it hardens the heart without filling it.

Try to grasp this: I alone give joy. I alone. They imagine that I crush My people with sacrifices, whereas it is the sacrifices that give you wings. My child, you know that My yoke is gentle? Then tell them about it; they won't listen to Me. See that you mention My Name often in your conversations. You did this today, didn't you, and you noticed that it was like sunlight. It was so simple and yet so deep. Above all, don't count on yourself; count on Me in you.

When you went into that café to collect the rent and the men surrounded you for a chat, you noticed how, right away they spoke of God, of the life beyond, of death. Was this your influence? No, it was I in you. Poor people who think only of the pleasure of drinking and so becloud this thought that would rise to Me to love Me a little.

A little... big things begin that way. Love seizes. Love carries off, without a moment's warning, without waiting, without asking. And if you surrender and let the Spirit flow in, you give joy to the saints in heaven and glory to the Father because you have begun to understand His love. Oh, My child, give the Father the best of yourself.''

July 10 — *Holy hour.*

"Read a few sentences from our conversations every day. You find a little strength and love in them, don't you. Is it too much to ask you to do this once every morning and twice more during the afternoon? To keep us together — you understand? To discover Me in the sacrament of the words.

Oh, how I long to give Myself to you, and how diffident I am to ask you to receive Me! You see there's always this respect for your liberty.

Talk to Me. Don't be afraid to appeal to My feelings. Seek to console Me. Haven't I consoled you many times? Tell Me the things that you think would bring Me balm. Of course, this is reality not make-believe. I am the God-Man, sensitive to your marks of tenderness. Above all, believe this. Oh, if only you believed more... we should be more closely bound together, and you would experience great joy, since you would have come closer to bliss.

You know, don't you, that I am your bliss. Very few understand. Try to explain it to them. Speak for Me. I know that you don't work for a reward but only to please Me.

Oh, My child, create a climate of love within you. Unceasingly. There's where I want to live in you, in all of you, right to the moment when you leave this life. Then you will leave it so serenely. You will breathe forth: that is the true description of the last of your gentle sighs.''

July 27 — *In my bedroom. It was three o'clock in the morning and I was thinking, ''What prayer and what praise would be pleasing to Him in memory of His death?''*

''Say, 'Father, forgive them for they know not what they do'.''

July 29 — *Holy hour.*

''Aren't there sentences that pierce you like an arrow when you reread our books? The words speak all over again. And with fresh meaning; the Christ-consciousness sheds new light on them. In the past you had not been fully aware. You were younger and the chalice of your mind was only partly filled. Now it's as though the you of today met the you of yesterday. You see, the grace received and made fruitful fashions the new soul. You want to come nearer to Me, to be more understanding? Then open your soul to receive more. And when you have received, bear fruit like your well-watered trees. Nothing is lost of the care that you give your soul. You don't see it, but heaven sees it — all heaven. That's the only audience you should want to have.

In a little way, humbly, practice the great art of the silent stage. The applause and the glory are for later on. Be strong enough to wait. Have a patient genius for work. Didn't I have it with inimitable love? I may well have a little right to ask you for long courage — the courage to live, the courage to die. And if your faith paves the way with your devoted acts and generous words in this atmosphere of tenderness where I have placed you, how could you fail to find the way short? And how could I keep from going half way to meet you?

When will you do Me the honor of expecting from Me much more than you ever ask or think? Since I am All-Power and since I love you. Weigh up your unworthiness. Can you weigh up My compassion?''

August 6 — *The Transfiguration.*

''Do you remember when you were little you said to Me, 'Be transfigured, be transfigured before my eyes, Lord.' You trusted Me. Off you went to the mountain of solitude and you heard My voice. You saw Me then in another way. It was also love that transfigured Me before My apostles. Always see love at the source of everything that comes from God. There is love and there is hate — nothing else. Two roots: God and the devil. Man with his free will takes his choice of the fruit.

Be on the watch for the motive of your actions and

remember that I am stretching out a helping hand. And keep watch on your lower nature, the part that runs down your neighbor made in My image. Give the kind of affection that comforts. You know what I mean — the word, the glance. I am in all ways of loving, just as Satan is in all ways of wounding. You see the source? You see the fruit? Choose, and always be ready to choose Me. This is what it is to be always in love. It's the direct route to Me. It passes through death and leads you into My arms."

August 13 — *The old house is full of people.*

"But you are Mine as though you were alone. You give yourself to everyone and you find Me there. It's only your duty that changes. Your Master is the same gentle Master. And you have your nights. How well you know that the evening conversations are the most intimate; when your thoughts merge with Mine.

When you find it difficult to talk about yourself, the Spirit interprets for you, but you're not aware of that. You don't know that your humble, childish stammerings become hymns of glory for Me. Haven't you the intention of glorifying God? Prolong this intention throughout your whole life. Intensify it."

August 19 — *In a moment of depression.*
"Keep going. Be steadfast."

September 6 — *In the empty house.*
"I am always crucified before the Father, who sees all time in a single instant. I am always the Lamb of God who takes away the sins of the world. And since I am yours, why don't you offer Me more often to heaven from the depths of your heart? It is always now. Didn't you understand that when you were in Jerusalem and prayed on Calvary.

Tenderly offer your sacrifice for the world. Aren't there others weaker than you? Can they rise up without Me? If you wanted to save a person very dear to you and this beloved person refused your help, how much you would suffer! I want to help the world, and the world refuses My help. Speak to the Father about His Son on the cross, so that He will let Himself be touched and send light to these hardened ones who do not even look at Me. You know how one speaks to a father who is watching his son die? Won't this father hasten to carry out his child's last wishes? Remind Him of the words 'Forgive them for they know not what they do.' It is always now.

And if He forgives, what will He not do? Do you know the outpouring of any love like His? A love as vehement, as faithful, as all-consuming, as full of delicate and incomparable sweetness. A love that is all readiness. It is now this love. It is always now.''

September 9 — *''Lord, I rack my brains to find ways of loving You and I don't succeed.''*

''I am all simplicity. Love Me simply.

When you think about Me, feeling sorry at not being able to do better, you love Me. When you act rather from duty than from inclination, you love Me. When you belittle yourself in your own eyes and before others, you love Me. When you want to pray and you deplore the distractions that make your thoughts wander, you love Me. When you hunt for words without being able to express your desires, you love Me. When you forgive a wounding remark; when you give pleasure for the sake of giving Me pleasure; when you cease to think of yourself in order to try to reach Me; when you attempt to leave everything as though it were the day of your death; when in thought you join the angels and saints, like one who arrives ahead of time; and when, in the evening you welcome your tomorrow morning that will unite us, you love Me.

It's all very different from what you thought you ought to do in order to love Me. Oh, My little girl, simplify yourself sweetly in My Presence, your love wide-awake. You know very well that I am always there.''

September 16 — ''My little girl, nothing exists but your Christ. Then could anything keep your heart from Me? Could you yield it to a mere nothing? Don't you feel that since I am all perfections I should attract you right to the very inmost depth of your being created for immortal beauty? Unwind yourself from your self. Fall in love with your God — this glorious Reality. And if you are in love with Him, you will think about Him more often. It is this remembrance of Me that I want in you, this desire to please Me, this fear that people offend Me, this joy in My kingdom. I want to reign over each one of you. Keep your heart yielded, not by force but by love that fuses two wills. Learn to meet Me the livelong day. And can you meet Me without greeting Me with love?

When a lonely stranger travels through a distant country, he sometimes finds it painful not to see an affectionate recognition anywhere but to go on his way as one among the dead. I am this stranger when no remembrance of Me passes across your souls, when they are sealed and lifeless. But I call you by events, by some circumstance.

'That's chance' they say.

Who will say, 'That is He'?''

September 30 — *Coming back from a magnificent autumn walk, I was admiring the clouds in the form of gigantic animal heads. ''Lord, they are as beautiful as if they were Your first Creation.''*

"But each day is a first creation. Not one is like another. I never stop creating. And it is all for all of you. If I didn't hold you up, you would cease to exist. Will you love Me enough to thank Me for it?

This continuous creation of your body and your power of thinking comes from My everlasting love. So sing praises to Me. Sing with your body and your mind, as though you had begun this song at your birth and meant to continue it right to the moment of your death, only to take it up again for all eternity.

You saw the expression of that father's face as he listened to the song composed for him by his child. He was smiling at the little one, longing to put his arms around her. That was only a human father; he hadn't given his child her soul. Your Father in heaven is the life of your soul. He is your soul. You are My breath. I give it to you with every second that passes. And My breath is My love. Breathe Me with great eagerness to this one end: that you may live only to love Me.

Pray for those who receive My gifts without wanting to know Me, to love Me, and to serve Me. They too would cease to exist were I not holding them up. So I wait for them. Pray that they may seize every opportunity of returning to Me. I am always thirsty for them. Let them come to Me and like little children say, 'Forgive. I won't do it again.' All will be forgotten. And immediately there will be great rejoicing in heaven. If they only knew...! The Feast of My heart will be even greater. Ah! the tenderness of a God!

I am at the bottom of the stairs of your life and I'm listening. Will your feet approach or will they go away forever?"

October 4 — "Today you will contemplate My beauty. Already this morning you saw that deep flush of color arrowing the eastern horizon, and as you passed under the trees you stopped to admire the long October spider webs festooned from branch to branch and spangled with drops of dew like rows of pearls in open necklaces. Then as the sun rose, the crickets that had been vocal all night long in your cherry tree suddenly ceased their singing; the Loire mirrored one hue after another in a rich medley of unearthly colors. And the herons passed over, streaking the violet sky.

If you have eyes to see, every hour of the day holds its splendor. It comes from Me, from a fragment of Me. For you, of course — so that you may learn the lure of praise, the joy of adoration, the love of Love. And I vary my spectacles every morning to rejuvenate your hearts.

Have you anyone else so ingenious in his ways of pleasing you? You have someone to carve the clouds into the shapes you love, haven't you? And an engineer to swell the tide so that the water reaches the wall of your terrace? What tradesman placed the birds in your trees and so many butterflies around your flowers? And this morning, was it a dealer in tulle who unfolded that chiffon scarf of mist right across your island, turning it into two storeys.

Whose hand plucks the yellow leaves of your linden trees with such grace while your strawberry-plants offer you their long rest for the fruit of future years.

Open your eyes wide and look at Love. It is He who is passing by."

October 7 — *Holy hour.*
"After living through these glorious autumn days, these days with My grandeur and My power, would you like to live with My extreme kindness? You can come across it in each of your days, can't you? Again this morning you met just the one you needed most at that moment. And when the mail arrived, didn't you

receive the letter necessary to encourage you to continue the good work you had begun? Once more this was I.

And yesterday, at that social gathering when the conversation begun by you unexpectedly opened out into a topic of general interest to everyone — one that held them spellbound — you were aware of My help, weren't you? Your words flowed so effortlessly.

This joy too, that sometimes comes to you in little gusts, this refuge that you find up above the earth, as though you escaped from the life below, this rest, this blissful peace, this comfort that you draw both for yourself and others, doesn't your faith tell you that it is I? (....)

Tell Me that at last you believe in My immense love ever-present in you, that you are always sure of it. My grace would increase in proportion, even to the point of miracle, for what is a miracle but a token of love's simplicity? Believe that I love what you give Me, when you think of giving it to Me. Of course, it is I who put the gift into your hands. But it is you, a beggar maid, who has offered Me something. Thank you for having thought of Me.''

October 14 — ''Stay with Me even if you go out into the world. Stay with Me.'' *(I was going to a reception at a friend's home.)*

''Stay with Me all the way there, and when you are inside the house, abide with Me still in the depths of your heart, so that you will give Me the joy of knowing that you are more at home with Me than with them. If your hearts sometimes experience this pride of having a friendship for yourselves alone, an almost exclusive friendship, don't you believe that I hope to be the One above all others for you at all times, I whose love is always greater?

And for fear that you may get away from Me in these worldly distractions, I would gladly throw the fowler's net over you to hold you captive, as in a spell, in the stillness of the Christ-consciousness.''

October 21 — *The priest who had directed me for part of my life had just died and I felt the touch of his blessing still.*

''Believe that in Me My children remain united together. Members of one Body have only one heartbeat. There are spiritual heritages held out across the walls of the tomb, and everything comes through Me for the glory of the Father.

It is because they all belong to the same family and the same home that this oneness between the living and the dead is so great. The home is My Father's, and the same Blood, — Mine — flows in all the children.

Stay very close to your departed ones. They are close to all of you. Increase your trust. Venture out beyond the little earthly dimensions and take up your residence in the womb of God. There's nothing in this world that can hold you back, so lose sight of the world more often. You're traveling to eternity. Oh, My child, when you *know*...! That's when you'll understand the hymns of praise sung by the All-joyous Ones and their exultant cries of thanksgiving.

Win the right to see Me. Let this secret longing be your constant thought. I say 'secret' because it is still feeble. Ask Me to make it grow in you, so that it may be light and warmth to those who come near you; and they too will understand that I am the End. The End of every beginning day.

And when at last you close your eyes, hope that they open only to see Me, your very gentle, your most loving Savior.''

October 27 — *Holy hour.*

At the Angelus they sang, 'He has lived among us.'

"I always make My home among you. You see My house — the tabernacle? I wait for all of you. In the world you have a day 'at home' when you receive guests. Every day is an 'at home' for Me. And nothing is lacking in My home; you know that, don't you? Neither the banquet, nor the Spirit, nor the affection, nor the gifts of My graces, and you don't have to wait to be received. I am the One who waits. I know some who have never come. I don't mean who have never come to My feet to confess their sins; I mean that they have never even come to greet Me.

Others come for certain ceremonies, but without the slightest thought that I am there waiting for them. They leave as they entered. Nothing in them has been stirred. My eyes follow them sadly... with My sadness of Gethsemane...

You who come every day to My house, speak to Me for them so that before they come for the last time carried in a coffin, they will give Me their living bodies, their faculties, their entire being. With what warmth I shall receive them and respond to their trust!

I have another temple — your soul in a state of grace: a state of Me-in-you, since grace is your Christ. Who can ever know the joy it gives Me to be loved there, even if the love is feeble. Do you know what it is to feel at home in a soul? To be the One waited for, the most loved, the most understood, the Head of the household even though I am so ready to fulfill the desires of this one who lives for Me alone.

Beloved friend, ever joyous and ready to please Me, eager to listen to Me, eager to deepen the love that it finds so fleeting, poor, uncertain and fragile; so fearful of falling into the same faults as yesterday... Let us close up all the portals of our home so that we shall no longer hear the howling of the wolves. Let us forget the earth and its little things, and in the innermost sanctuary, which is within your own heart, let us speak our language. Without words.''

November 4 — ''I knock at your door. You don't believe that I need My children, do you? And yet My God-Love needs your love. That's how it is. Always.

You remember My words, 'I thirst'? I am always thirsty. If you knew this thirst, more intense than the thirst of men, you would devise every means in your power to quench it. That is why I knock at your door.

Do you remember the heat of the Sahara? The desert burns less than I. Can you understand My thirst for your awareness of Me, for your desire to be pleasing to Me, for your gratitude for My pitiable sufferings, your compassion for all the disgrace, the filth and the hatred I received during the night before My crucifixion and on the morning of My death? And for the blows, and the torture of My body and mind. Do you sometimes think of it?

Can you measure this love that made Me give Myself up when I could have escaped into the invisible? It was My love that went out to meet the torture.

Don't you believe that I paid for the right to have at least your friendship? You recall what the thief said: 'Remember me when You come into Your kingdom'? And I say to you, 'Remember Me during your life'. Place Me as a lighthouse in the center of your mind, not just a lighthouse that illumines, but one that gives warmth.

Where can you be where I am not? When you are hunting for Me, I am already there, and when you love Me, I love Myself in you.

I am your Source. Give everything back to Me in joy and simplicity. So few stop to think about this.

Then tell Me now, do you want Me to knock at your door?''

November 11 — *Holy hour.*

''Practice being more attractive for love's sake. You could do immense good with an affectionate look and a smile. If you keep yourself for yourself, you are your own slave. But if you go to meet people with delicate thoughtfulness, you bring peace and rest; you give the balm of Gilead. How a smile from you would have soothed X this morning if you hadn't shut yourself up in your ivory tower. There is a demon called the spirit of contradiction; he fraternizes with the spirit of self-seeking.

Remember that love is not puffed up with pride and that it will never pass away. What you do for yourself will perish miserably. What you do for others, for the love of Me, will go on re-echoing throughout all eternity.

Have you tried to see Me in others? Have you understood that I live in that old crippled woman on the 'sunken road' and all others like her? Couldn't you bring Me a little wood for this winter, and some clothing? Won't you give Me something to eat? Suppose she is bitter and doesn't thank you, what difference does it make? Since I am the One who receives, and I am rich.

Don't be shy when you give. Be daring in goodness.''

I was thinking that I should be ashamed to wheel a barrow with wood in it right to that place.

''Perhaps. But I shall not be ashamed of you at the last judgment. Don't run away any more from what costs you something, and you will be among the happiest people. Besides, I've done so much for you... You are free though. You will not even commit a fault by not going. I'll just have the sadness of wanting something without getting it."

"Lord, I'll go."

November 18 — *Holy hour.*

I was thanking Him for having given so sweet a perfume to a palm branch that I was bringing from the garden.

"You may be sure that it is for you that the Father Creator made all these things that charm you in nature. His goodness is exuberant in creating for His children. Who ever thinks of thanking Him? And yet if He has prepared such magnificence in nature for all His children, He has also done so for each one, just as if each one were His only child. Oh, this love for everyone and for one alone! God knows all the ways of loving and all are adorable. Thank Him for His way of loving you, for His special thought for you, for what He has put in your heart and not in the heart of another: for having chosen you; and for all the favors that you must recognize as coming from Him. Isn't it a favor that He has watched over you from all eternity? Doesn't it make you feel more than ever His child and happy to have such a Father?

What could ever harm you? You are God's child and Christ is your Brother. Isn't that a wellspring of joy? Escape from yourself. Forget all earthly cares. Return unceasingly into the Eternal Womb that bore you. Give yourself to the Spirit. He will quicken you. He will interpret you to the Father. You can't understand this; so knowing that you know nothing, give yourself all the same, and the smaller you are the more the Spirit will exalt you. Go over your deficiencies. You would like to fly and you do not even know how to walk.

Then hold out your arms and the Spirit will take hold of you."

November 19 — *"And my faults and failings, Lord, so many of them!"*

"Weep in your heart for them. People don't cry enough over their faults. Some make a show of them. But My friends know what they cost Me, and they are sad for My immense sadness. They despise themselves, and from this their love is born, a love eager to make amends. After that all their poor little actions are meant to repair the wrong so that I may forget. As for Me, I use the ugliness of these tear-stained sins to make soul-splendors.

Believe in the matchless beauty of a humble soul that shows Me its wounds and hopes in Me alone. I clothe it with My merits. How could I ever do otherwise?"

November 23 — *After Communion.*

"You remember in the gospel it is written that only to touch the hem of My robe brought healing.

And you feed upon Me; you possess Me utterly. What is not My power in you to heal you, change you, completely transform you in a single instant? Believe that. Do you really believe it?"

November 25 — *"Lord, I am here before You like the dry ground upon which the prophet called down the dew."*

"I am the Prophet and I am the Dew. My Word is meat and drink, have you noticed? It offers itself to you; you accept it and immediately it begins to grow. This is the Dew that falls from heaven. What a banquet, My child! What new transports of delight!

Set off again. You understand: no halting place. Run straight to God as you used to run along the road to meet your father. How happy he was, this earthly father... Your Father in heaven is more so, for eagerness is also love — love, faith and hope. Do you think that God would turn a deaf ear to the calls of His darling child? He will multiply His gifts, for His treasures are as great as His desire to bestow them.

Poor little ones, you have such a false idea of your Savior. Do you think He would redeem you and then abandon you?

Don't set limits to your confidence. He sets no limits to His favors. Hunger for God and you will receive. If you don't call Him, how can He come? Do you go to see people who don't want you?

"Never stop coming, Lord, I never stop wanting You."

"And when you call Me, believe that I come."

December 3 — "Have you taken a long look at My goodness? Have you seen the details in your soul, in your possessions, even among those around you — because they are around you? It is the quality of goodness to diffuse light. And if it shines on any point, everything that touches that point lights up.

Don't compare the goodness of God with man's goodness which is nothing but a rough sketch. But try to equal the boundless goodness of God. Have you fathomed My favors? You notice how delicate they are. Then imitate this.

This morning someone came to ask you for information and you cheered him. Don't you find that I often give the impression that you are all part of my family, part of the Holy Trinity? Then why not give others the impression that they are part of your family? Isn't this a reality? Aren't you all God's children? But what a long way there is to go, My child, before this feeling of brotherhood reigns in the world. Be on the watch for opportunities of showing it. Do good below the surface — in hearts — and the good will be done to Me. Doesn't that thought alone encourage you?"

"Lord, where will I find the means of intensifying my zeal?"

"In Me, your Lord and God. Ask, just as one does 'en famille'. Let Me live where you live, every moment. Let nothing carry you away, and may nothing ever cause Me to be estranged from you. Keep Me in your center like the sun at the zenith, and your days will be divine."

December 9 — *In my bedroom.*

A cloud that had caught the sun's rays lit up the entire room. "Beloved Lord, help me to reflect You."

"Lay hold on God. What are you without Him but nothingness? Give Him all the room. Whether you think or speak or act, take care of Him only and He will take care of you.

Your time on earth is so short, so evanescent; at least may it be all for Him. Didn't I live for you — in Bethlehem, in Nazareth, during My public life and at its distressing close. Place Me before each one of your actions. What is your goal? Is it I? What is the object of your love? Be sure that it is not you yourself, poor little finite one. And if you are filled with Me as a sponge submerged in living water, how could you fail to decrease in order to increase Me — to give Me to others. You will decrease by sacrificing your withdrawal into yourself, your silent solitude, your life of seclusion, your preferences for what is exclusive.

I often say to you, 'Get outside of yourself'. Be outgoing for others. If you approach them without affection, you fall short of your purpose. But if you act in a heartwarming manner, you win them. And to win someone for Me... do you realize just what may come of this?

Spare nothing. Don't keep anything back. Look at Me, always drinking My cup of suffering to the very lees. And be joyous. Joy is the hallmark of love.

Go, My child; walk with your head in God. And

your heart? Are you in love with yourself or with Me?''

December 21 — *I was coming back from Paris and I thanked Him for a grace.*

''Wasn't this what you asked Me for every morning when you offered Me all your actions? I too know how to give pleasure. Learn every kind of thoughtfulness from Me.''

''Lord, my faults deserved punishment instead.''

''Imitate Me. When you correct others don't humiliate them. Show them new tenderness; then they will humble themselves. In everything imitate your God. Ask Him to help you to understand Him better. Until your soul leaves your body you will not have seen God, but you will have come to know Him better than by sight, and from this knowledge will be born an immense yearning to possess Him. Oh, be possessed of this eagerness to possess Me! Let it be like a glory that you offer Me or like a play of the light of your love flashing back the fires of My own. People believe so little in My love. Do you always believe, My child? Some think it's a weakness to do so. Blessed weakness! How it rejoices My burning heart! So don't be afraid to believe too much. Don't be afraid to love Me too much. Go still further, as though you had done nothing up till now, and I, who have loved you boundlessly, shall begin all over again like a new proof of infinite love. Oh, My child, learn to love Love! Love to learn Love.''

December 22 — *After Communion.*

''You see, in the past there was the law of fear. Now it is the law of love. Doesn't the beautiful Feast of Christmas make you feel this deeply? From now on, won't everything in you be love — above all, your sorrow for your sins? Use your faults as a springboard to love Me better. And don't think this is a small thing. Love is never small. Love is transfiguration... You carry it with you from morning till night like a beacon, and each of your thoughts and feelings and actions become *light* that mingles with the *light* of heaven. Aren't you one with those who live in eternity? Aren't you one family, the children of the Father? And isn't there joy in union? Draw freely on the common treasury of merits while you are still on earth: you will not be alone then.

Love is not selfish. Love never calculates. It hastens to help. In heaven there is nothing but love. And I bring it to the earth, whereas the Evil One sows hatred. There are two camps — choose. And if you choose love, don't remain shy and on the outskirts as it were. Enter into the arena with the strong ones.

Look at the cycle of My life. What have you loved the most? My humble birth, My hidden life, the public revelation, or My shameful death? Wherever you look, can you see any other hallmark than love? Love for My Father, for My children, for you, My child. So be full of joy. Respond to the avalanche of My gifts.''

December 30 — *Holy hour.*
I was entirely occupied in taking in the Christmas rents.
''When you come close to Me in thought, see that you put away every little earthly worry so that you can be really all Mine. And if you often repeat this loving effort of your mind, you will get the habit of living more with your Creator than with any created thing, more with the unseen than the seen. You will get to the point where you use the things of the earth and relations with people only for the love of God's kingdom and for His glory. That, My child, is pure love — never to think of oneself but of God and how best you can

please Him. Oh, this loving gesture of a generous heart in a direct ascension!

You know very well that everything that is of time is short-lived. So stretch out your arms to eternity. Long for eternity. This puts you on a higher plane, your heart forging ahead to this unknown, undreamed of country. This is the way to get a close-up aim at the goal.

As the hunter cautiously and silently approaches his prey, close in on your remembrance of God. Silence your memory of the earth and let your prayer fly straight upward. I, your Lord, tell you this. I shall not resist the arrows that you shoot with all the strength of your will. I shall fulfill your longings, for I alone know how to satisfy.

To be completely at peace, ask yourself at this close of the year: 'Have I hurt someone?' This 'someone' is My image. So go to that one, and speak as a sister. If his face displeases you, look at Mine through his.''

1949

January 1 — "The keynote? Serve. Find your joy in serving God and your neighbor."

January 6 — *Holy hour.*

"Who is like God? My little girl, can you find any comparison? Have you a greater Friend? A Friend more tender, more wealthy, more powerful? And if it is impossible to compare Him with anything that you know, how can you fail to give yourself wholly to Him? You hold something back, don't you? Why are you afraid to abandon yourself?

In life as in death, stretch out your arms to My all-loving immensity. You see the picture — one going to meet the other.

I want you to realize that I am grateful to you for flying willingly to Me despite the gravitation of earthly things. I am the Benefactor who feels happy when someone is eager to accept His gifts.

You remember that Canadian who offered you a handsome gift and said, 'Thank you for the honor you give me by accepting it.' You were utterly taken aback. Then when I offer Myself to you, repeating the same words, humble yourself. Be filled with gratitude. You find it difficult to believe in the generosity of your Lord. 'He... I... Can it be possible?' you ask.

Everything is possible in love. So come boldly. You will always find Me waiting for you."

January 13 — *Holy hour.*

"What is lacking is loving desire for My glory — enthusiasm. Your thoughts and actions are monotonous without this intention of pleasing Me, of giving Me your love as one stretches out a caressing hand. This would be living for Me and not for yourselves.

You lift up your heads, but then you fall back again on your self-center. Even the best of you do this, and I am the One who is set aside. Sometimes I'm the Sunday One. I want to be the One of all your moments.

I am your Root. Long for the blossoming I'm preparing for you. Long for the fruit — so that you may distribute it. Keep watch on your influence. If you don't share with others, should I give? Serve others even if they don't serve you.

Even were I not to love you, love Me. And love Me for Myself, not for yourself.

Offer Me all that I have given you. My tenderness is so great that I'll have the impression that everything comes to Me from you.

Take a look back over My past; you'll understand Me better. See Me as a child on earth — My candor, My faithfulness, My spirit of sacrifice. And yet I was only a child among other little ones. Your soul is only a little soul. Keep it very simple. Why be complicated? Respond to the simplicity of your Lord, and come every moment, unceasingly. Have you discovered what hinders you from coming? Discover and destroy."

January 20 — *Holy hour. Flu.*

"Use these discomforts for My cause. Offer them within My sufferings. The divine essence will make them fruitful. And what better fruit, what fruit more urgently needed than those of the mission that will soon take place in your parish? Use your body and mind for it. Ask Me to shower new grace upon everyone, the aged and the active, women and children. And when you ask in the Name of the Son, believe that the Father grants your request. Keep on asking and I'll keep on giving. While Moses prayed on the mountain, his arms raised toward heaven, the armies fighting in the plain won the victory. But when he grew weary of asking the men on the field lost ground.

God wants a mediator. He wanted even His Christ. You My brothers, continue My work. Work for your neighbor. You should love him as your own body and mind. And if he sees your loving concern for him, what will not be his astonishment and joy! Won't he be ready to do all that you tell him? Don't you think that at least three quarters of the people who do wrong fell into their way of life because they were not loved enough? How much an affectionate look, an outstretched hand, might have done in this or that circumstance...

Acquire the delicate art of letting your neighbor feel that you stretch out the arms of your heart to him. Should this be so difficult if we think of God in him?

It is late... the hour of conversion has struck many times for this parish. So many priests, so many retreats, so many Easters. I am there, and I am waiting. I am patient, for I am eternal. Even if all who are expected don't come. Even if half of them are not there, if a single repentant sinner were to find heaven again, your prayers would be changed into joy as the tears of the woman who has given birth to a Son.''

January 27 — *Holy hour (at home).*
I was adoring Him in spirit during the Forty Hours at St. Donatien.

"Are you sure that I alone count in your life and your death? What means most to Me is that My children give Me the preeminence in the life of the soul — this first life that they offer Me before their own, so that outside of Me nothing exists for them and they consider only their nothingness. These people enthrone Me everywhere and in everything. Their heart is ingenious for My Glory and there I truly find My rest — this rest that I call My delight and that makes Me forget the insults of so many.

My child, give Me the first place and that is enough. This assures Me of you, and you feel Me to be greater than all the powers within you. The first place for Me. Ask the Spirit to establish this order in you.

It's the order of creation.

It's the order of revelation.

It's the order of love.''

February 3 — *Holy hour.*

''Fan the flame of your confidence. Don't you need it along your way? Keep it burning in Me. I want you to be happy, so come back again and again to this feeling of trust until you are never without it. Trust is an aspect of love. Don't you grasp the fact that if you love Me and believe in My love, you surrender your whole self into My hands like a little child who doesn't even ask, 'Where are you taking me?' but sets off joyously, hand in hand with his mother. How many blessings this happy confidence wins for you My children.

Keep going blindly. Take delight in knowing nothing about the future for the sole purpose of seizing an opportunity of abandoning it to Me. I know how to lead the blind by the best paths. And when this blind person knows that he is My son, won't he be glad of his infirmity, since it is his power over My heart? As for Me, I'll be tempted to thank him for his trust which is like a pledge of his love — a special favor.

In all this, see My tenderness. It is everlasting.

This life of ours: I-you — is a life without death. Cultivate it. Do your part. Call it forth often by your loving desire. Let it be like your very breathing. And don't find this is too much. As for Me — and I am in you — I always ask, 'Is it enough?'"

February 10 — *I was giving the response: 'That we may be worthy of the merits of Jesus Christ.'*

"No one is worthy unless it be those who keep themselves unwaveringly in My love, because you see, it is I who am your worthiness. Then strive to the utmost to make our union straight-forward and faithful at every moment of the day and night.

You are Mine — Mine without any interruption. Then why should you create these interruptions in your love, in your silence and adoration, in your intention to please Me? Don't return to yourself. Since you gave yourself to Me in the morning and throughout the day, make Me your dwelling place. Shut yourself in and give Me the key. So that when you speak to your neighbor you will still be speaking from your home in Me, and your words and actions will spring forth from your inner life with more perfection and love.

My child, even the angels envy this beautiful life of ours — this oneness. Oh, this intimacy in time that leads straight to eternity... this heartwarming way of consoling your God! Since you love Him, could you ever fail to make every effort to cultivate this life with Him by the help of His grace? There are the weaknesses of your nature, of course; sometimes you are careless. I know all about this. But don't be afraid. I am your Creator, your Savior. My suffering was complete. May the joy you give Me also be complete. It's not difficult. You know very well that I look at the soul's intent in every action rather than the action itself. What I want in you is a spirit of love and humility, one that is constant and independent of created things, freed from the earth and ready for heaven at my first call. Joyously ready. Without joy the departure would be without love. Joy is the song of departure that leads to the élan. The soul already rejoices even though the body still holds it back.

Death with joy — this is the death worthy of Jesus Christ.''

February 23 — *After Communion.*

"You forgive Me for wanting you to be wholly Mine? I need all of your faculties as though they were necessary to My faculties as a man. Remember that I was a man among men even though I was also God.

I need your acts of self-denial too, your discomforts and your bodily sufferings, just as though Mine were not complete and I had to wait for yours in order to bring salvation to the world. You see My need for union? You see My love? Perhaps you cannot understand it yet. But know this, that My power is restrained by your will. Of your own free will you come to Me or you fly from Me. I say 'fly', so speedily do some go away when they hear Me call. And so I dare not return for fear of adding to their fault. I wait... because I know how to wait for that moment of remorse that sometimes comes with the fear of death. You see, My child, the sufferings and hopes of the garden of My agony? My hour had come. But that hour is always now before the eyes of the Father, who sees all time in the eternal present.

Offer Me, in offering yourself. I offered you as I offered Myself — you, My intimate friends, for our brothers, the prodigal ones. Your brothers, whom you should carry every day in your love, as I carried you with My cross.

There was the visible cross of Good Friday. But there was also the invisible cross of all the days of My life of thirty-three years. Haven't you yours too, My beloved children? Oh, in this world of suffering, may these forests of crosses lifted to heaven with Mine in the midst, be in the eyes of the Father, an appeal for grace for those who don't believe in Him!''

February 24 — *Holy hour.*

I was waiting for His words. ''Tell me if you want to speak to me, Lord, and I'll listen. But if You would rather I prayed, I'll pray. Above everything else I want to do Your will.''

''And I'll accept your loving will as a very tender tribute to My Father. So often My life said 'Fiat. Let it be so since You have wished it.'

You see it is your first intention that gives a new color to your entire day, your entire life. Since you have this intention, be more trusting than ever, more certain than ever that God loves you. Isn't that magnificent? Nothing on earth can ever be compared with it. Try to enjoy it in all its fulness and you'll be richer than a queen. And can you believe it? — you will enrich your God. If you could only keep thinking of this joy, what new glory you would offer to Love that is not loved.''

February 26 — *My birthday.*

''You will draw water joyously from the Savior's springs.''

March 3 — *Holy Hour.*

''Look at Me often. When one is in love, what sweetness there is in a look! As for Me, I keep you always before My face. Tell Me that you long to give Me the same love-token. Oh, I realize you're carried away by a hundred and one things in life. But make it your first concern to be with Me. As though your roots, plunged into Me would give the flowers and fruit of your actions a fragrance that would rise to your Christ.

Come nearer and nearer to Me and bring others nearer. What new meaning this gives to your brief life on earth! I often call your attention to the swiftly passing days, because this is a reality, both for the days of repentant deeds and those of wrongdoing. When the end comes, what joy there will be for those who have tried to live only to please Me. And what remorse for those who have lived only to please themselves. The end does come, and with the speed of a torrent that carries off everything at once.

My little instrument, never serve yourself before Me, and you will find that it is I who serve you. As I did yesterday. Wasn't it surprising — that meeting with your businessman, and that other one with your tenant just when you needed him, and all that came of this? I have all the threads of life's weaving in My hand. I can look after everything. Do you firmly believe this?

Even without any thought of reward, serve Me for the joy of serving Me. Be the very little servant of My heart: the handmaid of the Lord.''

March 10 — *Retreat*.

''Such showers of grace are being poured out in this parish at the moment. Ask Me that each soul may benefit generously, humbly.

If, with immense love and a great longing to give joy, a wealthy man took pleasure in enriching poor people and they looked upon His gifts somewhat contemptuously, wouldn't the benefactor be deeply wounded? He would have the right to ask Himself whether it was a good thing to go on helping such ungrateful people, wouldn't He. But if some responded with zeal and devotion, the benefactor would continue to give to all just because of the dedication of these few souls. If you but knew the power of a single elevated soul over My heart! Didn't I choose only twelve apostles to convert the world? You remember what I said, 'You are the salt of the earth'. So don't be timid when you speak of Me, but love one another with a love full of peace and great warmth. Isn't the life of God something you share?''

March 17 — *Holy hour.*

"Don't you feel new yearnings? The retreat is coming to an end. Come close to your goal. Isn't your goal union with God at every moment of your duty, and in all your relations with others, whom you love for My sake? Close in on your goal so that you may be more sure of attaining it. Open your eyes — your physical eyes and the eyes of your heart. Have foresight and aspire with all your powers.''

March 24 — *Holy hour. The angel Gabriel's feastday.*

"Do you remember this prayer, 'Pray for me so that, like You, I may serve God on earth'?

Is that the way you feel too? Take a good look within yourself. Do you give joy to everyone you approach as the angel Gabriel did? He consoled Daniel, the three children in the fiery furnace, and Zacharias. He filled the heart of the Virgin with divine happiness when he announced the coming of the Savior.

Have you offered material or moral help to others? Do you weigh the word you should speak and the one you should withhold? Are you quick to do a favor? Are you full of loving enthusiasm for the glory of God? Do you keep yourself constantly before His face? Singing in your mind, 'Holy, holy, holy'? Ask the Archangel to teach you to sing, to serve, to scatter joy — the joy that is God-Power. But ask often. What keeps you from persisting if you believe? He is like a father. Be thankful. Isn't to believe the greatest happiness of all?

Oh, My little children, what a grace faith is! Could

you ever compare yourselves with those who have lost it? You who are rich, give to the poor. Give them all your power to pray and to love; and your longing to love more.

'How can one love more?' you asked the missionary. And he replied, 'By living only to please God.' Mirror this often within your heart. Do I live to please God or to please myself? All the distance between heaven and earth is there, all the distance between Allness and nothingness.''

March 28 — *After Communion.*
''When He shall come to judge the living and the dead... That will be the day of the great judgment. But now is the time of great mercy, and I come to love. Above all, live this present moment.'' *(My mind was going back to the past or on into the future).*

March 30 — *In my bedroom.*
''My child, ponder more often on the value of the present moment, the danger of going back over the past and the uselessness of gazing into the future. Just live the little moment that you hold in your hands. Simply and lovingly.''

March 30 — *Holy hour.*
''Take note of your thoughts. Don't you see that they occupy the greatest part of your existence. They belong to an interior realm that you must learn to rule since from them comes what is worthy and unworthy in your days. Keep them constantly in the climate of God, of His glory, His will, His mercy and all the qualities that make Him what He is. Live with these qualities and you will get to know Him better and attach less importance to yourself. You remember... 'When shall I be perfectly one with You, Lord, and so lost in You that

I shall no longer be aware of myself?' It is with thoughts of our oneness that you will discover your duty to give happiness to those I have placed around you. Don't believe in chance, but learn to see the hand of your Father, your Friend — the One who never leaves you — in everything that happens.

If, instead of giving joy, you were to hurt others, if you failed to diffuse the Light of Christ, the Comforter, would you have the right to think that you have placed your mind in the mind of God? Then see that your thoughts are all goodness and indulgence; see that they be full of loving enthusiasm for My cause. You are free to control them and it is your duty to choose Me. If you didn't choose Me, could you call Me your greatest Friend, your most beautiful Love, your beloved Being who never ceases to live in your being?

You don't see Me but you know I'm there. And since you know I'm there, give Me the loving thoughts of your blind trust.

April 7 — *Holy hour.*
''Why should you be astonished at having a soul ordained of God since I, your Brother, am the eternal Priest? I came to earth to offer worship to My Father, and you share in it. You have a share in everything that I am. Worship, you know, is adoration, obedience, love that leads to zeal and the desire to win others.

When your mind is busy with My Father's affairs, can it be occupied with the things of the earth that matter to you personally? Aren't you so impressed by the magnitude of this thought that you want to submit everything to Him? The Father will accept your efforts made with the earnest desire to please Him, and He will make you feel His action. Not that feelings matter except as encouragement for a child.

301

Surrender yourself to the Father as if you had received the unspeakable sacrament of ordination, knowing that you belong utterly to God.''

April 14 — *Holy Thursday.*
''Stay very close to Me today. This is the day of My great love. Celebrate its anniversary in your simplest, most affectionate way. See love first. Give love first. Seek love first, and you'll fulfill My desire for you. My poor little girl, all the rest is nothingness. Don't you feel this? Make others feel it, and you will advance in your vocation of apostle.

What a joy for Me if all your moments were filled with love and what a reverent response to My life on earth! You see I can't talk to you about anything else today. Have you ever thought of the burden of love that made Me institute the sacrament of the Holy Eucharist — this perfect harmony between that which is within and that which is without. I burned with desire to belong to all of you, to remain in your possession right to the end of time, to be something you could take, eat and drink. To be shut into your church to wait for you there, to listen to you, to console you in the most intimate union of all.

Won't you love Me more for that? What language must I speak to make you understand Me? If your faith is too weak to find burning words, ask Me to speak to Myself in you — Myself to Myself. Place your heart between My fingers as a harp with its strings tuned and stretched and I'll make music that will ravish earth and heaven. Would you like to be that instrument again?''

''Yes, Lord, and with such joy!''

''Our voices will blend together in the same tones, 'O Father, we give You thanks for having made this day dawn'.

And you will repeat it like a poor child learning the alphabet of love.''

Good Friday — ''Why should you use long sentences and difficult words to speak to Me? Just talk with the utmost simplicity as you do with your family and intimate friends. I belong to the inner circle don't I?''

April 21 — *Holy hour.*
''Today you wanted to live with My lovingkindness. Keep it by you all day long. Adore it. Love it. Let it be your very gentle companion, so that those around you feel the effects of it. Express it by smiles full of goodness. Try to judge no one today. Say all the good you can about others and don't mention their faults. My child, how I long for you to be holy and above what you are now. How My heart yearns for you to become My sister through gentleness and humility.

Learn this science. Delve deep into it and don't ever grow weary of doing so. When a pupil is learning his lesson, you know how often he goes over it in his memory until it becomes part of himself. Poor little pupil studying goodness... Don't lose time. Progress, progress. Pass your examination this evening with Me, near Me. Don't be afraid of the effort it costs; just look upon it as nothing. Think of the prize-giving day.''

April 28 — *En route to Paris.*
''Think often about Me, My little girl. Think often. With so little you give Me so much joy. Your free will with all its opportunities will no longer exist in heaven, you understand? Here you may choose; you may be for yourself or for Me. You think, perhaps that this very small thought that comes winging to Me is of little importance? But for Me it is the keynote of an entire life. A thought is a soul's glance. Let yours be natu-

ral, warm, frequent. You can never come to an end of thinking about Me. Do you know all My lovingkindnesses? Try to see them. And My sufferings? And My love? Adore it; hail it.

Believe that everything in your life is arranged expressly for you. Believe and you will honor Me. If you never grow weary of looking at Me like this, you may be sure that it will be like an allurement to you to imitate your Christ.

May this look at Me, form as it were a divine being in you. You know how a mother takes care to keep herself in the presence of beauty so that the child she is carrying may take the imprint of it?

Then be saturated with Me in My life on earth where you can follow Me. Your earthly life will not go on much longer. Make haste to join Me.

Be to others what I was. Be your Christ for others. Give yourself because I gave Myself. I am your reason for living; let this be enough.''

May 12 — ''When you come to Me, come quickly, with that warmth that is the heart-beat of love. If you are slow, if you find it difficult to tear yourself away from what you are doing, where is the joy of love, where is its eagerness? Don't keep me waiting — I was going to say 'too long', for I'm always waiting for you. Are you ready to leave yourself to come to Me? Don't deprive Me of the pleasure of calling you. When you wait for a friend, aren't you full of the joy of anticipation? But if she didn't come, if she had forgotten, or if she had preferred to go to see someone else, wouldn't you have been disappointed and hurt? I am still more sensitive, My friend. You know those hurts that one hesitates to speak about because they are too distressing.

Love Me for yourself. Love Me for others, as though

you gathered many loves within yourself and gave them to Me as one.''

May 19 — ''Do you think that you could keep going very long without Me? Don't you feel that you should cry out your need to Me? Don't you understand that I need this cry of yours?

I am here with treasures. If you don't ask Me for them, how can I give them to you? If you didn't tell Me often that you love Me, where would be My joy? I am the Father, the Bridegroom, the matchless Friend, and My heart claims life that comes from you, from you alone to Me alone. Each one of you has a direct ray that no one else can give Me. Don't fail to give Me yours, for no other ray could take its place. What you give Me is everlasting. The presents you give to one another on earth disappear. But what is given to Me becomes part of Me, and in Me nothing dies.''

May 29 — ''Do you know what I'm going to ask you today? To learn to speak of the good in others. It's a sublime habit. What an example you would set! And how it would please Me! There are always good points, even in those who seem to be full of faults. Would you like to try today and go on trying all through your tomorrows until your death?''

''*Yes, Lord, but I don't know how to go about it. It's always the disparaging words that come first.*''

''You remember those high carriages with two wheels? When the horse bolted, the driver took a grip on the brake and tightened the reins. In the same way, take a grip on yourself and hold your thoughts in check. It will be for Me. Can anything cost too much effort when it is for Me?''

June 2 — *Holy hour.*

''Don't you have the impression that you still think of Me as being the distant and severe One? Smile when you speak to Me, believing that this makes Me happy. And if you think of the joy you give Me, won't you come closer and more gaily to Me, as though you were in My heart?

You see, you mustn't expect happinesss from the things of the earth, but solely from your way of communing with God.

Of course it's not pride to believe that I always follow you with love, and that as I watch you live I love every gesture you make with the thought of pleasing Me.

Look simply at the depths of My tenderness. Don't be like those children who keep at a distance from their father for fear of being punished. Be like those who find such joy in flinging themselves into His arms.

Now that you are writing down My words, try to receive them as though you were leaning on My heart. This was John's gesture. Again yesterday, didn't you see couples full of love for each other living like that and finding great comfort in it?

Love grows by loving. Don't calculate; practice the direct outpouring of the heart whether you pray or thank, or whether you ask for My kingdom and My glory. There is no pride in this, since everything comes from Me. Doesn't it calm you to gaze on Me. It's as though you entered into My peace.

Thank Me for having invented this beautiful story of Creation. And for your second life — the life of heaven in this oneness with Me. There are so many ways of saying thank you. Let your love flow out to meet My tenderness. It will be the repetition of the first symphony heard by God and Adam.''

June 8 — *Traveling.*

"Up to the present, your union with Me was 'as though it were real'. One step further now: be one with Me in reality. No longer the realm of imagination, but the assurance of faith."

In the train.

"I fathom each heart. I read every motive. Nothing ever escapes Me. I take what you give Me and I keep it. You will find it later on in My heart, adorned by My merits.

When you pray for sinners, imagine that you are stretching out your right hand to Me to help Me."

Paris. In the 'metro'.

"Of course it gives Me more pleasure when you come to Me in the crowds than when you are alone in your room. The crowds in Paris leave Me alone as though I were still dead."

June 9 — *At a 'taking of the veil'.*

"See the simplicity of love in everything, even in the very little things. Why shouldn't the little things be as precious as the big ones if they belong to your Love-life?"

June 10 — *Anniversary of my first Communion.*

"Thank you dear God, for all the blessings of that first Communion, and for all the others right up to this morning — twenty thousand times, perhaps?"

"And perhaps more?

When I give Myself entirely it is for always — unless I am refused. Then do you find it surprising that I want you in your offering of each little moment of your lives? If we are everything to one another all the time, we have great joy and nothing can take it from us.

My life was spent entirely for others. I loved and I saved. You child, love, and save the honor of My Name of Savior.

Win souls. Work for souls. Prayers, yes, but also sacrifices. Few of you think of this. Many laugh at it. And yet it is the money that buys and redeems. But do everything in a gladsome way. Be joyously in love.

Love is like a sacred forest where secluded paths lead out to the cross-roads of joyous union. The high green foliage sways in the gentle breezes of the Spirit, and song birds moved by His divine inspiration complete the harmony which is but happiness in the sacrifices of the moment. How fleeting and small the earthly sacrifices are! Do you know that the saints in heaven would envy you: their time of sacrifice is over.

Don't lose any time, since you told Me that everything was for Me.''

June 16 — *Corpus Christi (As I awakened)*
''Happy Feast Day, my dear God.''
(....) ''Can you seek Me and not find Me? Here or there, am I not always waiting for you? Since I love you so dearly, just let yourself be loved and come to meet My love. Then it will really be Corpus Christi, My feast.

You know, there need not be any interruption between Corpus Christi on earth and Corpus Christi in heaven. The procession never stops. The last Altar of Repose is in heaven — the Heart of God where My blessed ones live. So begin right now to sing and thank and adore. Do you know what an Altar of Repose is? It's an élan of love and joy, an outburst of enthusiasm. So put altars of repose into your life, into each one of your days. Take a moment to love Us better. To talk to Me about yourself, above all about your weaknesses. I know them well, but in telling Me about them you wipe them out, just as though you wrote them on the moving sand of the great desert that the wind never ceases to restore, smooth and unwrinkled. This is what

My love does. It never ceases to act. Leave yourself to Me. Be the clay and let Me be the Potter. Often — I was going to say, 'always'."

June 23 — *Holy hour.*

"You and I. Together we make only one.

It is time to see Me in a new light — the powerful light of reality.

Even when you are doing the most ordinary things I am with you, because while I am the greatest, I am also the humblest, and nothing is ever deadly dull to Me. What is most obscure and despised only attracts Me more. So don't be afraid that I'll leave you at certain moments, for I love you all the time. Tell Me that at last you do believe in the faithful company of My love. Keep strengthening your belief by the little words of your heart; they are like the wood that you throw on the fire. And I quicken.

You realize now, don't you, that without Me, your End, your life is empty. So meet Me more often. Enter more gaily into your Savior-God. Oh, if only you could remain there forever! This solitude of ours is such wealth that even the angels envy it — they who have never received Holy Communion. Your entire being is saturated with Me. Consecrate yourself in your heart's outpourings and I'll bind you the more closely to Me — even to unity.

Why shouldn't you come to Me as gaily as you go to meet a very dear friend?"

June 28 — *From the garden came the exquisite notes of a blackbird.*

"You know why he is singing so sweetly? Is it because the sky is blue? No, it's because he's answering another."

And I heard the voice of the other bird in the distance as I thought of the voice of my God in my heart.

In the street I was saying, "Praised and loved be the Eucharistic Heart."

"Every time you express that wish, I feel impelled to answer you. It's as though I increased My glory just to please you."

July 4 — *After Communion I said to Him, "I'm most ashamed to think that you are placed on a useless and often unkind tongue."*

"I know it, but I come all the same. Even when you don't believe in all My grace, I give it. Even when you are quite unaware that I'm appearing in you, I appear, for I am in you. Even when you stammer out your short-lived feelings to the Father, I prolong them. This is my rôle as Savior. You don't see it clearly, but the elect know about it. As they gaze on Me they have a true understanding of their redemption and cry aloud for joy, praising Me. Join in their praise from time to time as you ponder on My work in you. Try to discover it in My life and yours.

Oh, precious faith! Use every manner and means of increasing it. Seek it as one who beams a light into dark, unexplored corners. Faith is what brings the Creator and the creature in touch with each other. And when you have affirmed all the powers of your faith, your hope and love increase to tighten the bonds of union. Then you are faithful in the little as well as the big deeds since we are one and share everything. And all is so simple in the ever-present God.

We're together. We're together. Say it over and over again like the rhythm of love's breathing."

July 7 — *I was thanking Him for blessings He had given to my neighbor.*

"Thank Me, if only to show Me that you believe that they were sent from Me in answer to your prayer.

Don't you pray every day, 'Lord, may torrents of blessings never cease to flow to those who need them'? I hear you and I love what you say to Me as a father loves to listen to his child. It isn't so much the words that matter as the child who says them. Believe this, and you will come to Me more sincerely and gaily (you notice how I repeat that word) because you will realize that you give Me joy.

A man had two daughters both devoted to him. The elder was actively engaged in her father's business not only for the love of him but also for the love of the work, which wholly absorbed her attention. The other daughter was so closely united with her father, her mind constantly in tune with his, that her work never hindered her from thinking of him with ever-increasing tenderness. Which of these two daughters, do you think, was the greater comfort to her father?

Nothing is more precious to Me than My children's remembrance, this remembrance of Me when you stand and when you sit. Many times a thought from one of you is a cry, and I listen to it. Oh, cry often so that I can answer you, My very little ones. My Benjamins all down the centuries, believe in your Listener so much that you give thanks even while you are asking, and everything will be done to give you the joy that you yourselves have given Me.''

July 14 — ''My little girl, there is nothing to be compared with My joy. And every joy comes from Me, even in the midst of suffering if you suffer for My sake. The pleasures of the world diminish man; My joy increases him. It gives him new power and love. Do you realize that I love man so much that I am ready to thank him for learning to savor My joy? For to savor My joy is to savor Me.

Ask Me for this hunger for Me. It will increase your

zeal in the service of your God. Can you evoke the Name of God without a feeling of mysterious charm? What perfection could be lacking? Then what can you not expect from Him? And if you depend on God for everything, never cease to call Him so that He may act and speak in you as the tongue of a bell, the breath of a flute or the vibration of a harp string.

Be willing for Me to be in you. Yearn for this. Sometimes the spirit of the world seizes a man and lives in him in spite of himself. The Spirit of God bends to man's will. Love — expectant... waiting... Oh, the vehemence of a love that waits before seizing!

My child, if you could only comprehend these transports of desire for God — this unutterable longing to possess Him — the meeting would be simple and you would never cease to lay hold of Him.

Place My Name before you, and... en route!''

July 21 — ''You believed in the affection of your mother and father. Then believe in Mine; I am both Mother and Father. I gave them what they gave you. Imagine My joy when you believe as I want you to believe! Just the wish to give me this joy could help you. Say often to Me, 'Lord, I believe; increase My faith', and I'll answer you. You know that I pay attention to what you ask Me. Even before you speak My ear is against your lips. As for My heart, there is no one on earth who can listen to you as avidly as I. No heart but Mine could ever know how to treasure your words, complete them and make them more beautiful. Doesn't everything you say to Me need to be intensified, purified, amplified? And who can do this if not the one who lives your life? Don't you ask Me every morning to make you live? I died for My own so that My life might live in them. Then don't be afraid of anything, but abandon yourself often to the wisdom of the One who in-dwells you, because He loves you. All these things that are beyond your understanding — He takes them and looks after them. He is forever merging with you. You belong to His human nature. You are one of His family. You're descended from Him. So look more often at the closeness of your union with Him and hope for everything from it. Have boundless hope.

Let your upsoarings of love and trust be greater than any you have ever known before. What a beautiful loss to be lost in Me, never to find yourself again! Since I enfold you, don't hunt any further. You've arrived.''

July 28 — *Holy hour.*
In my bedroom in the country.

''Do you know what you mean to Me? You were My reason for living and dying on this earth. It is you, little one, who tore Me from the splendors of My Father to go all the lengths of human shame.

When I look at you I see My horrible sufferings again and all the cruel inventions of My love even before you were born. And now that you have received the breath of God and His likeness what are you going to do for Me in the few days that remain for you on earth? Are you going to awaken your heart to a new life so that it turns toward Me? Or will you keep to your ordinary little trial flights without ever showing Me other upsoarings warmer, more direct?

I lived so strenuously — I was going to say, so painfully — for you. Then you can understand, can't you, how deeply I long for the loving response of your life. I have an absolute need for the return-sacrifice of your body, and much more, of your faculties that you received from Me. Above all, of your thoughts; they move your heart and make you act for Me or without Me. Your thoughts can lay hold of Me and keep Me and they are proof to Me of you. They can lead you to heroism and enable you to put Me on as raiment that fits you in every detail. And when your thoughts reach Me, joyous because they are tender, what wouldn't I give you for their confidence!

I didn't leave you during the thirty-three years of My life nor throughout eternity. Then may I not ask you never to leave Me deliberately, to stay with Me right to your last moment on earth, that moment of our meeting? How well you will understand then that to quicken your heart-beats you had to hold Me closely in your very breathing.''

July — *I was having great difficulty in accomplishing a work of charity.*

''Don't you want to begin to be happy to suffer a little for Me?''

August 3 — *After communion (absent-minded)*
''I'm here.'' *(In a tone of gentle reproach)*

August 4 — *Holy hour.*
''When you are at My feet praying or meditating, why not be one in spirit with all the pure in heart who are praying and meditating? You aren't a little church all by yourself. You are part of the great activity of Christ in the breath of the Spirit. And in isolating yourself you would break the chain. So be linked together with other fervent people and aware of My desire for you all to be one. You remember My seamless robe?

Become humble enough to lose yourself in everyone else and eager enough for merits to seek to benefit by the merits of your brothers, since I permit this. I am the Father who has found a way to help His children get rich quickly. And having explained this to them, I wait for them to profit by it, for I suffer more than they do from their poverty. My little girl, you don't see how poor you are. If your eyes were opened, how careful you would be to cover your dress with someone else's garment in order to be pleasing in My sight.

Do you want to think more often of this daily union with all My Christians in the world at this moment? The suffering ones, the persecuted, the abandoned, those in exile and in prison, those who are martyred for My Name's sake, the souls in ruined bodies who continue to bless Me, to serve Me and to call Me with all their love right to their very last breath? Unite with them so that you may lose nothing of all this. Try to grasp the fact that these new treasures bring you ever nearer to Me. This is your goal: to reach Me. And I am so eager to have you that I stoop down, stretching out My two hands to you. Don't turn away. It's the proud who refuse a free gift. How I long for you to do Me the favor of accepting My help. I'll be even tempted to say, 'Thank you!'''

August 11 — *Holy hour.*
"Isn't it as though you had two different houses, one outside and one inside. And don't you find balm when you withdraw into the rooms of secret intimacies to wait for your Beloved who is waiting for you to wait for Him so that He can be there with all His gifts? Don't you take a present when you are invited to a friend's home? And if your wealth were unlimited wouldn't your gifts be fabulous? Mine are like that. And as a friend who is fearful of burdening another with too great a sense of gratitude, I offer them so delicately that you take them for granted without always appreciating their value.

Your interior wealth should shine through you and make even the outside beautiful. You have no right to bury My light. It is time that the King's secret reach from soul to soul so that the heart of the King be better understood and loved. These words of Mine are not for one alone, even though one is as dear as all. My flames are like a prairie fire. They sweep along with torrential speed setting alight as they go, in order to reach the outermost parts of the earth. Only then, as a hunter satisfied in the chase, shall I rest in the rest that souls will find. My task as Savior will be ended. At the last day, the day of triumph, I'll appear before My Father in the midst of these sheep of Mine fed in My pastures.

My child, outside and inside, let everything about you speak of Me, give Me, make Me understood among the ignorant, the baffled, the hungry, the fearful and the suffering ones. Tell them that I am there for every state of soul. Tell them to come to Me and I'll never let them go. A God who loves... Just think of it!''

August 18 — *There was a question of a surgical operation for me.*

''Whatever happens, what does it matter? Since you are Mine, since you live in My love? And since your pathway on earth leads to everlasting life, let everything take you to it.

Ask Me to go this last part of the journey side by side with you. Make it the most intimate and the most joyous, since we'll be going at the same pace. You have your marching song — the will of God. No other song can raise your spirits like that one. We'll sing it together.

You know very well that I don't go away when My friends suffer. My presence is such a comfort to them that some want to suffer always. So keep Me very near you. We'll travel along better that way. O beautiful road that leads to eternity. Don't be sad; it would pain Me if you were, since to die is to come to Me, and in losing yourself you find Me. You are eager, aren't you, to come face to face with Me at last?''

August 25 — ''If you are weary, rest. But take this rest on My heart. In no other place will you find the same love. Am I not the eternal response? I bought it with pain, you know, when I gave Myself up. I've known everything. I've earned everything. For you. Then since it is for you, don't be afraid to accept. Don't be so timid and heedless. Offer My merits to the Father just as though they were your very own. How few make use of them. How few desire them. Yet they are there for the taking — all of them.

If a man had sent out an invitation to every passerby to come to a sumptuous feast which he had been to great trouble to obtain, wouldn't he be wounded in the depths of his heart if, instead of eagerly accepting his invitation, people overlooked it with contempt?

And if those who called themselves his intimate friends came only on rare occasions because of their forgetfulness (forgetfulness is in itself a wound to love), don't you think that this generous man would be deeply offended and that he would have every right to close his door?

I am this generous man. But My banquet is free to all right to the end of time.

Then come, all of you who have not yet felt the tenderness of the invitation, and bring your friends too. All of them. Come and take My riches and give to the poor in confidence, the poor in desires, the poor in vision, for they think they are rich. The more you give, the more munificent your part will be.

My merits never come to an end. They are fitted to everyone's needs. They only multiply as you take them. For My merits are Myself.''

September 8 — *At the hospital after an operation.*

"I could have come for you, couldn't I? And you would have let yourself be taken joyously. But you still want to do a little work for My glory, don't you? Gaily too? Isn't it true that nothing is worth living for except service for Me? And do you believe that I wait upon you so that you may wait upon Me? I'll keep on giving you all you need in your mind and heart. Have I ever failed you? Don't fail Me.

Together we'll weave the last threads of your life-pattern. Together... always. Isn't that power?

When you feel weak as you do today, take your Brother's power to love, to praise, to thank our Father. Don't deprive Him of any smile. A smile is a happy amen. And give the same to the people around you. They need joy and kindness so much. Don't ever have to accuse yourself of having given begrudgingly, but go eagerly, go with power. Go as though you were going to God."

September 15 — *Convalescent. Holy hour.*

"Let your return to life to be a return to love — a love that keeps closer to Me and that never wanders away. I've asked you for this for a long time, haven't I? Don't you think that a little effort of your mind is all that is necessary, and that this very little effort would bear much fruit: uninterrupted union, transforming your life like magic fingers that light up everything they touch.

The law of love is to keep on growing. Don't you feel a burning regret for the little that you give Me for all that I have given you? This fire that sometimes torments you is love itself. You must accept its torments and its joys, for to long for one or the other is the same as to long for love. Don't limit your longings. Desire to desire. Ask for this thirst, beg for it, let it be part

of your life. Don't breathe without it; you could lose it.
Take great care of your love, since it is I.''

September 22 — *The priest came to hear my confession in my sickroom.*

''You see, I came right here to pardon you. You needed this new enfolding of My love, didn't you? You don't know all My kind attentions. But they never surprise you, do they? Recognize them with the same joy you had the first time you noticed them. Aren't they always new? So it is with My grace. You might think that it was always the same, but the truth is that just as the sun, at every instant, sends out the right ray for the delicate posture of the flower, so there flows from Me to you exactly what you need for each passing moment. Oh, My child, what all-attentive love! How it anticipates your desires, sees each detail, is ever on the lookout for you! Nothing in you escapes it, because it knows you better than you know yourselves.

Get the picture of My love brooding over you as the Spirit brooded over the waters.''

September 29 — *Convalescence.*

''You see the difference, don't you, between the life you offered Me before the trial and the one you want to offer Me now? Wasn't it good for you to feel yourself approaching the end of life so that you could see in the full light of reality the difference between life on earth and eternal life?

You can believe, can't you, that your God used this trial as a new way of getting your attention so that you would take a firmer grip on Him?

My child, how creative My love is, how I long to take hold of My children swiftly, and how many slip away and escape Me. But you — let yourself be taken captive. And exhausted as you are — for you have suffered

— rest on My heart. Do you think I don't know about the trial I've asked you to bear?

The main thing, you see, is that you didn't doubt love and that you said 'Fiat', abandoning yourself to whatever might come. And that's where God lets His children prevail against His power. It is you then who lead heaven by your complete and perfectly trusting surrender.

Now we shall no longer leave each other. I close your life in on all sides. I am your globe. If you burn, it is in My fire. Your footsteps are mine. I am your breathing.

You see how a joyous acceptance of My will can melt a soul into a new mould never before suspected. You see how necessary it is to say 'Thank You' with all the strength of your heart, and to let Me have My own way in your lives. For in the path I have prepared for you there are sudden turnings that you never dreamed of. And when faith or Love's look at you has made you understand, you offer your Father a joy that you know nothing about — this Father, who in your times of sorrow or happiness is Love and Love alone.''

October 6 — *I was trying to hold back someone who was being carried away by a terrible passion.*

''You can't succeed alone. Call My mother. She will see Me in this man. She will take hold of him. But pray.

How much you need to ask for the salvation of souls. All your little unused minutes — give them to Me for your brothers in danger. Be one with those who pray on the earth like a society of souls that draws its strength from Me. Be one, as the Father and I are one.

Be like God. Always strive to be the faithful image of Himself that He sketched in creating you. Do you make every effort to do this? Do you ponder on your living Model every day in order to reflect Him? He keeps His face before you. He gives you a glimpse of

His qualities, ever so gently, so as not to overwhelm you. He is humble enough to make Himself smaller in order to help you realize how accessible He is, like the fowlers who devise ways to avoid startling their prey.

Take a long look at My face when I was redeeming men — the face of One who wills to give His life. You may imagine what love it can express.

Outreach yourself. Reach Me.''

October 13 — *Holy hour.*

''My dear Christ, once again I've fallen into the same pride and the same selfishness.''

''Why are you astonished, My child? Hasn't your life always been one continual beginning again? I love you this way, humbled, but ready to do better for love of Me. It's then that I come to your help. And the Spirit fills you because your eyes are open to your own worthlessness, and empty of self, you are ready at last to let Him take complete possession of you.

Take a look at your usual incapability. Acknowledge your poor judgment. See how little you are inclined to make any effort, as though you lost interest in My glory. Show Me your inadequacies, especially the most discouraging ones, such as your lack of perseverance in keeping watch on your bad habit. Tell me how it distresses you, but be sure that this distress is because of My distress. Then try to make amends with words of love, silences, upsoarings of your heart, repentance in your simple, sincere way — with new resolutions. Take My mother into your confidence. She'll help you keep watch. It will be easier with both of you, won't it?

And take a long look at Me. Doesn't one love to gaze at the face of a matchless Friend? Isn't there power in a look at Him? And if this Friend is your ideal in every kind of virtue, if He is the resplendence of every perfection, each time you look, won't you find strength to imitate Him? Won't you be lured toward the highest good, not because of anything in yourself, but by His tenderness and affectionate pity?

Love... You realize, don't you, that the hallmark of every Christian life is love. But you haven't yet heard all the tones, all the symphonies — not just the unfinished ones, but others not even begun. Discover a new love with every day that dawns, a love as yet untold, a love that will conjure up within you impulses and feelings you have never known. It will be as though you were speaking to a new God, seen and adored in another light, a God who would reveal new aspects of Himself to you each morning, to exploit every last note of your heart's music in vivid concertos of union. For God is infinite.

Enter into Him as into a deep forest where silence full of mystery thrills in the depths of your being.''

October 20 — *Holy hour.*

''Lord, my perseverance slips away like sand between my fingers.''

''Aren't you a poor little girl? Should your weakness astonish you? Don't you see that you must give Me your hand continually? That you must call Me and accept the joy I bring? Joy is power. Sing in your heart. That's the way you should go to meet a sacrifice — singing. I recited the Psalms and it was like a hymn within Me rising to My Father.

My very little one, don't be afraid to come and drink at the fount of My power. It never runs dry; nothing ever comes to an end in Me. Does anyone diminish the ocean by taking water from it? Doesn't the next tide often rise higher than the one before? What riches do I lack? Do the blessings I give now seem to be fewer than the ones I have been giving since the beginning of Creation? Would I be God if in giving I became poorer? And because I have been generous to one of Mine, does that mean that I shall not give him any more? Should he remain shy and aloof? Let him only venture to think that what he has received up until now is nothing at all for Me, and that I find My happiness in showering blessings upon him 'according to My means', as people say. Let him strive to meditate on the length and breadth and height of these means which cannot be compared with anything on earth. And if that child suspects that besides the power, I also have the longing to give — for what lover is not happy to adorn his beloved — he will lose his fear of imposing upon God's kindness or of being too daring with Him. Fully aware of his littleness he will understand His joy in being great for him.

How often I have had abundant treasures in My tabernacle all ready to give, but no one came to ask Me for them. Yet a good many people came into the church for a short visit — absent-minded and aloof, as though My body were dead in the Eucharist and My soul still in heaven.

Make an effort to think of My Real Presence; it will help you to love Me. Does the life of stillness within you need your senses? Aren't you beginning to be more sure of the invisible than the visible? Aren't there moments when the certainty of faith suddenly breaks in upon you? It is at those moments that We descend into you, because you respond to Our purpose in creating you.

A man will leave everything — every material thing — to follow God alone, the One he loves without having seen Him. This, My child, is the whole secret of the delight that a soul can give its God.''

''But, Lord, even when I speak to you in faith within my soul, my poor words are not very beautiful.''

"What does it matter, since it is you?"

October 25 — *(On the terrace)*
"Don't be like the October butterflies that can't fly any more because it's autumn and the wind is intractable. As your life goes on, go higher, ever higher."

October 27 — *Holy hour. In my bedroom.*
"When I see that you are looking for Me, do you think I'm going to run away? When you call Me anxiously, won't I answer? Have I changed from the God I was in the first mornings of Creation? You remember how the first man, splendid and upright, waited to pour out his heart to Me and found unutterable fulness of joy in those first conversations with the Father of his body and soul. And there was Moses too, on Sinai. And the prophets. And the Man-God in his nightly and daily solitudes. Didn't I come close to them with My fatherly comfort?

And since the Man-God allowed Himself to be crucified in cruel torture for your sake, don't I see Him still in each one of you? My Christ, My only Son. Your voice and His; Jacob taking the place of Esau. My blessing descends on all of you forever if you are faithful to Me. Then believe with all your heart and don't deprive Me of any call. Could you ever bear for Me to desert you? Can you conceive of even half a day without Me? Or a morning without Communion? Or a joy without sharing it with Me? Or a heartache that you couldn't confide in Me? And yet — just think of it — in the world at this very moment there are beloved children of Mine who want to be total strangers to Me. Pray for them in their terrible poverty. Pray with the riches that you have received expressly to help others. Think of it and pray for them as though you were praying for your Christ.

It's a strange thing, isn't it, but all My children are other Christs. Ponder on this. You don't work for conversions because you don't see them. But the day will come when these people who enter heaven by your help will cry aloud their love and gratitude to you, for love reigns in heaven.

Oh, My child, honor the body of Christ. Take care of His members. Glorify His bride, the Church. There is nothing in the whole world greater, or more precious or more excellent than the holiness of the Bridegroom and the Church, His Bride, if not the splendor of the Trinity that enfolds and illumines everything belonging to It.''

November 3 — *Holy hour.*

(....) *''Lord, I have loved You so long, but I don't know yet how to love You.''*

''To love the Father and the Spirit, borrow My heart, and to love your Christ, offer Him His passion.''

November 10 — *Holy hour.*

''Lord, there always seems to be a thick curtain between You and me, that hinders me from running to You.''

''Fix it firmly in your mind that this presence of Me in you is not an allegory or a fantasy or a metaphor. It's not a story you listen to or something that might have happened to someone else. It has to do with you and Me. It has to do with a reality to be lived.

Then live with assurance and gladness. You will find so much happiness in this and you will give Me so much joy. Greet Me in you often in your own way, in all sorts of ways. I'll love you in every one of these ways of yours.

Run after Me in you. Never give up the chase. Seek Me as Father, Bridegroom, Savior. See Me looking at you. You know I'm waiting for you. Don't be heedless of the moments. Take a flying leap in your free thinking, just as you would if someone said, 'The gates of heaven are wide open.' Heaven is Myself. And it is I who am in you. Do you thoroughly grasp this?

The saints live for Me alone. Get used to living now as you will later on among the All-joyous ones. Make an effort. Come out of your five senses. Seek fellowship with Me in your heart-center. Submit every earthly tie to Me, since there is still time and since it would please Me. There are always two paths, one that goes down toward selfish distractions and one that goes up to Me, for Me. The choice is yours: either you or I. Ask the saints to help you to come very close to the One who loves you so much and to make your home in Him. You know of course that you can go in without knocking? Aren't we both at home together?''

November 17 — *Holy hour.*

''Why do I ask you to pray? Because prayer is to grace as the lighted match to the candle. You get the picture: the first effort is man's; then comes God. Always oneness. Never God alone. Never man alone. But God and man working together. This is the law of My love. Isn't it beautiful? Why should you try to escape it? Wouldn't you find greater joy in hastening our re-union by your calling desires and your cries of love? What delight it gives Me to be invited by your hearts!

So don't be reticent. If you want Me, tell Me so. I mean pray — sink deep down into the remembrance of Me and talk to Me in a direct look. That's what prayer is — the prayer that asks, the prayer that praises and thanks, the prayer that loves. Don't you think that the direct look of love is very eloquent?''

''Lord, what we miss, is not seeing the One we love, so that we love almost in the twilight.''

''Don't you have a detailed account of My life and

My death? Can't you lay hold upon Me in this or that page of My gospels? Doesn't your faith need practice and opportunities to win victories? Blessed are those who believe and love without ever having seen. I belong to them — I, who am the kingdom of the saints. And what can be said of those who have helped others to know Me? The missionaries, the preachers, the writers? They will find as it were two banquets — theirs and that of their beneficiaries. Even the one who has taught the Our Father to a single child, who has taught him to say, 'My God, I give You my heart' — that one will know My joy and gratitude. He will experience a new heaven because he will have increased Me.

O My child, pray without ceasing. Remember your Christ in His life. For whom did He pray? You too, pray for others and God will take care of you.''

December 1 — *Holy hour.*

''Concentrate on going higher, always higher in the Holy Trinity. This is your Family, your End and your Center. Your Home, too, so you must take up your residence there. (....)

Be grateful to be invited to it. Dwell on the thought of it with praise and song, remembering your nothingness and the tenderness of the invitation. It's a long time since the invitation was sent out, isn't it? Don't you think you should respond by focalizing all your desires on this one end? What a blessed Home — the heart of the Trinity opening up all its unutterable delights for you in the love untold of the Father and the Son! How can you refrain from thinking of it every day with impetuous longing?

Ask your heavenly mother who understood better to lead you there. She is the bride of the Spirit, the mother of the Son, the daughter of the Father on whom her immaculate heart was forever centered. Let her go with you before the Holy Trinity to whom you belong, free though you are.

You are thinking, 'But these three Persons are so great. What can I say — I, who am so little?'

Have you forgotten that it is your weakness that attracts your God? Then give Him your utmost confidence — boundless trust, you understand? He can give you everything. He owns everything and is only waiting for your call. Be sure of Him. Aspire to reach Him. Thirst for Him with a thirst that can never be quenched. Your loving insistence honors Him greatly. Don't be like the silent ones who consider themselves too unworthy to ask for magnificent favors. I tell you, they will never overcome their unworthiness. Be like the humble ones who expose their poverty and count on their Christ to transform them at each confession, because He hears their cry of regret and turns it into a hymn for His glory. Don't restrain your heart's upsoarings, My child. Come more often into the secret place of the Most High. That's where your permanent home will be.''

December 8 — *Holy hour.*

''Why don't you offer everything by the hands of your mother, by her sorrowful and immaculate heart today and in your living and your dying? You know that she loves those two titles because I gave her, first her very pure conception, then suffering for the greater part of her life. And everything that God gave her she received so very humbly with love and respect. Then you can believe, can't you, that the three divine Persons must have lived in her with all the joy they anticipated in creating her, so perfectly did she respond to Love's demands. And for this she attained to heaven's royalty. Child, give yourself to Mary so that you may walk in her ways. She is ready to help you because she knows God and His desires and she knows you in your difficulties, almost all of which come from human pride. So give yourselves often from the depths of your heart. You must admit that with such a Father, mother and Brother you are greatly helped along life's way.''

''Lord, grant that I may never forget this. My thoughts are forever carried away by the trifling things of this world.''

''Draw the curtain across your interior stage. You know how important it is at the theater for the curtain to fall at the right moment? In the same way, let the curtain come down between the moments for the temporal things of the earth and the moments for God alone. Your mother will help you — she who above all knew God's moments. Then fill each instant for your God with perfect love. Come to Me to buy perfect love for I possess it. You will purchase it with longings and prayers and with intimate love. You see how we always come back to the same words: 'intimate love'. This is what I want from you, for this love of yours is My joy. And it's the entire program of life from birth to death. Even the fear of Me wounds Me-in-you. I need your gesture of total surrender and trust, My beloved and intimate friends.''

December 9 — ''Couldn't you put an end to all these little useless thoughts that do nothing for you or your neighbor or God, and substitute others of loving adoration, or desire for My kingdom, or zeal for the salvation of your brothers? All of this would be like the plants that brighten up reception rooms.''

December 11 — *End of the novena to the Immaculate. I was deeply moved by the Mass sung in five parts.*

''What will you say in heaven when you hear My praises sung in billions of parts? Each of the blessed ones has his own particular melody.''

December — *I was hearing of the enthusiastic remarks made by readers of 'Lui et moi' (He and I).*

"Thank You, Lord, for all these choice graces that You are scattering about in secret."

"You don't know them all. Only in heaven will you learn about them and what joy this will be for you! I like to explore hearts by means of our little book. Many people read and are pierced by one of My straight arrows. Others dare not believe in so much love and remain on the border of reality. A few close the book without wanting to understand. But believe Me, many are utterly astonished and try to imitate this intimate love that never strays but seeks all ways and means of charming, consoling and rejoicing Me with new tenderness.

I told you, didn't I, that when it comes to Me, you can never exaggerate, even if you seem foolish. Didn't I love you beyond all reason? And could you ever respond in the same way?

Near as I am to your hearts, I am so poor. There is so much indifference, so much hostility that those who understand Me better try to enrich Me every day, even if only by a feeling of pity. It takes very little pity from you to comfort Me. Even the desire to come nearer to Me brings Me heart's ease. An upsoaring of love, however momentary in the midst of your activities, pleases Me. And if One of you reaches the point of living for Me alone, I heap that one with favors even in this life, for he offers Me a refuge on earth. But don't imagine that there are many like that.

Read the gospels. Look at your Model. From the love of others draw zeal for the Father's service and oneness with the Spirit so that He may breathe upon you when He wishes and as much as He wishes. And if He tests and tries you, don't say, 'That's enough!' Surrender your whole being to Him so that He may take you where He wishes. And he will lead you to the heights.

Since you have found Me, don't you wish to honor Me with your gentle love? Even in the midst of visits, travels, distractions, open the door to the tabernacle of your heart. My throne is there."

December 15 — *Holy hour.*

Coming back from Mass in the dark at 7 A.M. in the freezing rain. "This too, Lord, may I offer for Your sinners of this Marian year?"

"I take all sufferings little and big, and place them in the treasury of the Church — the treasury used for the making of saints. You forget your past sufferings, but they continue to bear fruit in My sight. You have already forgotten your travel weariness, weather annoyances, desert thirst, the fears, exile in distant countries, the slow journeys back, the long tests of endurance, times of illness. But remember that you offered Me everything and that I've kept everything.

You love to look at the precious jewels in your mother's jewel box, or your favorite books in your library, or the unusual souvenirs given to you during your long tours. Often it's only a trifle, something that hasn't cost the donor much. You remember the Moslem's terebinth, the Indian's moose glove and the pressed leaf given to you in Larache? You treasure these things because those who gave them to you wanted to please you. For the same reason I have found joy in all the little presents given to Me by My children. Even if they have not cost you very much, even if you gave them to Me only because My Father put them into your hand by some circumstance other than your own free choice, you offered them to Me like good and affectionate children. And so I treasure them as though they were a part of you. Such is your power over Me! You bind Me to you by a single hair of your head. And the more you believe how utterly disarmed I am by your love, the more My unfathomable tenderness overflows to you. The great wrong is to lack faith in it.

Then offer Me everything — every gesture, every thought.'' (....)

Looking at the preparations for Christmas.
"Thank You, Lord. How could You come down to earth, knowing that You were going to suffer so much?"

"And if I had not come down, should I have had the joy of instituting My Eucharist where I remain right to the end of the centuries?"

December 22 — *Holy hour.*
"Lord, may nothing in me hinder your voice from reaching others!"

"Echo it back with all your loving warmth and you will give them joy. And this very joy will make them much more sensitive to My voice, these poor people, so often troubled with regard to Me or consumed by earthly worries. How much more freely they will breathe if you talk with them about Me!

I'll be there, though unseen, and you will feel the sweetness of My Presence. In heaven it is I who am the center and circumference for everyone, and the blessed ones exult. Isn't it from the fullness of the heart that the mouth speaks? This is why I rejoice when you mention My Name. It's like a cherished secret that you disclose because you can no longer keep it. It's as though you said, 'Let us talk about God, the One who is my entire life, the One who alone is worthy of my every heart-beat. This glorifies Me, and to glorify Me is to love Me. You're thinking. 'Religion is always love, nothing but love.' Haven't I explained to you that you will be judged according to the measure of your love — on that alone?

Every sin is a mockery of love, just as every virtue is the choice of love. And I am Love. Try to understand the greatness of the principle. Get rid of your small self. Be My Self. It's as though I said, 'Don't think of yourself any more. Think of Me.' The saints thought only of Me all their lives. Accept the help of My mother for this, and think of Me with all the tenderness of which you are able. Tenderness honors Me more than reverence. It consoles Me. I was going to say it pays Me.

My tender care is ever around My children. But they don't see it. They look upon all the happy incidents in their lives as only natural and are inclined to attribute them to chance. Yet a word of happy thanks would bring Me such joy that My joy would redound to them in new gifts.

Oh, when evening falls may they think of coming to My embrace, their hearts overflowing with gratitude, asking Me to come again with new blessings. And I will come again. And in this way we shall approach the end of life and the last of My blessings.

For this last blessing, My child, give Me your tender thanks now.''

December 29 — (…)

''Lord, I should so love to put into practice all that You have told me this year. Instead of running, I'm dragging along.''

''Do you remember this sentence: 'The weight of your favors has been part of my burden'? This is because the more I give, the more clearly you see your wretchedness, and this is the light of reality. Be sorry that you have reached only this poor impasse in your efforts to do better. But keep trusting, since you can do everything in your Christ who strengthens you.

And remember that I want your perfection more than you do. Do you ask Me for this every day? Those who are thirsty never stop asking for a drink. Are you saddened by your usual mediocrity? If you weren't, how could I help you? Your cry, full of hope would be music to Me. So learn, learn to cry to Me, My child. Rouse yourself from the apathy of lifeless souls. Say to Me, 'Lord, let me sacrifice myself with joy for You. Let me live in You, in Your sight and in the sight of others. And let me treat them with the same great kindness that You show me. In this way I'll reach You.'

Yes of course, every time you go to others to speak to them about Me, I'm there among you and you feel the ever-increasing overflow of My tenderness.

Never doubt My power. Never doubt My love, my poor little creature; you don't look at Me often enough.

Listen carefully to Me. I'm always there.''

1950

January 1 — "The keynote:

Hope in your God — boundless hope."

"Lord, may these words inscribed by You on these white pages, as on solid walls, be as many springs of love where my brothers and sisters on the earth may quench their thirst."

January 5 — *Le Fresne.*

Looking out on the Loire River and a leaden sky.

"You see how the trees and flowers await the sap that is preparing to bring back life. Everything is gloomy and dead now. But ever so gently along comes the spring.

Give yourself up to grace. Grace and you: the sail billowing in the breeze, and the boat. What a gentle alliance!

You hear the murmur of the Loire as it flows beneath your walls, and the breeze brushing the window panes. But you don't catch the sound of the divine power that carries you along when you put the rudder of your life into His hands. Sometimes you stop and say to yourself, 'Isn't that He?'

It's always I...

Then be like your trees, like your flowers. Be all-expectancy for My life-giving powers. Look for ways of reaching Me. Hold out your life to Me. There are still blank pages in it. Ask Me to guide your hand and we'll write in it together. That's how it was when you were little? and you are always little."

January 12 — *Holy hour.*

As I was marveling how quickly the first edition of 'Lui et moi' (He and I) sold out.

''That's because I wanted it to be so, and the sorrowful and immaculate heart of My mother shared My desire. Do you know what we're doing in writing these pages? We're removing the false idea that this intimate life of the soul is possible only for the religious in the cloister. In reality My secret and tender love is for every human being living in the world. There is not one who does not have a mysterious yearning for it. And how true it is that each one wants to see someone live My love so that he may discover the means of reaching Me.

My child, what a joy for Me and for you if at last all people became My faithful friends, trustfully calling for Me and offering Me the most secret chamber of their hearts for My permanent home. You can imagine what outpourings I'd draw from their souls' depths — there where so many things have been instinctively hidden, awaiting the coming of a friend worthy of their esteem.

When they have understood that Christ, the Savior, not only could be, but longed to be their unique Friend, this Friend whom no words can ever describe, this Friend who begs and thanks; when they have guessed at His happiness at being welcomed by His child whom false humility has kept at a distance, what transports of young joy they feel as they fill their life to the brim with love to honor the God who lives in them! How they keep on begging Him to increase their poor, weak love which seems but of yesterday, exposing it like ice close to a furnace, no longer counting on themselves but trusting boundlessly in Christ who watches tenderly for the feelings of newly awakened souls.

Beloved children, you who are still afraid, dare to believe, dare to hope, dare to love. Lead other souls into the chain of love. And may this movement go on right to the end of time, gathering more and more speed like the last wave of the sea.''

January 19 — *Holy hour.*

''It's a long time since we loved each other — I mean in the heart to heart communion of a holy hour: eight days...

Take many a moment for spontaneous and joyous outpourings of your love, as you did when you were little. You jumped up to throw your arms around the necks of those you loved when you had a little recreation. And when you left the city for your beloved country home and reached it some beautiful evening in your holidays, didn't you recapture all the enchantment of your youth as you caught that first glimpse again of the Loire and its islands?

So when you put aside the duties of the world and material things to enter into your heart for a few moments, give Me the joyous effusion of your spiritual childhood rapidly, lovingly, wholeheartedly, going away afterward to continue your work among others for My service.

Don't be timid when it comes to loving Me since you comfort Me for the coldness of others. I may have been counting on you for a long time. Are you going to disappoint Me? Don't forget that I am Man also. I too have My dreams and hopes. May I say to you, 'Respond to all My dreams for you, for your pilgrimage among men and for your influence, as though you took from Me to give to others.' Even the stars impart their light to one another; have you noticed this?

When you keep yourself before Me, My Gabrielle, look at Me with great tenderness and think that it is just as sweet to be seen as to see.''

January 26 — *Holy hour.*

The cold was intense and to honor the Holy Year I had not lit my fire.

''What a small deprivation, My child, if in exchange you bring back a sinner to Me!

You don't feel yesterday's cold any more and you can't yet feel the cold of tomorrow. So it's only a question of this present moment. And what is a moment of discomfort in exchange for the salvation of a soul who will praise Me eternally? You too will know that person's joyous gratitude but you will give all the glory to My compassionate heart, since you know that without My help you could have done nothing.

It is for you all to catch My inner promptings, to let them unfold in your minds, to ponder over them and strive to your utmost to fulfill them gratefully. Then the Spirit will come and remind you of all that I have told you.

In this present century people forget to make these acts of self-sacrifice. Wouldn't it be better to do them of your own free will than to be compelled to do them? Always be joyful about it, for joy is the luster of self-denial. It is love's sweet intimacy.

A bride had done a long piece of work for her bride-groom, and as it required the utmost patience and perseverance, he expressed all his surprise and admiration for the many weary hours she had spent on it. 'But I loved you so much in every moment of fatigue,' she replied, 'that my joy outweighed all my suffering.

Isn't that a little the way you feel near your empty hearth? (....) Can you guess what I feel for you, My little sister-companion in work? The embrace of the kiss of peace.''

January 28 — *At a big reception.*

''The more you suffer, the more you serve.''

February 2 — *After a meeting in a room full of friends.*

"You've noticed, haven't you, that it's not so much what you say as the way you say it that gives weight to your remarks. It's like that when you talk to Me. So discover the loving way within you, the delicate shade of trust — and I'm vanquished. Since you know what your special weapons are, why not use these instead of any others? At this moment I am like the man who put into the hands of his enemy the sword that could wound him more deeply. And I say to you, 'Aim straight.' Quicken your feelings. Tell Me of your sorrow for your shortcomings, not so much because they have sullied you as because they have pained Me.

For you had the sad courage to hurt a Man-God who gave His life for you. And yet you knew... You disregarded it, and before His eyes that followed you with distress, you resisted His will and did what you pleased.

Feel grief for it — tearless grief — and your renewed resolution will lead you to humble love and a sense of your nothingness. Then I'll swoop down like the eagle and carry you away to the secluded paths of the 'garden enclosed'. When you try to speak to Me of the past, I'll place My hand over your mouth and you will hear words of tenderness and mercy that will melt your heart. You will thirst for a new life and be ready to run in search of it. But humbly now, fully aware of your dependence on Me, you will surrender your faculties to Me one by one, all your faculties. And we'll walk together, patiently striving day by day.

My very little one, understand Me: it's the patient daily efforts that give value to small things."

Holy hour.

"You don't ask Me for enough. Why are you so timid? Why don't I hear your voice? Don't you yet understand the joy I have in making your cup run over? But even if you don't understand, try to go deeper into the reality. Some explorers travel on the run, while others stop to study the details. Explore the boundless needs of My heart in order to seek the better to satisfy them. You will find that I'm waiting for your requests on a bigger scale — humble but powerful, contrite but full of assurance.

Be My delivery messenger, standing by until your arms are filled. My angels will carry the gifts from door to door. But it must be you who procure them. There are the sinners I'm waiting for you to lift from the mire again and again. And there are the missions — the pagans in France and other lands. My priests too need your help to persevere in My likeness. And My bishops, so that they may be fatherly. And all the people in your time, to that they will desire to be intimate with Me at every moment. Haven't I deserved it? Haven't I suffered more atrociously than words can describe? If you could only know! But at least remember this: a word of love pays Me. And when you bring your lives close to My life and to heaven and the Eucharist, I cannot but carry you in My arms and cover you with My merits.

Each person has his own way of asking. Let yours be warm and long, joyous as though you already had the answer, loving because you are sure that you are loved, generous as always, and charming, since you are full of My gifts. Be repentant too, but audacious, because it is in My Name that you are asking.

I'll listen to you such joy that it will flow over into you, and this will give you new courage to call upon Me for victory after victory. And when you ask even more than your highest hope, speak to your Christ-Man and your Christ-Man will make your wants known to God the Father by the Spirit of love. After that, can you ever imagine that your requests will go unanswered?''

Paris. On the boulevards.

''Am I not your Friend? Then why don't you speak to Me joyously?''

Auteuil.

''It's in the evening of your life that you'll begin to live, just when you think that you are going to die.''

Paris. On awakening. ''What's new today?''

''God.''

Paris. In my bedroom.

''When you have just heard My voice, the silence that follows is still full of Me.''

The chapel in the rue de la Source. At the Sanctus.

''You who have asked Me to do what you do, do what I do surrounded by My angels:

Praise: 'Holy, Holy, Holy.' Adore. Love.''

At the Louvre.

''Imagine how I say your name within Me and try out the same love as you say Mine within you.''

Alone in the streets.

''There is no solitude anywhere since I am everywhere.''

Notre-Dame des Victoires. Near someone who was praying.

''The soul... what was the use of giving that one a coat of flesh. You can see, can't you, that it can never be imprisoned there?''

Paris. Window shopping.

''Never allow futile things to clutter your mind to the point of hindering it from seeing Me. It would be like wearing a mask on your soul.''

Among the orphans of Auteuil.

''Don't be just half saintly. This would only prove that the other half was full of defects. To be a Christian is not only to be born of God. It is to be reborn to Him unceasingly. It is not just to live in His sight. It is to be His living and His dying.

When a saint comes into the world, he comes to the entire world.

Never stop having desires and ask Me for whatever you lack. Whom else would you ask?

How can men who know the joy of being a father ever forget that they are also sons — sons of God?''

February 19 — *The Luxembourg Gardens.*

''Don't you think that I love you a great deal more than you ever imagined? Can you compare My powers with yours? This is why I so often say, 'Love Me with My love.' We'll act together always in future, won't we? Isn't it I who live your life? It's so simple. A Father... your entire being is of His very substance. And this is better. Up until now what made you think you were alone? Why did you want to be alone? When I was burning with the desire to make all your actions divine?

Never forget that without Me you are nothing. Are you ashamed of this? But since it is your extreme poverty that attracts Me... Count on Me moment by moment. When you call Me, I'm there. Scarcely have you pronounced My Name when I hear it. It's like a memory, as though you had called Me long, long ago. Always I yearn for you, do you understand? Forgive Me for often finding you late. It's as though I said, 'Forgive Me for loving you so.'

Never grow weary of Me. Don't become accustomed to our conversations. I want them to be always new to you, as new as that first day when you were not sure... and so amazed by this sudden contact that you trembled as though you had done wrong. Moses trembled too, before God. And in the presence of Christ, Saul fell to the ground. Who can escape Me when I want to take captive? And yet I respect your freedom. And when you yield it to Me it is the greatest gift that you can offer Me and the one that gives Me the greatest joy. Your freedom makes Me think of Mine that I yielded so utterly to you when I was on earth. Listen to what I have to say. You will sacrifice your freedom even more completely to Me at the moment of your death. That will be love to the uttermost: its supreme effort. And I'll receive your death as a palm.''

March 2 — *Holy hour. Nantes.*

''I plant everything you need in your thoughts. So take them one by one as you pluck off the petals of a daisy, and from Me they will go to others, filled with My life-giving fragrance. You know what this fragrance is? It's the feeling that God loves you and that He looks after all of you with the greatest care. Every line in our book tells about it and awakens your trust. The confidence of His children is God's glory. And their love is His kingdom.

Understand this: When you say 'Lord, I love you', you can go no farther, for you've said everything; you can only repeat. And the Lord reigns over you. When the whole earth has declared its love, then His kingdom will come and 'the times' will be fulfilled. But you must pray. You don't yet know the power of prayer. It's like a strong arm helping Mine since I allow you to help Me. You remember Simon, the Cyrenean?

Together, you with Me. My tenderness is imperious, isn't it? You have seen mothers hug their children as though they wanted to lock them in their hearts? What is that compared with My love? Haven't I asked you to eat Me every day? Poor little ones; you don't understand. At least offer Me your good will and try to love Me a little more. Come a step nearer every morning. Picture My outstretched arms. Who is keeping you from covering the last distance between us? Oh, may it not be fear!

Call Me and I'll take hold of you as I took hold of Peter. You remember? I had called him 'Man of little faith'. And I said, 'If you had faith even as a grain of mustard seed, you could move mountains.'

Never cease to quicken your faith and hope, and you will never leave Me again. Can anyone leave Me once he has found Me?''

March 6 — *Nantes.*
''How free you are, My child, when you are sure of God!''

March 9 — *(Very busy)*
''The more you advance in life, the more I want you in Me. You know how much swifter the little streams flow as they get near the sea — just as though they were in a hurry to lose themselves. Come to Me in the same way, gaily, in your wholeness as though you said, 'I take You. I give myself.' And in this way you rock your soul in God as a child rocks in its cradle, and you bind yourself closer to Him.

Keep on enlarging the picture that you have of God. See perfection in all His qualities and powers. See strength and grace. See His will to be good to His children in measureless measure. You are sure of this; you have the details of His passion. What you can't see is the munificence of His rewards for your poor little acts of good will. So give Him your boundless trust. Expect the infinite — in other words, expect Him. What else would you expect but love? Don't look for more, for love is fulness. Give thanks and give yourself.''

''Lord, I find nothing in myself worthy to offer You.''

''Haven't I told you that I'm a collector of miseries. I am like one who mends china and is only happy when he is practicing his art on the thousand and one fragments of some beautiful object. I'm like a painter who takes pleasure in touching up the colors of a faded canvas. I'm a surgeon who has put together broken limbs. Nothing, no one is beyond My care. And it's all free. I'm paid when My people pay attention to My commandments and say with simple and childlike tenderness, 'Thank you, dear God.' Is it too difficult?''

(In the depths of my soul:)

''Lord, live in me. I need You, but you don't need me.''

(Quickly and eagerly:)

''Yes, yes, I do need you. My love needs you.''

March 16 — *Holy hour. (Tired)*

''When you feel weak, give Me your weakness. I take it into My power and unite it with all My weariness on earth. Even before My crucifixion, in My journeyings and My work I suffered much physical fatigue, sometimes moral depression too, in the midst of so much human misunderstanding. So, weak and depressed, come close to Me as though you had chosen to be at the end of your resources just in order to reach Me. We'll be like two patients in the same room, praising the Father, longing for His coming, joyously listening and wondering whether the bell will toll for you soon.

You remember when the last siren sounded on the great liners, you used to think, 'To leave! to leave is to live.' Have this same thought as you leave the earth. You are going away to live and to live in the real New World. It is waiting for you. Its people are waiting for you too. In New York the people were on the pier — a cheering crowd of them. That was only the world's poor welcome. But the ecstatic cries from the heavenly city, the love, the radiant joys — who could ever express it in the language of men?

345

So be filled with joy at the thought of approaching it, as you were in the airplane when you asked, 'Shall we be arriving soon?' And someone said, 'Keep on looking at the horizon and you'll be able to tell when the plane is about to land.' And if some of your dear ones were waiting for you, your heart leapt with joy. My child, the One who is waiting for you is your Creator and Savior. Go gaily to meet Him as if you were going to a festival. Lovingly prepare your 'going away' costume, the one ornamented with the jewels you have received from Him. And besides this, borrow the radiant colors — your heavenly mother's and your Beloved's raiment. You must take the habit of adorning yourself in them every day. They are holding them out to you because they want to see their own beauty in you. Give them your humble smile, the smile of a child happy to be going home.''

March 24 — *Ill.*

''How good it is for you from time to time to feel near the gate leading out of this life. Your vision of the past is so clear now, isn't it? Things have lost the gloss of the world's opinion. You can see the real motive now — usually selfishness, indifference to the glory of God when that alone should be your goal, unconcern for the salvation of your brothers when the desire for it should set your very thoughts on fire. What sadness, My child, if you were to arrive alone! Provide yourselves, all of you, with a cortège of companion-souls saved because of your solicitude, whether they be in far away missions or close to your home. In the luminous evenings of the East, as at Nazareth, when you were meditating on the terrace of the Franciscans, you noticed how some stars slipped alone into space and others seemed to be set in discs of light. If only your souls could each become one of a constellation led by you into the home of the Father of the family, what acclamations there would be!''

''What must I do?''

''Mention their names often to Me: your protégés, your unbelievers, your deafmutes, I'll hide them beneath My seamless robe steeped in My blood.''

March 30 — *Ill.*

''Why not use this time of solitude in bed as though you were in adoration before the Blessed Sacrament. What is there to hinder you? It only takes a little effort. And why not transmute these thirty days of prison into thirty days of joy, since all sickness destroys your body a little and brings your soul nearer to the gate of Life.

Why not offer the Father your steady decline so that your words and writings may bear fruit and nourish your brothers? Somewhat in the way that I wanted you to feed on Me and take strength in My power. And you were fed by Me too, in the first stages of My agony when the moon shed its white light on the garden awaiting My sweat of blood...

May even the far-off first fruits of your death bring help and joy to your brothers. You can imitate Me in so many details, My dear little ones, so distracted by the world. And if I want you to try to imitate Me, it is because this brings us closer and you are more Myself. When will they be able to say, 'To see a Christian is to see Jesus Christ'? What a powerful example, what a silent testimony! You remember what I said: 'He who has seen Me has also seen My Father'? When I said that don't you think that My voice was filled with an all-engulfing love?

Oh, My child, rise above your little ways. Gain altitude. Give to God directly, without the slightest human fear.''

March 31 — *The Communion of the sick.*

"I illuminate the nothing that you are so that you may have a clear picture of your nothingness."

April 6 — *Holy Thursday.*

In bed, I was mentally visiting all the altars of repose in the city, the country and foreign lands.

"A Host — both of us."

April 8 — *Holy Saturday.*

"*I have only little things to offer You since I am ill.*"

"A little thing with great love adds up to a big thing."

(Later in the day) (....) "Go in search of sinners and bring them to Me. Take care of My Mystical Body. Offer Me in the tomb where I lay, broken for all the unfortunate ones who are afraid to be Mine."

April 13 — *Ill.*

"Is there a day or an hour in your life that could be kept from Me? Can you set aside this week or this month? Don't you see that My requirements as Head of the household extend even to your quarter-seconds? And don't you feel a burning desire to surrender yourself utterly to My ownership?

In the grip of fever suffer for Me. In your interrupted sleep, rest in Me and find a flame of courage."

April 20 — *Ill.*

"I'm placing all these acute sufferings as flowers in your crown. There must be roses on your head as well as thorns. Unite your oppression with Mine. I suffocated in My agony. I suffocated when I was bound by the soldiers; and when they made sport of Me at the court of Annas; and when they mocked Me at Herod's palace; and while they scourged Me beneath Pilate's judgment hall. I suffocated as I carried My cross. And when it was planted upright, and all through the hours that I hung upon it, there were the suffocations of the battle with death, right to the very last gasps, right to the cry of all-triumphant love that carried away My soul.

In this illness when your body lacks air, oh, may your soul breathe God. Yes, My friend, take Him to give Him. He will give you your share.''

April 25 — *Fever.*
''See Me above everything and see Me everywhere.''

April 27 — *Still in bed. ''As you wish…''*
''It is good for you to abandon yourself to My tenderness. Life or death, what does it matter? You are in My heart. You are in My will. It isn't enough just to accept; your acceptance must be charged with the utmost love. Unfold this love like a flexible cloth to the very extremity of My desire. Then your work and Mine are one in the Father's sight and you are all-powerful.''

May 4 — *The seventh week of illness.*
''Lean upon my courage for your courage. Remind yourself that alone you are nothing. Can you acquire this beautiful habit of always being with Me? Together always…

Invite Me often to be present in your life, as though you gave Me a ticket for a concert. And keep Me a place of honor in the front row, as if you were concerned that I miss nothing of the spectacle, this spectacle of your daily acts, all lived for Me.

Dear child of My heart, what beautiful things we'll do together. Keep this word ever before you: *'Together'.*''

May 5 — *Suffocations. "Lord, is this the last illness?"*
"Magnificat."

May 6 — *Suffocations.*
"Why be anxious? You know that it is I. Offer this present moment with all the power of your love — this little moment that you can't even hold in your hand. Borrow My love, My mother's love, that of all the saints who are still on earth, and offer it all to Me with your present moment. I'm waiting for it as one who waits for the love of a beloved child."

May 12 — *During the Anointing of the Sick.*
"You are all hidden under the robe of My merits and that of My mother's. Doesn't that give you a sense of security?"
Weaker.
"Lord, is your cross big enough for me to stretch out beside You?"
"My poor little child, just think — I call the whole universe to it."

May — *"Lord, is this my last holy hour on earth?"*
"May all your hours be holy hours now. There are so few before the last.

You are white as snow through the Anointing and its graces. (....) My love has washed away every stain. (....) If I love you at all times, I am even more moved in this great moment when the last visitor comes. May she do all she should for you. But rest in My arms while you wait for the final moment when the very last veil will be rent.

Now, My friend, here is your work: Regret, regret, regret your sins. And love, love, love ever more and more the One whose name is Love."
"Lord, take my little flame in Your fire."

May 13 — *Weaker.*

"Yes, I take your body like the wheat to be ground. It is for your brothers."

"For my brothers — with You."

May 15 — *Weaker.*

"Most tender Lord, give me Your arms. I am returning to our home with the tiny steps of a small child."

May 18 — *Ascension Day.*

"Don't love's preparations already bring joy to the heart of love? (....) What are you going to say to Me on arriving? What am I going to say to you? Oh, this moment of the Meeting! Put your whole soul into it. Believe in the infinite tenderness. You realize that you are too timid. Then venture out on My love. Hope. Come, My beloved, come and tell Me everything you have not dared to say."

May 23 — *Communion of the Sick.*

"Poor little soul, you've waited to the very last minute of your life to believe in My boundless compassion, in the final forgiveness. Have no more fear of anything. It would wound Me if your were afraid. Surrender your whole being to love, my beloved."

May 24 — *"No more strength. I can scarcely see. I'm scarcely able to love You."*

"Take My eyes. Take My voice. Take My love."

May 25 — *"Have I come to the end of my life? Is this the moment when I celebrate my first and last Mass? Where are You, loving Presence?... And afterward, what will it be?"*

"It will be I. It will be I.

   Forevermore."

Achevé d'imprimer sur les presses de
Imprimerie H.L.N. Inc.,
2605 Hertel, Sherbrooke, Qué. J1J 2J4

PRINTED IN CANADA